The
CONCENTRATION
of POWER

The
CONCENTRATION
of POWER

Institutionalization, Hierarchy
& Hegemony

ANDERS CORR

The Concentration of Power: Institutionalization, Hierarchy & Hegemony
© Ottawa, 2021, Anders Corr, First Edition

Published by Optimum Publishing International a division of
JF Moore Lithographers Inc.

Library and Archives Canada cataloguing in publication

Trade Paperback
ISBN: 978-0-88890-319-8

Hardcover Edition
ISBN 978-0-88890-322-8

Digital Version of the book is also available
ISBN: 978-0-88890-323-5

Names: Corr, Anders, author.
Title: The concentration of power : institutionalization, hierarchy & hegemony.

Printed and bound in Canada
US Edition Printed and bound in the USA

For information on rights or any submissions please write to Optimum:
Optimum Publishing International
144 Rochester Avenue
Toronto, Ontario
M4N 1P1
Dean Baxendale, President
www.optimumpublishinginternational.com
Twitter @opibooks

It is the hope of great monarchs to make a single city of the entire world.

—GIAMBATTISTA VICO, C. 1725

CONTENTS

INTRODUCTION: *The Concentration of Power*   1

PART I: THEORY OF HIERARCHY AND HEGEMONY   27

CHAPTER 1	Theory Introduction	29
CHAPTER 2	Theory of Hierarchy and Hegemony	35
CHAPTER 3	Defining Hierarchy	43
CHAPTER 4	Origins of Hierarchy	57
CHAPTER 5	Functions of Hierarchy	69
CHAPTER 6	Structure of Hierarchy	75

PART II: COMPETITION BETWEEN HIERARCHIES   101

CHAPTER 7	Competition Introduction	103
CHAPTER 8	Competition Between Hierarchies	115
CHAPTER 9	Division of Power	123
CHAPTER 10	Conflict Between Freedom and Organization	127
CHAPTER 11	International Hierarchy	133
CHAPTER 12	Domestic Hierarchy	155

CONCLUSION: *The Deconcentration of Power*   179

ACKNOWLEDGMENTS   189
BIBLIOGRAPHY   191
NOTES   215
INDEX   261

INTRODUCTION

The Concentration of Power

On January 6, 2021, a red-white-and-blue mob descended on Washington, DC's American Capitol, the most powerful symbol of democracy worldwide. A thin police line blocked the rioters, but the Proud Boys, a "patriotic" group acting in quasi-military fashion, took the lead in muscling past, breaking the dam through which a deluge of approximately 10,000 protesters then flowed. A police officer who sought to protect a door to the Capitol was pulled from the squad and brutally beaten with a hockey stick. Air Force veteran Ashli Babbitt, a Trump supporter, was shot in the neck and died after trying to climb through a broken window close to the House of Representatives chamber. A Trump supporter discharged chemical spray at Officer Brian Sicknick, who collapsed that evening, and died the next day from a stroke. Three Trump supporters died from medical emergencies at the riot, and almost

140 officers were physically injured.[1]

About 800 protesters made it into the Capitol Building itself. Average protesters at the building that tragic day were not like the Proud Boys, however. They were typically middle class and middle aged, and from a geographically representative sample of America's counties. They believed they were standing up for liberty and the Constitution. They believed the election had been stolen. And, they wanted to right that perceived wrong to democracy.[2]

Hundreds of millions of people around the world watched the events at the Capitol, but they viewed and judged from their own perspectives, colored by the positions and identities to which they subscribed. Democrats tended to be outraged. Many Republicans, aghast. Europeans, shocked. But some Republicans—whose industries had been shipped to China decades ago and who voted for Donald Trump in the hopes that a strong American president would turn the tide of America's "decline"—might, like many of the rioters, have felt righteous or cathartic. African-Americans and other people of color who had lived experience of extra-legal police brutality, including that promoted by President Trump,[3] might have felt a mix of fear and foreboding at the many current and former police and soldiers, now wearing civilian garb, mixing with rioters sporting Confederate and military paraphernalia, and doing literal and symbolic violence to the nation's Capitol Building.

Having been influenced by years of Trump's attacks on the media as "enemies of the people," the mob turned against the press, destroying equipment and threatening reporters. One was manhandled and thrown over a wall. Pipe bombs were found at the national headquarters of the Republican and Democratic Committees. Even after the rioters (some would say insurrectionists) breached the steps of the Capitol at 2:07 p.m., and the entrance itself at 2:16 p.m., President Trump tweeted inflammatory words against Vice President Pence, who was then overseeing the electoral count in the Senate chamber. A scaffolding and noose were erected as public "art." Only at 3:36 p.m., about ninety minutes after the breach, did Trump authorize the National Guard to intervene. It took an additional forty minutes for him to finally heed the urging of his advisors and tweet to the rioters to go home.[4]

President Trump had, an hour before, inflamed the crowd with claims that "this election was stolen from you." In his fiery speech, he said the word *fight* twenty times and the word *peace* just once. A week after the riot, on January 13, Trump was impeached, but not ultimately convicted, for inciting an insurrection.

In prior weeks, Trump had remained silent, even supportive, with respect to his ally General Mike Flynn. General Flynn had promoted martial law to rerun the vote under military guard. One of Trump's corporate allies was seen entering the White House just five days before the inauguration of Joe Biden, with notes that appeared to advocate utilization of the "Insurrection Act *now*" and "martial law if necessary."[5]

Five months before the election, Trump had entertained the idea of utilizing military forces to oppose Black Lives Matter (BLM) and Antifa riots. Anti-racist and anti-Trump protests were largely peaceful, but organizers tended not to acknowledge the bottles and rocks thrown at police or the fires lit on the fringes of their protests.[6]

Adding to concerns leading up to Biden's inauguration, Trump gutted his own administration on numerous occasions, including Secretary of Defense Mark Esper, who resigned under pressure just five days after the election. Trump then filled positions at the Pentagon with loyalists. America was polarized, on edge, and Trump appeared to be entertaining plans for martial law that threatened to stitch the country, which was ripping apart at the seams, back into a monster of its former self.

That did not happen. A peaceful transition of power occurred on January 20, when Biden took office. Democracy worked. America's democratic institutions of over 200 years, including the Constitution, were upheld. The global public heaved a collective sigh of relief, thinking of the post-election atmosphere of crisis as an anomaly.

But considered over centuries rather than years, it was not an anomaly. It was the most recent failed step in a global concentration of power that has been ongoing for millennia. Sometimes this power concentration served some public good in response to a crisis. Sometimes, not. American presidents have been draining power from Congress since the Civil War. Brussels, in the name of the European Union (EU), is gradually absorbing the power of nation-states, like France and Germany, that have existed for hundreds of years. In Asia, the Chinese Communist Party (CCP) is increasingly powerful, with its leader, Xi Jinping, now "emperor for life" and attempting to push US military forces out of the region.

Not all readers will agree with every paragraph of this book. In fact, they should not. The book is not liberal or conservative, left or right. It looks at empirical evidence from prehistory, through the ancient world of Greece, Rome, and China, to the consolidation of states and empires in the nineteenth century, and makes a case for a particular theory of history in which power concentrates over time. It argues that power is concentrating increasingly in Beijing, Brussels, and Washington, DC, and that to avoid a future in which one country controls the world will require a redoubling of efforts to resist illiberal forms of hegemony.

One of the causal arguments in this book is that the concentration of power acts like a ratchet. It concentrates when conditions are ripe and force is applied, but due to ratchet mechanisms like subsidies, transfers, and corruption, power does not easily return to an unconcentrated state when conditions are not ripe. This book thus takes a position against historical theories of progress toward an egalitarian future, or an oscillation of power concentration throughout history, with equal periods of power aggregation and disaggregation. The evidence points elsewhere.

Even when power is concentrated in order to defeat power concentration—for example, the presidential powers that Franklin Delano Roosevelt acquired to defeat the Nazis—that power tends to stay in its aggregated form after the threat is defeated. The pawl in the ratchet engages to stop the disaggregation of power.

The pawl is typically some form of incentive or disincentive that those at the top of hierarchies offer or impose upon those lower in hierarchies, in order to keep them within the hierarchy and thus maintain the concentration of power. For example, Denmark imposed a trade monopoly on Greenland in 1776, closing the island to foreign access. In the 1940s and 1950s, the US, Canada, and Denmark increased the building of weather and defense installations that were used during the Cold War as a base for nuclear-armed bombers, bomber interceptors, jets, and missiles. However, both Greenland and Denmark are democracies without a law against secession. This weakens them as states. Greenland has the opportunity to break from its foreign and defense union with Denmark, which provides opportunities for internal or external powers—including the US or People's Republic of China (PRC)—to influence the politics of both Greenland and Denmark, and potentially encourage their division. Conditions are therefore ripe for the disaggregation of Denmark's power over Greenland and the reorientation of that power toward foreign capitals. To forestall this, Denmark makes an annual transfer of $623 million to assist in the financing of basic services in Greenland. Without this money, which acts as the pawl in Denmark's ratchet, Greenland's mainly Inuit people, numbering 56,000, would have to seek another source of income and might vote to secede. So public opinion in the country tends to persist against secession. This matters to geopolitics, because Greenland's territory continues to be used by North Atlantic Treaty Organization (NATO) countries in their defense, including utilization of the strategically located Thule Air Base by the US military, and attempts by the US and Denmark to keep China from opening a weather station and rare earth element mines on the island.[7] When the threat of China's expansion into Denmark decreases, and conditions for the expansion of NATO's alliance are again propitious, the ratchet theory described here would predict that Danish subsidies could be withdrawn and diverted toward the further concentration or institutionalization of Danish, NATO, or democratic power more generally.

The utilization of incentives and disincentives to maintain power concentration acts to regularize and institutionalize hierarchies, including national and alliance hierarchies, which stops the deconcentration or disaggregation of power during times of stress. Other hierarchies globally follow the same defensive strategy but revert to the offensive when opportunities arise. Over thousands of years of history, we can observe the sustained concentration of power through this two-step mechanism of the ratchet: 1) pull toward power concentration by human avarice and bandwagoning, in which those lower in the hierarchy are incentivized to support those higher up, punctuated by 2) engagement of the pawl in the ratchet to stop deconcentration through the provision of incentives and imposition of disincentives by existing hierarchies on those parts of it lower down that threaten to break off. The successive political, economic, and knowledge hierarchies that result are geographically broader, more peaked in their power concentrations, and more invasive to individual freedom.[8]

One might deduce from this observed trend that the world is headed toward illiberality and global hegemony. Such a deduction would not be teleological. There is no divine, natural, or ideological purpose that is drawing history in the direction of an illiberal global hegemon. Rather, the theory presented here is the identification of causal mechanisms that explain micro- and macro-historical trends in that direction, and enables—through knowledge of these mechanisms—a prediction that, all else equal, we as a global community are headed in the direction of an illiberal hegemon.

But all else need not be equal. Understanding these mechanisms and the direction of history allows for remedial action and a different future, of diverse and sovereign democracies, to be reached by a more concerted form of collective human agency and intervention. I return to this argument in the conclusion.

My argument in the body of the book is not strictly evolutionary, though there is an evolutionary argument to be made. Certainly those non-cooperative and static political and economic units that fail to utilize the ratchet mechanism for defense and expansion—following a strategy of expansion when expansion is possible, and stasis or even contraction when necessary—will be outcompeted by cooperative and dynamic units. But even if all units follow this strategy of cooperating with friends in the competition with adversaries, the ratchet and variations in power lead the system to trend toward larger units and more concentration of power over time. That the progress of technology, and economic power variations, frequently makes the aggressor or initiator more likely to win than the passive defender, introduces aggressive action into the political, economic, and military systems that results in the consolidation of power for the victor. This is not purely an evolutionary argument, then, but one that argues that the concentration of power results from a ratchet mechanism in history. Conditions that support concentration lead to concentration, but conditions that support deconcentration, because of the ratchet, do not usually lead to deconcentration because of the ability of power concentrations to incent and disincent likely disaggregators and secessionists. The ratchet, which sometimes slips, thus leads to a punctuated equilibria of power concentration over time. A key point is thus that conditions that one would expect to lead to deconcentration of power, in fact, do not usually do so.

While the trend toward a global hegemon is concerning, we should also note that the hierarchy that is part of the trend's mechanism is not all bad. The most dangerous of hierarchies—such as fascist or communist dictatorships—are typically fought through the aggregation of power that most effectively takes a hierarchical form, such as the democratic use of economic and military force. Fire is used to fight fire, during war, when voters grant to the central democratic government increased, almost autocratic, powers such as conscription and control over a nation's strategic resources, including key sectors of the economy. But in the process, years after the war is over, we typically fail to notice that the house of democracy is becoming more hierarchical. The return to a decentralized state of power is not happening because we do not make it a priority, and we do not typically plan institutions, such as sunset provisions in laws, that automatically deconcentrate power after its necessary concentration during emergencies. Democracy is slowly burning down, and in its place in societies around the world are rising more hierarchical and consolidated forms of state power, including in the US, Europe, and China.

Sometimes the burn is fast. A preemptive coup against Biden's presidency could have happened on January 6. Had Trump ordered the military into the streets against BLM and Antifa riots in the months prior, he might have gained the military's support in vacating the November 2020 election by force. Had he succeeded, there could have been massive riots in the US, or a civil war. Some of Trump's supporters were talking about a civil war well before the election. Some still were, as late as Inauguration Day. Trump could have used that sentiment to violate the Constitution and drive the country toward fascism. Similar far-right or nationalist movements in the West, aligned with Putin's Russia, have used loose talk of civil war, right-wing riots, martial law, and coups that are destabilizing or erosive of democratic institutions in contemporary France and Turkey.[9]

The 2016 "coup" in Turkey was actually a hoax, according to two professors at the United States Air Force Academy. It served as cover to eradicate the political opponents of President Recep Tayyip Erdoğan, who was in the process of turning his country away from its NATO membership and toward a closer alignment with Russia. They write:

> Since the 2016 coup hoax, Turkey has purged many of its troops on circumstantial evidence of being "too secular." AKP rhetoric about the U.S. and CIA backing the coup was meant for mobilization purposes. From this legitimizing narrative, Turkey has ceased partic-

ipation in numerous NATO programs, such as the Euro-NATO Joint Jet Pilot Training program, despite 35 years of involvement. Turkey's purchase of the Russian S-400 ADS fundamentally compromises the rationale and logic for NATO membership. Moreover, the arbitrary jailing of Westerners in Turkey to be used as political bargaining chips, should make NATO policymakers wary of the idea of continuing an alliance with Turkey.[10]

Turkey's drawing away from NATO is an example of the disaggregation of one hierarchy for the benefit of another, led by the China-Russia alliance. What appears to be disaggregation is not always so when it is for the benefit of some other, more powerful, hierarchy. Disaggregation of smaller units can be a necessary part of a trend toward some larger aggregation of power.

Some of the actions and symbology of the new pro-Russian group of far-right leaders in the West have parallels with fascism. Trump's lies, grandiosity, extreme forms of anti-communism, inculcation of violence and hero worship, and requirement for absolute loyalty among his followers were reminiscent of the rise of Benito Mussolini to power in Italy during the 1920s.[11] Had Trump gotten his way on January 6, autocracy might have resulted, extinguishing the moral high ground that the US occupies against China. There then might have been no American democratic institution left that was strong enough to counterbalance the growing power of Russia and China. Democracy in America, and therefore democracy in the world, had not faced such a combination of threats since World War II.

Yet, the concerns of Trump supporters about the growing weakness of America—including deindustrialization and economic weakening, as well as the political and economic links between not only the Biden administration and China but also establishment Republicans and China—are very real.[12] America has been weakened by its leading establishment politicians on both sides of the aisle, who are scratching the backs of global corporations in return for campaign donations from billionaires. Those global corporations seek incredible profits in China, which some have likened to a massive Ponzi scheme. As China sucks in more and more capital, it has enough to dish back to Wall Street, and then some. China thereby enriches itself and improves its strategic position to the point of "too big to fail." Global banks and corporations have invested so much in the country that a failure of China would mean a failure of many of America's biggest financial institutions. Global corporations will therefore work hard to stop any such eventuality. Add to this increasing social services in the US, at the expense of military and economic competitiveness, and we see the economic basis of democracy's potential decline in what President Biden has acknowledged is a global "competition" with China. The controversy over use of that word, long after it was appropriate, is itself an indicator of America's ignorance, lack of strategy, and decline in the context of China's rise. America is still stuck in China's trap of framing US-China relations as a purely economic game in which we say, "May the best man win." But the US-China conflict is not a game and has never been one. China knows that it is a deadly serious war of alliances—ongoing in cold and hot forms since the middle to late 1940s—between market democracies that anchor one side, and powerful dictatorships that anchor the other.

There is no apparent end to the accelerating gravitational pull of China's GDP growth. As it gets bigger and more powerful, China's economy is giving the country outsized political influence globally. China is using that influence to promote itself as a responsible regional power, here to fix the world's problems caused by the chaotic and disorganized democracies, including—paradoxically and ironically—America's supposed attempt to achieve global hegemony, as opposed to its actual attempt to lead a peaceful alliance of democracies. China, therefore, has a powerful message and strong propaganda apparatus to increase its soft power as a shield while the CCP itself seeks to use its military and economic power to acquire global dominance.

China influences the world through not only global corporations, but the politicians, academics, and think tanks that the corporations and their billionaire founders support through donations and lobbying. Like our use of the term *competitor* instead of *enemy* to describe China's attitude toward democracies, politicians remain quiet or de-emphasize the threat to democracy of over five hundred billion dollars' worth of US-China trade every year, along with the donations to politicians, universities, and think tanks that that business generates. EU-China business is even greater. International corporate corruption threatens American and European democracy just as much as Trump's insurrection. But, that corruption is slower, less spectacular, and more insidious.

This is all occurring behind a fog of partisan and factional politics in the democracies, a sensationalism of violent videos, and claims of fascism, communism, and racism that steal headlines and keep the public unaware of the house that is burning down around them. As with different names for the insurrection, all sides tend to discount the other's version of reality, the better to smear the opponent and climb into positions of power in Washington, New York, London, Paris, Berlin, and Brussels. The infighting is leading to a failure of democracy in America and Europe, whether through heads of state who turn toward autocrats and fascistic symbols, or a more subtle acquiescence to the corporations empowering autocracy through business in China and Russia. The infighting and political polarization is erosive of hundreds of years of democratic institutions of liberty, equality, opportunity, and diversity that struggled to take root as power concentrated throughout history. Risk accumulates, and constitutions and common law that developed over centuries could eventually be blown aside as so many scraps of paper in a fiery whirlwind of collapsing democracy. Over time, more and more democracies could fall—and autocracies take their place—in a removal of an international democratic superstructure built upon ideas, economies, and the preponderant military power of democracy that emerged, luckily, after World War II.[13]

An autocratic coup in America or Europe, a US-China war for global hegemony, or the subordination of the US or China through corruption by the other superpower are all consistent with the theory and predictions in this book. I do not argue that such events will occur this year, or this decade. Nor do I argue that it will be the US or China that, in ten or one hundred years, will be the main protagonist in history. What I do argue is that political, economic, and informational power is concentrating in an accelerating manner, and that the trend and mechanisms of history are leading the world toward an illiberal hegemon with the preponderance of global power. Once such an illiberal country has the preponderance of power, it will be difficult for democracies—more concerned as they are with human life and avoiding war—to resist the dictates, brinkmanship, and bullying of the aspiring hegemon. Hegemonic power will become institutionalized, and thus made resilient to change, in new forms of hierarchy, and its use of the ratchet of incentives and disincentives to strengthen its structure, depth, and reach progressively over time. Avoiding this asymptotically increasing illiberality in history will require much more determined and collective efforts by each of us who believes in democracy.

The events of January 6 in Washington, DC, in which a strongman railed against communism and sought a legal loophole to increase his power, were not without historical precedent. The Russian Revolution of 1917, and the resistance of property owners (Marxists call them capitalists), lit a global fire that has blazed forth in a similar way on multiple occasions. The Bolsheviks lit this fire in the name of removing the concentration of economic power through a "dictatorship of the proletariat" that would control the means of production.[14] The response of the propertied—whose power, including political power, was thereby threatened—was to go on a war footing by sponsoring strongmen in Italy and Germany in defense of their own lesser concentrations of power. These strongmen institutionalized their power through totalitarian government, creating what became known as fascism. Mussolini's regime was the first major outbreak of fascism per se, followed by Adolf Hitler's Nazi Party, which won the German election of 1932, in part through an anti-communist message. The defeat of the Axis powers in 1945 by the Allies, including the USSR, did not end the fight between communists and the right wing, which calls itself conservative largely because it seeks to conserve a partly disaggregated distribution of economic power rather than allow revolution that aggregates that power in a communist dictator. And, after defeating fascism, communist countries like the Soviet Union and the PRC continued to seek to expand their authoritarian systems at the expense of democracy. The avarice of authoritarians of all stripes continued to drive the ratchet toward greater concentration of power.

In France, Charles de Gaulle took power in 1958, two weeks after a crowd of his supporters rioted, and sacked the General Delegation. The seat of France's highest civilian authority had fallen to a mob that sought to strengthen the French government through a new constitution and keep Algeria a colony of France. Between 1954 and 1962, the Algerian National Liberation Front (FLN, Front de Libération Nationale) successfully fought a war of independence against France, including through the support it gained from communist bloc countries.[15]

The right-wing riot in 1958 was followed by the founding of a military "Committee of Public Safety" in Algeria, and reports of French forces in Corsica planning a landing in continental France to force the government to fight the FLN and keep Algeria French. Two weeks later, de Gaulle was given the presidency. François Mitterrand, a socialist, publicly called de Gaulle's presidency the result of a coup. De Gaulle, of course, maintained that his unconventional path to power in 1958 was all entirely legal. After he switched his position in 1959 on Algerian independence—due to what he called the "tide of History" in favor of decolonization (a reading of history that obscures the post-war transformation of colonialism into American, Soviet, European, and Chinese business expansion through the use of local elites)—right-wing French colonists in Algeria opposed him. In 1960, and again in 1961, there were attempted coups, both of which failed. The coups were led by rightist retired generals in Algeria who claimed that French law prohibited Algeria's independence. They sought and failed to override de Gaulle and what they claimed were his communist supporters.[16] The threat of communist authoritarianism caused a reaction, or an excuse, for rightists in France to seek to maintain a greater French Empire even through a coup against French democracy. Fear of outside threats drives the ratchet forward, and keeps it from allowing the disaggregation of power.

Mitterrand, who served as President of France from 1981 to 1995, also had brushes with extremism. He was popular with communists and had a history of collaboration with the pro-Nazi Vichy government. When he admitted to his Vichy past in 1994, and argued that the French government persisted as a singular entity through World War II, some claimed that he was whitewashing Vichy collaboration with the Nazis, thus committing a "symbolic coup" that refounded France on a "Vichyist-republican" ideology.[17]

Whatever one thinks of such ideological acrobatics, there is plenty of authoritarianism in recent history, including the history of democracies. We do tend to look at history through an optimistic and self-serving filter, biased toward our own national and political identities and preferences.[18] When removing that filter, history becomes at once more complex, and simpler. Beneath the surface of moderate politics in representative democracies are extremist undercurrents of communism and fascism that occasionally come to surface. When they do, and fail, they are quickly forgotten in preference to an official history that depicts democracy as always victorious, and never at risk from internal instabilities and would-be autocrats. Democracy is, however, more fragile than we like to admit, and the concentrations of power within democracies are growing more robust, as are the concentrations without.

Contrary to de Gaulle, I argue in this book that colonialism and imperialism are on the rise. But, it isn't necessarily European or American imperialism, under the guise of international business, that will win. New forms of imperialism, emanating from Moscow and especially Beijing, are extraordinarily powerful. The new form of PRC imperialism is using an innovative mix of alliance, capitalism, communism, and totalitarianism to defeat the older democratic powers, which, in their time, defeated the yet older monarchies.

I write this not to support the new imperialism, but to warn of its coming, and to encourage a redoubling and unification of efforts in the defense of democracy, freedom, and equality. Factionalism in democracies makes them vulnerable to outside threats. Fighters for freedom against equality, and those who fight for equality without freedom, will not win this war. Fighters for freedom cannot fight against fighters for liberty and hope to beat the totalitarians. All hands—of whatever ethnic, religious, gendered, sexual, or class type—must be welcomed on deck for a unified fight against totalitarianism.

Democracy's defense—and the defense of the democratic values of liberty, equality, and diversity—will require a massive, coordinated, and concerted effort. Because, unlike what de Gaulle claimed, the tide of history is in the opposite direction: toward greater concentration of power, including of the military, economic, and informational varieties. The defense of democracy requires international action: against autocratic regimes like China and Russia, and for domestic institutional defenses; against would-be dictators; and against the more insidious and invisible concentration of economic power that has occurred as heads of state in Beijing, Brussels, and Washington—of communist, liberal, and right-wing bents—attempt to consolidate power through the granting of special favors and cross-border forms of corruption. They thereby ensure their own rise in the hierarchy, not thinking sufficiently critically about the steady concentration of power in the global system to which they are contributing, and which could end in a global form of illiberality that is unparalleled in history.

Democracies and democratic social movements must ally with, and work together, encouraging one another's independence and strength. The US and EU must support a militarily powerful and democratic US, Europe, and Japan, to serve as checks and balances against not only autocratic powers like China and Russia, but against any emergence of the US, or of Europe, as the sole global superpower. The emergence of unitary power in any state is a danger to all, given that, even in democracies, coups remain a possibility.[19]

Trump in 2021 and de Gaulle in 1958, with their uncomfortable parallels to Mussolini's rise, remind us that no single country, even of the democratic variety, is infallible. Adverse regime change from democracy to autocracy happens too often in world history to fully trust any global hegemon, even of the American democratic type. No single country can adequately protect the world's democracies from aspiring autocratic superpowers such as the USSR in the 1970s and 1980s, a strengthening China today, or would-be dictators in the US or Europe. The US and Europe must use their strengths to protect the international system, but they must also encourage other superpower democracies, including India and Japan, to ensure not only global stability, but the stability of American and European democracy should they experience adverse regime change and a return to the nearly unthinkable: an autocratic Europe or America.

I take these internal and external threats more seriously than most, perhaps, because in my studies, I found that history is an unfolding of the unpredictable, and there is plentiful evidence for an accelerating concentration of power toward illiberal governance and a single global ruler, or hegemon. I present the theory that has emerged from those studies, and some of the qualitative evidence, in this volume. The process of power concentration presented here constitutes the institutionalization of informational, economic, and military power to create enduring hierarchies in the international system. As noted above, the mechanism that drives this trend can be likened to a ratchet. That ratchet is sometimes prone to slippage, that leads to short-term disaggregations of power in the context of long-term power concentration. Thus, despite reversals, the ratchet describes an ongoing process, from prehistoric violence between bands, clans, and tribes, to the breakup of the Roman, British, and Soviet Empires, through to the present globalization of power and influence by countries such as the US and China, and institutions such as the EU, United Nations, and World Trade Organization. Empires fall, in part, because of the rise of these newer powers in the international system, with later powers invariably exceeding the strength of their now broken predecessors. Thus, the ratchet can momentarily slip—for example, in the case of a single state or empire—but almost always as part of the longer-term trend toward concentration by other more powerful states, empires, alliance systems, and international organizations.

These global powers and institutions are not necessarily bad, if they can be directed and controlled by free citizens to defend against totalitarian power and democratically flatten global hierarchies of power. But they are, at the same time, dangerous to democracy and diversity if, for example, they fail to disaggregate and devolve power once the need for defense is past, if they threaten to turn into the authoritarianism that they were meant to defeat, or if their institutional structures are vulnerable to influence by an autocracy that manages to hijack them for their own illiberal purposes. The many potentialities for the misuse of superpower status and international organizations by an autocrat or other illiberal actors to defeat democracies or human rights are insufficiently examined by the academic literature in its generalized enthusiasm and insufficiently critical treatment of "liberal" international institutions.

The theory presented here lays the groundwork for a historically informed criticism of the trend toward an interlinked economic, informational, and political globalization by focusing on hierarchy—including hierarchies in international organizations—as a mechanism for the concentration of power. I define hierarchy as the institutionalization of power.[20] This institutionalization can be good or bad, subtle or powerful, and is found from the granular level of individuals—including the destitute poor in the world's poorest countries—to the billionaires in the world's wealthiest cities. Hierarchy is found from the uneducated without access to the most basic forms of communications technology, to the super-educated in the world's elite universities; from unarmed villagers on the wrong side of military campaigns of ethnic cleansing— forced to flee and become refugees without a home except on the border between two unfriendly powers—to the presidents and generals who influence international organizations and lead alliances that deploy expeditionary armies to the opposite side of the globe.

Through the exploitation of mechanisms, opportunities, and inequalities in the hierarchy, power concentrates in the global system at the individual and institutional levels. Opposing this concentration of power and its institutionalization have been regular people joining in nonviolent social movements and democratic institutions with the aim of leveling political, economic, and knowledge hierarchies, and protecting their local political organizations against consolidation at higher levels, over which they will have little control. However, these social movements and political parties are often turned against one another by politicians and other social entrepreneurs who seek to use them by reifying factions for their own private or organizational purposes of climbing the hierarchy. Principled, independent, unified, and strong democratic organizations are needed that can simultaneously work toward diversity, equality, and liberty at home, while abjuring the influence of corruption and defending against the most aggressive and powerful hierarchies abroad.

This is easier said than done, as even good democratic citizens and countries tend to break down into self-interested factions that fight one another, rather than resist the trend toward global power concentration in illiberal capitals such as Beijing and Moscow. Joining one of the political factions that fight one another to take control of democratic governments is the surer way for an individual to rise in local and national hierarchies, and acquire material and non-material goods in the short term. And so, under the mantle of some cause or another, citizens are drawn up into these self-interested factional hierarchies that are more interested in gaining power than in diffusing power in a democratic manner. Over time, they come to be indoctrinated by their factions and start to believe that the other side—which fights for liberty rather than freedom, or vice versa, for example—is the most dangerous threat to democracy.

A lack of information and perspective also weakens these factional individuals and organizations. They typically see just a part of their own local hierarchies from their own perspectives, rather than seek to understand their part in the totality of global hierarchy and the direction it is taking. This blinkered view puts their organizations and social movements between a rock and a hard place. They can focus on localized infighting that destroys the democratic hierarchies that could protect them from more powerful foreign authoritarian threats. That part of the domestic democratic hierarchy they touch feels real and genuine, because they suffer beneath its grip and must respond to its carrots and sticks. But their movements are thus piecemeal, grappling with local symptoms and trivialities, rather than developing the broader principles and bipartisan alliances necessary to defeat the totality, and worst instances, of power concentration in time and space.

Added to this factional myopia is a confusion resulting from divergent means and ends. The way to defeat the world's most powerful hierarchies is sometimes to utilize the tools of hierarchy itself. The defense of democracy and its values both need hierarchy to defend against the world's most powerful emergent dictators, and are threatened by that same hierarchy that concentrates and institutionalizes power domestically. Thus, work to disaggregate power must take place simultaneously at the local and international levels, but in different forms and with strategic sequencing. The disaggregation of power at the local level in a democracy under threat from foreign autocrats should not be so extensive as to disable the democratic hierarchy in its defense against global authoritarianism. The social movement use of violence in democracies is particularly disruptive of their ability to identify, target, and defeat international authoritarian threats. At the domestic level, in a democracy, only nonviolent social movements work to make long-term positive change.

A Theory of Hierarchy and Hegemony

The theory developed here builds upon a little-known but important set of writers, usually not mentioned in the same breath. In 1957, international relations scholar John H. Herz theorized the expanding geographic size of nation-states and other political units due to increases in the range and power of weaponry.[21] The legal scholar Kimberlé Crenshaw wrote in 1989 of the compounding and intersecting effects of hierarchy across multiple subaltern, or subordinated, identities. Ascriptions such as race, gender, and sexuality interact with poverty to compound discrimination against those with overlapping subordinated identities, and the privilege of those with overlapping ascriptive benefits.[22] Biologist Peter J. Richerson and anthropologist Robert Boyd wrote in 1999 of a ratchet that drove increasing social complexity, constrained from backtracking by the pawls, or inner ratchet mechanisms, of population growth and knowledge retention. Richerson and Boyd assert that, "The tendency of population to grow rapidly and for knowledge of advanced techniques to be retained somewhere act as pawls on the competitive ratchet. Even during the European Dark Ages, when the pawls slipped several cogs on the ratchet, the slide backward [away from social complexity] was halted and eventually reversed in a few hundred years."[23] Social complexity does not always lead to power concentration and its institutionalization in hierarchies, but it almost always does.

Rather than apply the metaphor of a ratchet to social complexity, however, the theory presented here applies to a broader range of more specifically hierarchical types, including the reification and expansion of informational, economic, and political-military hierarchies, as well as identifies a ratchet effect that drives trends in the geographic size of political units (known as "polities" or "units") throughout history. Polities include clans, tribes, city-states, kingdoms, nation-states, empires, alliance blocs, and hegemonic spheres of influence. Viewed over thousands of years, it is clear that sovereign polities are trending toward larger geographic sizes.[24] This is one form of power concentration, facilitated by hierarchy in which intersections of individual privilege and intersections of subordination compound and accelerate the expanding geography of power, and thus the speed at which history is taking place. As power is institutionalized, it facilitates its own concentration into the hands of fewer and fewer people at an increasingly rapid rate. Concentration begets concentration, and is therefore exponential in its effects and growth.

Hierarchy and the incentives and disincentives it imposes are pawls in the ratchet that, more often than not, keep power concentration from slipping back into more decentralized forms when environmental conditions, including technological or political conditions, make such slippage most likely. Slippage does occasionally occur. Alexander the Great of ancient Greece and Macedonia conquered territory as far as present-day India. He left multicultural democracies and satrapies in his wake, and paid a price for his leadership with the wounds that he personally suffered in battle. Affected by pride from his conquests, and to appeal to his new Persian subjects, he took the title of king and sought to be honored as a god. When he made his subjects kneel, his habituated Persian followers readily agreed. He was thereby close to using his intersecting privileges of military and ideological power to accelerate the institutionalization of his territorial expansion into that of a far-reaching royal reign. But his Greek and Macedonian generals not only refused, they denigrated Alexander's pretensions to absolute authority through laughter and derision. The egalitarian values of Greece in that moment were more powerful than the kingship Alexander sought to project. Alexander's empire crumbled after his death into smaller kingships, each led by his former generals.[25]

Could these egalitarian values, then, and their apparent disintegrative effect on Alexander's empire, be the constraint on hierarchy that keeps the system from reaching the hegemonic status of unipolarity? They help, but they cannot alone protect diversity. The theory and evidence collected here indicate that egalitarian values over the centuries, and other potential restraints on expansionism, have not stopped human societies, states, and international systems from experiencing a long-term trend—punctuated by short-term reversals—toward greater power concentration and geographically larger political units.

In parallel with political power concentration, the concentration of wealth[26] and an increasing control of knowledge continue apace. Billionaires own the leading newspapers and social media companies that they feel free to influence and censor depending upon their political proclivities. Some of them today may be using their media power against autocracy, and to flatten hierarchy. But what of tomorrow? Will their children, who inherit media empires and big technology companies, be as benign? This is the perennial problem of benign dictators, which applies just as much to the billionaires of today, who wield dictatorial power over their own vast empires of the economic and informational varieties.

And what of nationalism? Might nationalism of the Ukrainian or Taiwanese types serve to slow the aggregation of power by illiberal powers centered in Moscow and Beijing? Yes, to a point. But even as national identities serve to protect societies against takeover by foreign countries, they create a global caste system in which, depending on the luck of birth, one is born into a wealthy country or has the ability to purchase citizenship in a highly desirable country. Conversely, the poor in poor countries are typically stuck in urban ghettos or trapped in rural areas, with little opportunity because of the domestic and international borders that serve as a constraint on the free movement of people internationally.

Our international organizations and prestigious universities are geared to support the easy movement of capital anywhere in the world. But not labor. People are born into the national caste into which they are born, and if poor, they are invariably stuck there. On a global scale, therefore, equality of opportunity is a myth. Instead, the well-born are free to live anywhere, invest anywhere, and purchase as many megaphones (e.g., advertising or entire media companies) as they please to drown out the free speech of those who question their privileges. Others, impoverished, are forced to stay put and listen. The feeling that regular people have no voice or control over the mainstream media and big tech that bombards them daily with information creates an anger that destabilizes even democratic societies.

More democratic freedoms, progressive taxation, and greater limits on the use of wealth for political and media influence, including by illiberal regimes, are needed. But, they are not on the agenda in most democracies, much less autocracies. At the same time, the US and Europe need to maintain or expand their economies through sufficiently low economic constraints such that capital is attracted rather than repelled. Capital and industry are needed in democracies to make their economies, tax bases, and militaries strong in the competition with illiberal regimes. If regulations and taxes on corporations are so high in the US and Europe that those corporations flee to China and Russia, or to international tax havens, democracies could, over the long term, be economically weakened and defeated.

If autocracies provide companies with politically subdued and non-unionized labor, few regulations, and perks for CEOs and investors that cannot be obtained elsewhere, global corporations could, at some point, decide to relocate their headquarters to Beijing and Shanghai. Even without these benefits, CEOs could be incentivized to move capital to China if they were compensated through innovative agreement structures with Chinese companies that front-load revenues over five or ten years while deferring costs to ten or twenty years in the future, thereby maximizing CEO compensation at the expense of long-term shareholder value. One way to do this is to trade technology for market access, which is a frequent element of many Western trade deals with China.

The theory presented here arrives inductively and deductively at the conclusion that there is a near-permanent lack of restraints on global power concentration. Yet, such restraints are desperately needed to avoid a global and illiberal hegemon in the future, due to the ability of dominant countries to expand militarily, buying off weaker and subordinate countries and corporations (including universities and media empires) in the process. Even billionaires are not safe if they have nowhere to run because the world becomes a patchwork of autocracies, ruled by one dominant hegemon, that can tax and regulate free enterprise into nonexistence. Some of these billionaires, if they think in generational rather than quarterly terms, are therefore natural allies of democratic movements that seek to advance diversity, freedom, and equality.

If we act strategically to institutionalize democratic values today, the global hegemon that emerges will be democratic and benign, or perhaps no hegemon will emerge, maximizing local forms of governance and diversity, allowing for some (not extreme) economic differentiation, and encouraging plural forms of democracy to thrive on every continent. Or, power concentration at the international level will yield a multitude of democratic superpowers—such as the US, EU, India, Brazil, Japan, and even China, if it can be democratized—that protect individual freedoms and exert a liberal and stabilizing influence in their neighborhoods.

If we are not strategic, the hegemon will be autocratic and prioritize its own control, including through violent imposition of global conformity to its culture, language, and political thought. For this reason—and because we appear to be risking the illiberal end of a historical process of political aggregation, or at least a major terminus of thousands of years of political evolution—it behooves this and coming generations to prioritize international politics and problematize other forms of high power concentration in order to guide our nations in the direction of diversity, equality, and liberty for common people.

Democratic hierarchies have a part to play in this defense of democratic values. Good hierarchies are bulwarks against those that destroy diversity and concentrate power. We must identify the best hierarchies among the bad; better protect them from corruption; strengthen their constraints on power concentration, internally and externally; and then throw our support behind them for the ongoing fight with expansionist autocracy.

Domestic constraints on power concentration that interrogate, transform, and strengthen democratic hierarchies into structures with more diversity, equality, and individual liberty will be critical to ensuring that these institutions are sufficiently attractive, and last long enough, to unify their citizens and defeat larger global forces of totalitarianism. In that spirit, this book seeks to understand hierarchy to defend against its worst, sometimes genocidal, excesses while at the same time, accepting it where it provides organizational, efficiency, and practical gains to defending the democratic values believed in by regular folks.

Hierarchy and the Ratchet Effect

This book started as an idea in a nonacademic environment, transitioned to an academic environment, where it picked up some academic baggage, and is now attempting the transition back to a general readership. As such, I humbly beg the reader to ignore or excuse those vestiges of academia found within, including whatever pompous language, endnotes, and theoretical constructs are left after the thorough pummeling the book took by the very reasonable and gratefully accepted edits of the general readers to whom I submitted the manuscript for advice. Please feel free to skip all endnotes and any boring paragraphs, sections, and chapters at will. The book is designed to be skimmed, and to deliver the general idea, which is common sense really, to you, the highly selective reader. Along with the introduction and conclusion, the book is organized into two parts, each of which is divided into six short chapters.

Part I, "Theory of Hierarchy and Hegemony," provides a general theory, divided into sections. The concentration of power is reifying in hierarchies that combine over time from the individual level of the family into meta-hierarchies, or hierarchies of hierarchies. This process is converging toward an illiberal hegemonic point that is not inevitable, but that, when viewed from the vantage of thousands of years of socio-political evolution, is rapidly approaching.

Power compounds at the polarized intersections of subordination and privilege at an accelerating rate, including due to domestic contestation of factions that facilitate the skimming and pumping of power from below, to more authoritarian and unitary forms of institutionalization. Because power begets power, the concentration of power accelerates exponentially over the course of history. We may not have much time before the system reaches the status of a global and illiberal hegemon. Static hierarchies, including political institutions, are an illusion that is dispelled when considering them in historical perspective.

Despite some slippage, the ratchet effect of incentives, disincentives, and hierarchies imposed by dominant units in political, economic, and informational realms ensures that, by and large, subordinate individuals and political organizations—including formerly independent nations—remain under the dominant unit despite opportunities to exit or break up hierarchy. Instances of slippage, or disintegration of weak hierarchies, are often part of the process of reaggregation of subunits by more powerful units as they enlarge by absorbing these disintegrated parts.

As units in the system enlarge at others' expense, they change names in order to signify their exceptionalism, and ease their rise above subordinated units that are thereby left with the false impression that their sovereign status as tribes, kingdoms, or states remains intact. In fact, they keep their names but lose their sovereignty, which is what is most important to them.[27] Dominant hierarchies skim power from mediate hierarchies by elevating or devolving authorities to weaker entities more tractable to the dominant hierarchy.

As the system nears unipolar status under the control of a single hegemon, international organizations emerge as both a tool and a constraint on the powers of the hegemon. But due to the intersection and concentration of military, economic, and informational power among elites—and factional infighting—they, too, are trending, over time, toward complete subordination to a hegemon.

The meta-hierarchy is composed of relatively equal and interlinking political-military, economic, and informational hierarchies. The power of political-military hierarchies is greater but less frequently used. The power of informational hierarchies is lesser but in near constant use. The power of economic hierarchies is moderate, as is its use. Variables that cause even minor power imbalances provide opportunities for increased concentration of power and reification of hierarchy.

True leadership by individuals is largely an illusion. Individuals must accept and accommodate the evolution of the system toward power concentration, or become crushed beneath its path. Hierarchies, when temporarily freed of constraints due to the absence of competing hierarchies, are in a state of drift due to leaderlessness. When a global hegemon emerges, this hierarchical drift will be profoundly dangerous to humans and the environment due to lack of constraints on the whim of the hegemon and the hegemon's arbitrary power.

The nature, functions, and structure of hierarchy are addressed, including the main outline of contemporary domestic and international hierarchies, and those of the US, EU, and China.

Part II, "Competition Between Hierarchies," examines how power concentrates in the context of hierarchies that compete with one another for commerce, influence, and territory. It shows how the levers by which hierarchy operates are divided, and examines how three main forms of hierarchy and power—namely; force, wealth, and knowledge—are interlinked and how lower levels of hierarchy, including that found in the family, are patterns for higher aggregations of institutionalized power.

The ways in which the different types and levels of hierarchy are separated or welded together, and how this creates a trend toward totalitarianism—only occasionally reversed by inadequate levels of devolution, federalism, and the separation of powers—are discussed. The dissolution of hierarchy through rebellion and revolution is also discussed, as well as the reinstitutionalization of hierarchy by supposedly revolutionary regimes that are, in fact, more hierarchical than their predecessors.

Part II also addresses the enduring conflict between those at the bottom who seek freedom from hierarchy, those in the middle who seek to protect the benefits of their own position at the top of sub-hierarchies, and those at the top of meta-hierarchies who seek to further institutionalize and aggregate sub-hierarchies and competing hierarchies beneath themselves. An enduring conflict in history is identified between a set of democratic values and their autocratic opposites; namely, diversity versus uniformity, freedom versus order, and equality versus concentration.

Finally, the physicality and frequency of different types of power and their effects on hierarchy are discussed, and the argument advanced that force, wealth, and knowledge have relatively equal effects on the development of world hierarchies over time.

Methodology

In mapping the world's most powerful hierarchies, tracking the direction and speed in which they are aggregating, and seeking to explain the causes behind their movement toward ever greater concentrations of power, the book is best seen through the lens of political theory, which inspires it and from which it draws. However, I am not a political theorist by training, but rather, something between a quantitative political scientist, an international relations specialist, a policy analyst, and a generalist. Add to that some real-world experience in military intelligence, business, and social movements, and I hope the reader will excuse my methodologically and philosophically diverse approach. One thing my graduate work did provide is a methodological prescription to start with theory. And so, this is a book of theory.

To illustrate the theory, the book includes empirical anecdotes, which are stories offered as illustrations rather than proofs. While the theory presented is entirely qualitative in nature, it draws from my prior formal theoretic work, including game theory and computer simulation,[28] to produce some theories deductively. Other theories are inductively derived. I attempt to take a long-term (*longue durée*) view of history. Within this, illustrative examples are developed into representative, revelatory, critical, and extreme cases, which I have begun to prepare for future volumes.

Some representative material presented here surveys the heights of twenty-first-century power in the international system; namely, those found in the US, Europe, and China, as well as the lowest points in hierarchy; for example, famine victims, and the causes for the failure of empires, including the Japanese, German, British, French, and Soviet Empires. These seven regions represent the peaks and troughs of twenty-first-century international hierarchy beneath which are (or were) not only their own domestic hierarchies, but also the influence they imposed globally on less powerful hierarchies in the international system, including international organizations, less-powerful nation-states, and through that nation-state level, individuals and organizations domestically. The examples presented here are, therefore, broadly inclusive of the highs and lows of hierarchy in twentieth- and twenty-first-century politics that affect all levels and types of power beneath them.

Some of the qualitative empirical data provided here will lend itself to causal process tracing. Revelatory illustrations explored in this treatment include, for example, instances of bribery at the highest levels of national and international organizational politics. These instances were not always previously available to scholarly examination, including those I discovered from my own government sources.

Extreme examples from which the theory draws include hierarchies within situations (for example, communist countries and hunter-gatherer societies) that are sometimes portrayed as egalitarian. If hierarchy and the concentration of power can be found in these situations, they can be found anywhere.[29]

PART I

Theory of Hierarchy and Hegemony

CHAPTER 1

Theory Introduction

In 1951, British officials in colonial Singapore issued an official dispatch: "On a moonless night in mid-July a party of Singapore Police, 'acting on information received', crossed the deep-drained vegetable-growing area off Lorong Tai Seng and raided the isolated hut which was a headquarters of 'Freedom Press', the notorious Malayan Communist propaganda organisation." Inside the hut was a printing press on which *Freedom News*, a Chinese-language underground paper published by the Malayan Communist Party (MCP), was published. It was the organization's only Chinese press, the English press having been captured in December 1950. "Two Chinese escaped, but a Chinese man and a Chinese woman compositor were arrested," according to the dispatch.[30]

When the police entered the hut, *Freedom News No. 24* was already set in type, with galley proofs hanging to dry. "The Singapore Police hit on the idea of publishing a single, final issue of *Freedom News* in the format its readers knew, on its flimsy yellow paper in red ink, but with a Union Jack in the top right corner of the front page beside the title." It was duly published on August 15, the paper's normal publication date, with assistance from the Singapore Public Relations Department. The lead article began with the opening sentences prepared for the original paper, "which make the point that revolutionary activities in Singapore at present are comparatively quiet, a state of affairs that might cause 'a loss of confidence in the victory of ruthless Communist dictatorship'." This part, taken from the original *Freedom News No. 24*, was in quotes. Ex-communists wrote the rest of the paper, including explanations of its capture and rewrite.

The official dispatch on the *Freedom News* operation is largely deadpan, but the officials who carried it out evidently saw themselves as exceedingly clever and funny. The communist leadership and arrested compositors likely failed to see the humor.[31]

The 1951 retooling of *Freedom News* by the Singapore Police illustrates the dynamics of force, wealth, and information in the concentration of power and expansion of hierarchy. Police used intelligence networks to find the location of the Chinese-language printing press, a rare item of wealth among the poor insurgents, confiscated the press using their preponderance of force, and then used the paper and ink of the original press to assert their symbolic and physical victory in ideological and military operations over the communists.

Such displays of dominance signal to individuals—both inside and outside of hierarchies—who must be followed, and what the consequences are of disobedience. Power concentrated in that moment of the press's capture, as power tends to do.

A lot has happened to global hierarchies since 1951, most important the final fall of the nineteenth-century European colonial empires—including those in Singapore and Malaya—the rise of the US-led international system until approximately 2008, and the replacement of the USSR by China as the most powerful challenge to that system thereafter.

Before 1951, the British Empire was the largest empire, by territorial control, that had yet existed. Getting to that point required millions of years of political evolution from bands, tribes, and villages, to city-states and kingdoms, toward ever-larger nations, states, empires, and alliance blocs. Indeed, most of human political history, about the first two million years, we spent in largely autonomous bands and villages. As the anthropologist Robert Carneiro notes, "Not until perhaps 5000 B.C. did villages begin to aggregate into larger political units. But, once this process of aggregation began, it continued at a progressively faster pace and led, around 4000 B.C., to the formation of the first state in history."[32]

Hidden within long-term political development and the tectonic shifts from small societies to nation-states and higher forms of polity, like empires and alliance blocs, is the concentration and institutionalization of physical and ideological power over not only territory but economic and ideological resources. Clues to the ongoing global trend toward the hierarchicalization of human beings can be found in a history of such trends that stretches back into the prehistoric family, ancient Rome and Greece, and the formation of nation-states consisting of thousands of previously independent kingdoms and city-states, from the medieval period to the nineteenth century.

This steady institutionalization of power over time occurs because humanity tends to accept the hierarchies around them as natural, useful, intrinsic, or just parts of the social order, especially when they serve an urgent and popular purpose, and when those hierarchies are supported through the ready imposition of incentives and disincentives on disobedient individuals and organizations. When such ideologies, purposes, and incentive structures are lacking, significant portions of humanity revolt and overturn hierarchies, especially where they become particularly oppressive and thereby surpass reigning norms. But such revolts are rare, and, when suppressed or not, serve to legitimize later hierarchical forms through creation myths of individual heroism and national independence.

While myths that support hierarchy generally emanate from the top down, hierarchy is almost always perceived from the opposite, local perspective, looking up, and around. Intersecting architectures of subordination, within which individuals daily find themselves, are perceptible as a 360-degree map of the hierarchy at least two steps immediately above and below our own positions. We study this map to provide the hierarchy with polite or flattering feedback, when asked, and to better climb those heights, or manage those lower down.

Yet, for all our fascination with hierarchy, and especially those at the top of the most powerful hierarchies, "Modern man is virtually incapable of fully recognizing [hierarchy]," according to sociologist Louis Dumont.[33] Rarely do individuals think about the entirety, dependencies, and accelerating pace of the multiple overlapping hierarchies in which they exist: family, workplace, town, nation, state, alliances, international organizations, and world; or how hierarchies have transformed, and are transforming, over thousands of years of human history into ever more concentrated forms of power.

This chapter theorizes these issues by surveying and building upon theoretical models of social and political hierarchies, and their development over time. Its admittedly ambitious scope spans from the interpersonal to the international, and across a wide range of historical periods from prehistory to the present. The general theory of hierarchy presented here argues for the existence of a similar and accelerating ratchet effect across all human hierarchies that explains the global and accelerating concentration of power that we experience today.[34]

Many theories of the long-term histories of power, order, and hierarchy lend themselves to optimism. Some modern political scientists see a historical trend toward less-hierarchical forms of government, such as democracy, rather than monarchy and dictatorship.[35] Some see the rise of social media as eventually wiping away authoritarian hierarchy. Marx believed that hierarchy withers away as it is driven by the successive unfettering of modes of production: from "primitive" communism to ancient slavery, feudalism, capitalism, a dictatorship of the proletariat, and, finally, to a communist utopia.[36] Some see a decrease in the incidence of violence, which is usually hierarchical, over historical time.[37] Still others believe that utopia—in the form of heaven or enlightenment—is theirs to enjoy in the afterlife, should they live a good life today according to the precepts of religious hierarchies. Hegel followed Vico in thinking that states progressed through an initial stage of monarchy that degenerates into aristocracy and democracy, only to reemerge in a secondary form of monarchy. Vico's initial monarchy was the family, and so its transition to aristocracy was not a disaggregation of power but a step toward consolidation of patriarchal family units into a hierarchical association. The aristocracy then dissolved into democracy, in the process of becoming unified as a civil monarchy.[38]

Most of these historical beliefs are mistaken, at least in part. As theorized here, and as I believe the evidence will demonstrate, power is concentrating and hierarchy is reifying in a gradual and symbiotic fashion over time. The optimistic theories noted above, while factually and historically incorrect, are part of the process. Political, intellectual, and religious leaders use comforting beliefs in future perfection to attract and mobilize followers, advance leaders' personal popularity, create new hierarchies with themselves at the top, and promote the goals of the hierarchies in which they find themselves or which they want to create for themselves. The empirical evidence for increasing egalitarianism, other than on an ascriptive or identity-based level that is more than overcome on economic levels, is lacking.

The evaporation or revolutionary overthrow of hierarchy is nearly non-existent when compared with other significant political events over thousands of years of history. Instead, small local hierarchies tend to aggregate into larger, more expansive concentrations of power, and concentrations penetrate ever more deeply and rapidly into individual lives to determine individual actions. While through this process violence may be made less frequent among individuals, that is not always the case. Sometimes violence against vulnerable individuals and unpopular groups is disguised and normalized by power to the point of genocide that takes years to recognize. When violence occurs between competing hierarchies, it is more destructive due to the increasing scope, lethality, speed, and range of military technology and human organization over historical time. The most obvious example is nuclear weaponry, but human organization is also a form of military technology, and with its increasing sophistication, politics becomes ever more lethal over time.[39]

This book not only describes the increasing lethality and expanding geographical size of political units over time, as did anthropologists Robert Carneiro and Louis Marano.[40] But, like Herz, Richerson, and Boyd,[41] it explains why this trend is occurring, and demonstrates how similar causal factors can explain change in the system during apparently different, and sometimes disjointed, historical "epochs," including prehistory, the ancient world of China, Greece, and Rome, feudalism, nation-building, and the age of empires.[42]

The trend that is easier to recognize in distant history, however, continues today. Just as the institutionalization of bodies of deliberation, such as parliaments and assemblies, can, over time, capture the sovereignty of a nation, the same can be true of alliance blocs such as the former Warsaw Pact, and now, the Shanghai Cooperation Organization (SCO), and NATO. What applies to nations in alliances, applies to their interactions in such international organizations as the EU and UN. Some of these organizations can be used for good, but they can, over time, also absorb the sovereignty of their subunits or lose their original liberal identities if captured by illiberal powers.

In this book, I discuss an equilibrium of increasing social unit size of various political and economic forms that is punctuated by brief and less-potent periods of disintegration, as some theorists noted previously. However, the book for the first time expands, synthesizes, and systematizes this into twelve interrelated causal theories of hierarchy and its evolution across the three primary and intersecting types of power: information, wealth, and force; and three main intersecting levels of hierarchy: personal, national, and international. When considering the above, the trend is unmistakable: a set of causal mechanisms that drives social evolution toward illiberality and hegemony on all nine metrics of the three types of power intersected with the three levels of hierarchy.

CHAPTER 2

Theory of Hierarchy and Hegemony

While this book is meant for a general audience, to the best of my knowledge it, for the first time, contributes twelve interrelated theories to the academic literature on hierarchy, world historical evolution, and political order. Together, these theories compose a general theory of hierarchy and hegemony that power of the political-military, economic, and informational types are concentrating over time in an interlinked and increasingly rapid manner. The theories are tools with which to understand subordination and privilege within the hierarchy, leading to the identification of relatively positive and negative hierarchies, and prescriptions for flattening positive hierarchies, and defeating negative hierarchies.

The theory is summarized in the twelve parts below, which are the most technical elements of this book. Following these twelve parts, the writing again becomes more readable.

The political-military, economic, and informational *concentration of power* is, over the long term, unifying nation-states and other types of polity, and causing a *trend towards more illiberal and larger geographic polity sizes*, with asymptotic convergence toward an endpoint that is a *single global hegemon of the illiberal variety*. This is an effect of the oscillation of power imbalances and the ratchet effect, which lead to ever more reified institutionalizations of power.

The *oscillation of power imbalances*—including temporary ascriptive, informational, economic, and political-military inequalities, as well as factional and partisan infighting—provides opportunities for the increased concentration of power and average geographic size of political units that the ratchet keeps from reverting to more egalitarian and diverse forms in future time periods.

A ratchet effect that utilizes hierarchy, incentives, and disincentives to subordinate individuals, entities, and polities restrains them from reverting allegiance to smaller or less powerful subunits and sub-hierarchies when conditions make such reversion possible. This leads to larger average geographic unit size over time. Likewise, the ratchet keeps economic and informational entities from breaking off from domestic economic and knowledge hierarchies. The ratchet is driven forward to concentrate power by human avarice for more power, fear of losing power to a competitor, and utilization of reason to construct hierarchy that institutionalizes power and thereby removes uncertainty. The same three basic human elements engage the pawl when necessary to stop deconcentration of power, with avarice appealed to through incentives, fear appealed to through disincentives, and reason constructing the hierarchy that removes the uncertainty that accompanies deconcentration. Those individuals and political units that fail to follow this rationality tend to be penalized by the hierarchy and selected out of the population.[43] At the national level, low taxes act as a ratchet in the concentration of wealth. The ratchet at personal, national, and international levels sometimes fails and slips, punctuating the general trend toward concentration and larger polities with temporary disintegration, decentralization, or stasis. However, the utilization of subsidies (a form of incentive) and imposition of penalties or violence (types of disincentive) by the dominant system, political unit, or polity, to the subordinate entities or subunits, serve as pawls in the overlapping ratchets that are usually effective at forestalling subordinates and subunits from taking advantage of slack conditions suited for those subordinates to break off in a process of unit disintegration. In other words, expanding dominant entities at the top of hierarchies, when necessary, impose—through utility or disutility—conditions such that subordinates are disincentivized from breaking off during down times in the process of the hierarchy's expansion.

The *disintegration of weak hierarchies is typically due to competition with stronger hierarchies, and is part of a two-step process of expansion,* in which such disintegration is the first step, breaking weak hierarchies into smaller, less-powerful hierarchies that are easier to digest and incorporated by stronger hierarchies. In this second-step process of *regestion,* the strong hierarchy digests (incorporates) the former sub-hierarchy that had previously been digested by the losing weak hierarchy. For example, when one empire defeats another, the defeated empire typically breaks up into competing factions or territories, making its subunits vulnerable to influence and conquest by the victor. The relinquished units were previously incorporated by the losing empire, which is forced to give them up, for example, by making them independent. They thus become vulnerable to *regestion or reincorporation* by the winning empire. The same occurs to bankrupt businesses (including universities and think tanks), whose assets—including groups of employees—are often broken up and sold to or hired in competitive markets. Stronger businesses take advantage of this competition to acquire the competing subunits at a cheap price, and thereby grow through regestion.

Concentration, disintegration, and regestion create a *concentrating but punctuated equilibrium* over long historical periods, in which there are relatively short-term downturns in the concentration of power, followed by ever higher concentrations of power in the long term. One step back, but two steps forward in the process of concentration. This process is often mistaken for a permanent power cycle in history between integration and disintegration, expansion and contraction, or concentration and deconcentration that over hundreds of years yields no average change in concentration. In these cases, analysis fails to identify the secular trend toward power concentration over thousands of years, often due to the narrow geographic scope of such blinkered analysis, failure to perceive how sovereignty switches over time to new units of analysis, short-time horizons, or normative bias (for example, an optimistic prediction of a future decentralization of power). The appropriate periodization—whether of centuries or millennia—differs depending on whether units are political-military, as in states and alliances; ideological, as in academic systems or religions; or economic, as in corporations or trade blocs. Economic downturns and political disintegration since the turn of the twentieth century much more frequently create failed states, bankruptcies, and foreclosures that benefit those with the greatest stores of military and economic power, ready to conquer or purchase—at low prices or with relative military or diplomatic ease—the broken territories and distressed assets made available through disintegration of adversaries.[44]

Over the course of history, what is called sovereignty and thought of as absolute and constant in a single unit of analysis, such as the nation-state, is actually in flux. Sovereignty is ratcheted from lower to higher political units as power concentrates in the latter, in a continual process of *sovereign flux*. For example, over history, sovereignty has progressively shifted from clans and tribes to kingdoms and city-states, and finally to nation-states and empires. Nation-states and empires have been with us for so long that contemporary analysts tend not to see the current shift of sovereignty from nation-states and empires to lead states in alliances and to international organizations. Sovereign flux creates overlapping and contested "sovereignties" in the process. Older forms of sovereignty lose salience over time, as newer, more expansive forms of sovereignty gain in power.[45] Yet the dominant unit's critical substance of *preponderant sovereignty*, or near-exclusive military control over a territory, is carried with it, or gradually transferred—from lower types to higher types of polity— causing an enlarging sovereignty of the most powerful over successively wider areas over history. In essence, only the political unit's scale changes as it absorbs weaker and smaller units. Subunits are left with their original *de jure* sovereignty and historically sovereign names to appease their sense of pride as they lose their *de facto* sovereignty, and eventually their *de jure* sovereignty as well, to broader, higher, and more powerful entities with new designations meant to assuage, and thereby prevent, revolt by these newly subjugated subunits. These *nominal upward shifts in the relevant unit of analysis over time, then, are a product of the very expansion and absorption of sovereignties for which they function to obscure.* Sovereign flux is the most powerful political effect of a more generalized power flux that includes a similar dynamic for economic and knowledge forms of power. Mega-holding companies absorb and transform other corporations but leave the latter's names intact. Leading universities, media organizations, and think tanks absorb the most powerful (but not necessarily the most accurate or least biased) academics, writers, and thinkers. Formerly independent universities, media, schools, teachers, and think tanks are, over time, absorbed into a subtly-linked knowledge hierarchy in which most of the intellectual and monetary resources flow to the top, with lesser flows to lower levels in an increasingly peaked hierarchy of knowledge.

Hierarchical skimming is the process in which dominant units at the top of a hierarchy skim off *de facto* power from mid-level units, either for transfer to lower-level units or for transfer directly to the dominant unit. *Hierarchical pumping* is the transfer of power from lower-level units to the top of the hierarchy. Leaders can grow their power not only through hierarchical skimming to the hegemon, but from a two-step process of hierarchical skimming, and then hierarchical pumping. For example, a king can skim *de facto* power from the aristocracy by separating it from *de jure* power, which is then extracted directly into the court, or drained into a national-level parliament of equals from which it is more easily pumped for the king's purposes.[46] The two-step process may be more efficient if the lower-level units to which power is initially transferred, for example, are more politically malleable than the aristocracy. *De facto* power can similarly be skimmed from a group of tribes or nation-states, directly to an empire, superpower, or international organization, and removed *de jure* to an imperial city or international institutions that are under greater *de facto* political influence by major power centers such as Rome, London, Paris, and Moscow (historically), or Washington, Brussels, and Beijing (today). Or, power can be skimmed from a state to its citizens through democratic reforms, causing new democratic states to emerge in which citizens supposedly have equal rights and liberty. Those states can then join alliances or institutions that, through pumping, come under the sway of, or even lose sovereignty to, dominant members of an alliance or international institution.[47]

There is an emerging and global *division of power between a legislative role for international organizations, alliances, and institutions, and an executive role for regional and unipolar hegemons.* This follows prior historical patterns in which, for example, kings who assert themselves as a first among equal sovereigns retain councils of those subordinated kings who have an influence on the king's deliberative and executive functions. The identity of a future global hegemon is still in dispute, but three current contenders are the regional and organizational hegemons of the US, the EU, and China. While history is, thus far, a near infinite succession of surprises—and other hegemonic candidates could still emerge—there is a strong likelihood that as power concentrates globally toward a single hegemon, international institutions may seek to check the hegemon's power. Depending on the nature of the hegemon, its influence among international institution member states, and its propensity or require-ments to share power with other nations, international institutions, and the states that send representatives to international institutions, those institutions will have a greater or lesser role in the determination and enforcement of international law, and thus the freedom of the hegemon to act unilaterally.

In what is here termed the *network theory of power*, the global hier-archy is characterized by power flows at the personal, national, and international levels that are networked with informational, economic, and political-military types, leading to nine level-types of power (infor-mational-personal, informational-national, informational-international, economic-personal, economic-national, economic-international, politi-cal-personal, political-national, and political-international). The power of information is more frequently exercised than that of wealth, which is, in turn, more frequent than the power of force. Interpersonal hierarchy is more densely linked than national hierarchies, which are, in turn, more densely linked than international hierarchies. Individuals are driven moment to moment by their understanding of the world in relation to the many individuals with whom they are in face-to-face hierarchies, which are conditioned by intersectional identities, and the interactions of domestic and international hierarchies of wealth and force. These densely linked personal hierarchies are situated in less densely linked, but more powerful, national and international contexts. The transaction of wealth is far more frequent than the utilization of force, even though wealth is dependent upon force for property rights at the national and international levels. The manifestation of national wealth through not only national assets but national sovereignty is dependent upon force at the international level, including the force of regional and global hegemons that enforce international norms of territorial integrity. Finally, recourse to force is increasingly less frequent and lacking in effect among those who are influenced ideologically and through wealth, including through the ideological power of hierarchy, independent of wealth and force. However, when recourse to international force is taken, the effects are increasingly destructive and stronger than other level-types of power. Thus, while informational-personal forms of power are the most frequent, they are the least powerful. Level-types of power get progressively stronger in their effects (but progressively less frequent in use) the closer that power gets to the highest rank of power; that is, the political-international level-type.

Following feminist and anti-racist theories of intersectionality, the *negative compounding of power* at the intersection of subordinated positions, including identities, and subaltern lack of informational, economic, and political-military forms of power, along with the obverse *positive compounding of power* at the intersection of privileged positions, *concentrates power at an accelerated rate throughout history.* Marginality and privilege are not only compounded at the intersections of identity, but in an increasing manner through the ascension of the nine intersections of the levels (personal, national, and international) and types (informational, economic, and political) of hierarchy. *The interactions of power thus have a multiplicative effect on power concentration and its institutionalization into more peaked international hierarchies based on physical power over historical time.*

A lack of leadership in the hierarchy describes individual leaders who do not actually lead but instead follow those higher up in the system. At the top, leaders follow voters, shareholders, clients, selectorates, campaign donors, or a mix of these influencing stakeholders.[48] In some instances, political and economic leaders simply follow their avarice and fear, driving them toward more power or wealth, however it may be acquired, while seeking the appearance of leadership. True individual leadership is therefore rare, and typically ineffective, invisible, ephemeral, and self-serving in a manner that leads to arbitrary outcomes for others in the hierarchy. The system is evolving, and individuals and entities within the system accommodate its rise, failing which, the hierarchy often destroys them and their followers. Thus, the hierarchy, rather than leaders, lead.

The hierarchy almost always leads toward the concentration of power.

Hierarchical drift is the way in which hierarchies drift, within the bounds of the trend toward a concentration of power. Drift occurs in terms of other goals or outcomes, driven by the capricious values of personalistic or demagogic leaders. Hierarchies do not drift when it comes to the increasingly rapid concentration of power over time, which is the direction in which the system leads. But, given the arbitrariness of leadership goals on other matters, the drift of hierarchy indicates an uncertain and potentially volatile future, in which power is not only increasingly concentrated, global in scope, and determinative of individual human agency and environmental conditions, but arbitrary, risky, and destructive as well—especially if it reaches unipolarity of the illiberal type. Individualism, domestic health, and the environment will increasingly be the victims if power reaches this state, and therefore has no outside constraints of ethics, electorates, coherent public opinion, or competition with other hierarchies. The individuals in which power concentrates in that state would be increasingly untethered from democratic and competitive constraints, and therefore from democratic and efficiency values such as diversity, individual incentives, human rights, freedom, equality, and innovation.[49]

The theories above will be illustrated, explored, and substantiated with evidence, including causal process tracing, in the pages that follow. As will be noticed, the focus of the theory as a whole is on the hierarchies and mechanisms that cause the concentration of power through its institutionalization and dynamics, rather than on a mere description of the concentration of power itself.

CHAPTER 3

Defining Hierarchy

The concentration of power is caused by hierarchy and its incentive-disincentive mechanisms of self-maintenance, which are therefore central to this book. The word *hierarchy* was coined in a theological context. According to anthropologist David Graeber, hierarchy "originally meant 'sacred or divine rule' and was first used by Pseudo-Dionysius in the sixth century to designate the orders of celestial intelligences (angels and archangels, thrones, dominions, and powers) that governed the cosmos. It was only in the High Middle Ages that it came to be extended to the ecclesiastical hierarchy modeled after it, and in the Renaissance, to the whole of creation."[50] Hierarchy is now defined in a more general sense by the Oxford English Dictionary (OED) as "a body of persons or things ranked in grades, orders, or classes, one above another."[51]

The theological usage is too constrained, and the OED is useful but too broad for the subject matter of human relations. It has no explicit reference to power, without which political and economic hierarchy—other than as simple descriptions—does not exist in human society. For the purposes of understanding human relations and societies, hierarchy is here defined as the *institutionalization of power*, which can be found in personal relationships as well as in organizations.

Hierarchy in the latter is obvious; for example, the institutional nature of the physical, ideological, and economic power that generals have over their soldiers, jailers have over their prisoners, landlords have over their tenants, managers have over their employees, and professors have over their students. In these human relations, hierarchy can be oppressive or murderous. Husbands can regularly abuse their wives (the vast majority of abusers are males who abuse their female partners). Officers can send soldier after soldier, year after year, to a near certain death. Employers can needlessly risk the lives of their employees, quarter after economic quarter, for small gains in profit.

Most of this book will be concerned with problematizing the most malignant forms of these obvious types of hierarchy. But there are benign forms of hierarchy as well, including some that are quite subtle. Consider a form that is so normalized, benign, and subtle, as to be barely recognizable as an institutionalization of power. When one partner in a couple, for example, does most of the driving because she is the better driver, this is a benign micro-hierarchy. Both members of the couple go to their respective sides of the car when they travel, without needing to discuss who sits at the wheel on each drive. Lack of discussion, in this case, is evidence of a regular practice or institution erected almost subconsciously by the couple. Yet, the driver has greater power in the driving process than does the passenger. What is normally benign can turn mildly abusive, if the driver uses her power to drive the passenger somewhere against his will; for example, dropping by the hardware store against his wishes on the way home from his ballet practice. The driver could use her power for a functional purpose, if at the ballet practice her partner injures himself but wants to dance on, and she informs him that the car is leaving the studio with or without him. He gets in the car, not because he would have stopped dancing without his partner's prodding, but because he knows it is his easiest way home. (The reader doubtless noticed that I am here reversing gender stereotypes, in this case to accentuate the subtlety of power relations.)

Egalitarian intentional communities can also include subtle hierarchies. Perhaps they include meals and shopping done collectively, decisions made by consensus, and meetings in which any whiff of racism or sexism—real or imagined—is identified and purged. However, if the deed to the land or building is owned by one particular individual, or if someone in the community is more organized, diplomatic, or eloquent, they tend to influence decisions and are turned to for leadership. These subtle forms of hierarchy that are less obvious in a couple or intentional community become more obvious and less consensual as they ascend the level-types to town, state, and international relations of the economic and military variety, where power is harder (less ideological), more concentrated, and more thoroughly institutionalized.

Embedded in the notion of hierarchy is the concept of legality, which is based on successive appeals from lower nested forms, to higher levels of authority, from local laws enforced in local courts, to state or provincial laws and courts, and finally to national laws and courts from which there is no appeal. Supporters of international law seek to absorb some of the nation-state's sovereignty into the international level of institutions, norms, and laws found in New York, Paris, Rome, and Geneva, with large doses of influence from London, Brussels, Beijing, and Moscow.

Considering the individuals who lead such hierarchies across not only political but economic and ideological levels, authority varies depending on the intertwined hierarchy, but can be abstracted as, in contemporary society, the head of the household; the city mayor, manager, and professor; the state governor, business owner, and university system chancellor; and the national head of state, secretary of the treasury or exchequer, and secretary of education.

There are, of course, many more relations of authority, including dotted-line (as opposed to stronger solid-line), linear, and exceptional forms, depending on the individual and state involved. But law, authority, and the state are all in the broadest sense based on the regularization, nesting, and expectation of authority that establishes an intertwining of political, economic, and ideological hierarchies.[52]

Not every action of a superior is legal. Where the president, general, jailer, landlord, manager, and professor use their power to break the law, they are operating outside the hierarchy should that law be enforced. If unenforced, they are using their power or positions in the hierarchy to operate in legal gray zones in a manner that could thereby be normalized into an institutionalized part of the legal hierarchy through custom, regularization, or legalization. Thus, the illegal or gray utilization of power can be, and frequently is, used to expand that power and its concentration.

States, superpowers, hegemons, and international organizations can use their positions of power to break or extend federal or international laws or norms beyond the intention of the represented, authors, or founders. Where they are defeated, prosecuted, or legally reversed, they are recognized as rogues in the national or international system. But where they succeed—and regularize new laws or norms, or found new nation-states—they are recognized, over time, as the makers of new laws or sovereignties. They can then institutionalize their power and, as victorious leaders, proceed to set the pace of a nation, bureaucracy, or international law, and, thereby, write their preferred history in order to justify themselves and influence future generations.

Hierarchy typically relies, at least in part, upon material goods, physical protection, and displays of submission to incentivize behavior preferred by the hierarchy. In close primate relatives of the human species, aggression by one member of a group—often by males for regular territorial access to females or food—is resolved through the institutionalization of power relations via regular shows of submission by those who thereby accept positions lower in the dominance hierarchy. As much as contemporary philosophers and social scientists might like to ignore biological effects on social systems, recent scientific evidence indicates that animals with larger cortexes relative to the size of the rest of the brain, have more complex hierarchies.[53]

Purveyors of ideas—for example, social scientists who center those ideas as the prime mover in history—do not like to admit to biological or "materialist" factors that explain parts of human experience. They sell themselves by reducing the causes of history to ideological constructivism, or the institutions that are themselves a form of knowledge. They tend to sound quite smart in doing so, at least to themselves. However, business and military professionals can, and typically do, quietly ignore such univariate idea-centered causal theories as they proceed to utilize the power of economic and military control to influence the course of events, including academic and media discourses. These professionals have their own biases, of course. But time spent outside of academia is useful in realizing just how limited are the effects and explanatory power of some of the social scientific ideas developed within academia.

Just as with non-human primates, much that is found in human hierarchy relies upon material forms of power, needs, and exchange through micro-incentives. To put it very crudely: guns, sex, housing, food, and money, and the exchange of one for the other, matter at the individual level. Individuals at the top of hierarchies, who control those hierarchies, are influenced by these factors, too. It seems so obvious as to be ridiculous to say so; however, in the white-washed halls of social science, these things simply are not mentioned in such a blunt manner in polite company. One doesn't need a PhD to know this, but one needs one to be able—through circuitous postmodern language—to deny it and then be taken seriously.

It should also be obvious that material assets can be traded for non-material goods that are typically already inherent to the hierarchy, such as influence, position, image, and status. But, material assets can also be traded for ideology and institutions, including through the founding, or influence, of think tanks and media organizations by donations or purchase, and the hiring of professors for consulting and speeches. In some cases, professors make twice as much from their outside income as they make from their regular salaries. Tenured professors at Harvard Business School (HBS), for example, can make over $1 million a year from outside consulting, according to an HBS source of mine, yet they make less than $500,000 a year in salary. The salary is guaranteed, as they are tenured. So their variable income, which is at risk, is not from their academic jobs. This monetary incentive thus focuses their production on acquiring and keeping outside clients, including by pleasing those clients through their public speeches, opinion articles in the *New York Times*, and peer-reviewed journal articles. Yet, Harvard professors (if the John F. Kennedy School of Government is any indication) are not required to disclose all of their outside income, or its sources, to the public. Thus, governments and corporations that spend big on Harvard arguably bias the output of Harvard professors.

Donors from China (including Hong Kong) were the biggest donors to Harvard from 2013 to 2019, giving a total of $255 million, according to Harvard's reporting to the U.S. Department of Education. However, this likely underreports the actual funding that is linked to the country, as it does not include the entirety of the $350 million committed by the family foundation of Hong Kong billionaire Ronnie Chan in 2014. While Chan has dual US-Hong Kong citizenship, much of his business revenue is tied to mainland China, he has links to the CCP, he tends to take a soft-on-China position politically, and, according to two sources of mine, he uses his donations to lever one organization to which he donates, the Asia Society headquartered in New York, to obtain his preferred soft-on-China outcomes. At least some of his donations are channeled through what appear to be shell companies in the British Virgin Islands and Monaco. After Chan's family donation to Harvard, he accessed numerous professors at Harvard's influential Kennedy School, according to a third source.[54]

As with tenured Harvard professors who seek outside income—and become dependent upon that income to support relatively lavish lifestyles typically hidden from the public—hierarchy is found in the dependence of one hierarchy or individual upon another for sustenance. This sustenance can come in a multitude of forms, including donor-recipient relationships, patron-client partnerships for jobs and contracts, senior-junior relations conditioned on inheritance; and in the material, not just ideological, realities of race, sex, and gender stratification, and their intersections, across the centuries.[55]

Primordial forms of hierarchy at the individual and family levels scale over history and serve as a pattern for hierarchies that grow from the levels of band, clan, tribe, and kingdom, to state formation and the globalization of power through empires, regional hegemons, and, finally, to the contemporary level of international organizations, superpowers, and the competition for unipolarity. These levels of hierarchy overlap, competing with like and unlike units over material goods, political power, and those non-material assets for which material goods can be traded. This is not to say that ideas do not matter. They do.

Ideology is the power that is held within the minds and knowledge production of the people over which hierarchies seek to extend their control. Ideas are powerful, which is why hierarchies seek to control them.

My argument here is that theory produced in academia has an understandable bias toward ideas as the primary mover in history, because ideas are what academia produces. And, those ideas are not immune to the effects of money, even at the world's most prestigious institutions.

Individuals typically accept or join hierarchies of knowledge because of the assets assigned to them, and because most people and organizations seek to climb hierarchies even when they find themselves at the bottom, and are poorly compensated. They gravitate into hierarchies even though they may feel the hierarchies that they join are inefficient, corrupt, arbitrary, unresponsive, slow, unintelligent, restrictive, dehumanizing, and ultimately meant to control, rather than liberate, the individual.

The primary demands of citizens are for jobs or other forms of wealth acquisition in the hierarchy, not the breakdown of hierarchy itself. Children are taught to climb and honor hierarchies both at home and in school, yearning to avoid being hit or sent to their rooms, or seeking the approval of the teacher and parent, with a golden star on their charts or a pat on the head. In the schoolyard and with siblings, children fight for toys and the front seat in the family car, a symbol of the power of the parent being ahead of the sibling in the back, or simply having the knowledge-gathering benefit of a bigger expanse of window.

At all subsequent levels—including the universities in which individuals train and find life partners, the companies in which they work, the nations for which they fight, and the international organizations that determine with whom they compete economically—there is competition for power and status, and all are inextricably linked through the globalization of power relations. The total non-acceptance of hierarchy would be an extremist political position and, when thoroughly acted upon, would quickly land one in jail or attract some other type of institutional violence, which is a form of force.

Power is defined here as the possession of force, wealth, or knowledge. Force can be applied as personal physical power, or through the control of thugs, the police, or military forces. Wealth can be gold, currency, real estate, securities, or other forms of property. Knowledge can be scientific, philosophical, moral, religious, or institutional. All of these material and non-material assets overlap and are fungible elements of power. They can be traded one for the other. Quantities of power beyond what one person can physically possess rely upon its institutionalization, that is, hierarchy. The institutionalization of power in hierarchy enhances, regularizes, and coordinates that power for the individual or individuals who benefit from the hierarchy, whether through coercion, trade, or influence.

Thus, the power of individuals within a hierarchy includes not only the power within their immediate physical possession, but the power that the hierarchy stores for the individual. A billionaire's power includes the wealth that the bank stores for the billionaire. A general's power includes the soldiers that the hierarchy stores for use by the general. A university president's power includes the knowledge stored in the form of professors, research assistants, and the students who pay the professors' institution in order to provide ideas to the hierarchy in the form of student papers, free of charge.

Hierarchy cannot exist without power. But one can have power without institutionalizing that power through hierarchy. For example, physically powerful children may not use their ability to take another child's lunch despite resistance, much less institutionalize it by, for example, regularizing the taking through extortion of lunch money. A farmer with a chest full of gold may keep it under the bed and never institutionalize its power by, for example, hiring a farmhand with that gold, through an open-ended contract. Some knowledgeable homeless individuals might never use their knowledge to acquire positions in the hierarchy. They might instead decide to spend all their time reading philosophy and ignoring the world. Power can be unused and unknown to others and, therefore, remain latent outside the hierarchy. Even when used, it need not lead to hierarchy if not regularized, ritualized, or institutionalized.

Trade and coercion are transactional manifestations of power, whereas influence is a non-transactional manifestation of power. Influence derives from the perception of power, which is status. Those perceived to have force, wealth, and knowledge at their disposal are given status in the eyes of a perceiver, because the perceiver hopes to benefit from granting that status through implied rather than explicit exchange or gift. Perceivers can be individuals or groups, as groups can benefit from providing status to an individual who provides, or may—because of such status—provide, a public good to the group. The perceiver typically provides status to the powerful through obsequious behavior indicating subordination. This granting of status and unspoken expectation of compensation influences the perceiver in two ways. First, as a follower, the perceiver subordinates the self in order to link into, and thereby rise with, a leader by helping the leader. And second, by participation in an unspoken lottery in which, by following a leader, some of that leader's force, wealth, or knowledge might fall like crumbs from the table into the perceiver's lap. The perceiver might even eventually inherit the position of the leader, especially if the perceiver manages to institutionalize their position relative to the leader.

Where leaders understand their status value, as they often do, and ask favors of their followers that are not explicit transactions, they enter a gray area between transaction and influence. Thus, influence can be traded, used for coercion, or leveraged for the compounding of even greater influence. But once power and influence are lost or hidden, status is also lost—unless that power again becomes known, institutionalized, and thereby regularly revived or maintained through hierarchy. To the extent that power is made explicitly through transaction, it is not influence or status, but exchange. This exchange can, but need not, be between equals. Monopsonistic or monopolistic exchange, for example, creates hierarchies where it is regularized.[56]

Hierarchy is most obvious where codified by written rules. But, it can also be regularized by unwritten norms. For example, a political party might routinely choose a candidate of a particular identity to appeal to that segment of voters. When choosing a new member, a board of directors often chooses a close associate of theirs to ensure loyalty, strengthen their business network, and receive like favors in future. Professors are more likely to footnote professors at more prestigious universities to appear more learned or make friends in those universities who can then facilitate their lateral moves into higher-status institutions.

Individuals cooperate to gain power through reciprocal "altruism," preferencing family (kinship selection) or cloaking their self-interest in an ideological veneer that appeals to a larger identity or identities of which they are a part. Unwritten hierarchies apply to the left and the right, to communist and market economies, to religious and scientific organizations, and to non-profit as well as commercial corporations. Despite what factions tell people about their own "principled" political stands, politics tends to be identity based, as opposed to value based, because this is how individuals define themselves and others, and therefore this is the primary lever available to politicians and social entrepreneurs to gain supporters.

Hierarchy grows from a repeated power relationship and the lack of anonymity between adjoining nodes of the hierarchy itself. Those lower in the hierarchy—the subalterns—must know whom to follow; though, strictly speaking, they need not know who is below themselves but unconnected or who is two levels above. They must know who is directly above and directly below them to function in the hierarchy's interests without being ejected or demoted.

Leaders' lack of knowledge about the hierarchy reduces the efficiency of the hierarchy for all involved. This is especially the case for their subordinates, whose needs, other than what is necessary for the benefit of the leaders, can be ignored with impunity. The hierarchy and its leaders—including mid-level leaders—can obtain what they want from subordinates through the utilization of not only incentives, which most efficiently cater to subordinates' needs, but disincentives, the use of which is the naked exercise of power.

This power includes the utilization of force, which does not always create hierarchy, though force without hierarchy is rare. Consider the example of a kidnapper who offers to return a child to a parent if the parent pays a ransom. This is utilization of force by the kidnapper, but, if not regularized, it does not create a hierarchy. If the kidnapper regularly kidnaps children from a particular village, however, and the village decides to provide the kidnapper with regular payments of protection money to stop the kidnappings, power has been institutionalized and a hierarchy is created. Along with hierarchy comes status, even if that status is one of infamy.

A lack of hierarchy provides no status to the user of force. Consider the category of an anonymous one-time killer.[57] Those who interact with him (because most murderers are male) later do not know that he was a killer, and so the killer does not thereby gain infamy, and perceivers are not influenced by his prior killing. Even if they do know he killed, if they believe it was a one-time event it may not have a strong influence. However, mass killers who are known—for example, crime bosses— more easily influence the behavior of those around them because they are feared and expected to commit violence again. That fear derives from the repeated threat that the mob boss wields and the boss's lack of anonymity to those who fear him.

Perceivers, therefore, use their reason to anticipate and avoid their fears while satisfying their wants. Influence can thus derive from the expectation of disutility that flows from infamy, just as it can from the expectation of utility that flows from fame.

Take, as another example, an insurgent group, any member of which is empowered to kill a deserter on sight. In that instance, the group is above and holds power over the choices of the individual considering desertion. All may be equal in the group, but they are jointly and severally above the deserter—*ex ante* in the idea of a deserter and *ex post* in his actual execution. This is an ongoing and known power relationship among and between the insurgents on one side, and the deserter, or potential deserter, on the other, and is therefore hierarchical and effective at maintaining group cohesion.

Relative to the exercise of force, wealth and knowledge are more frequently utilized and sometimes shared anonymously and on a one-time basis, making their exercise more frequently non-hierarchical. In these instances, they transfer power without creating a hierarchical relationship. Conditioning the transfer of wealth or knowledge on exchange is a transactional manifestation of power by the original possessor. Such conditioning, if for a single transaction, does not create a hierarchy. More often than not, however, the transaction is repeated, and any power imbalance in the exchange—for example, where one side is wealthier or more knowledgeable than the other—is thereby institutionalized. When systematized, ritualized, or regularized, such conditioning in the context of inequality creates hierarchy, including where a monopoly or near-monopoly, or monopsony or near-monopsony, creates a power imbalance between the transacting parties.

Using wealth to regularly purchase the labor of another where there is high unemployment, for example, or using rare knowledge to regularly influence a decision-maker who becomes dependent on that knowledge, creates a hierarchy in which those who have scarce knowledge or wealth are, in that sense, above the decision-maker. Examples of such a systematization of the power of knowledge are the influence that the Empress Dowager Cixi had over her adopted son, the Guangxu Emperor at the turn of the nineteenth century; Grigori Rasputin had over Emperor

Nicholas II and Empress Alexandra of Russia in the same period; Henry Kissinger had over US President Richard Nixon in the late 1960s; and, according to some reports, Steve Bannon had over President Donald Trump in his 2016 campaign and the beginning of the presidency that followed.

Striving to climb the hierarchy and acquire and maintain ever more power appears to be sufficiently common as to provide enough supply of climbers for a selection effect that emplaces avaricious but capable individuals into the upper echelons of organizations, companies, bureaucracies, and governments. The more avaricious, capable, and risk acceptant, the more likely the individual is to climb, or to die trying. Since a large supply of such individuals are climbing, many such risk-acceptant individuals can fail in their attempts with one of their number still acquiring the leadership position. Thus, the higher one gets in the hierarchy, the more likely one is to meet the avaricious, capable, and risk acceptant. Even lower down in the hierarchy, however, one finds striving for advancement. Few "untouchables" in India do not want to escape their caste or rise to a caste of higher level. Which student does not want to progress a grade? Which janitor does not want a promotion to manager? Which country does not want to beat its near peers in gross domestic product (GDP) and military power? Very few, I would argue.

As people and organizations progress up the hierarchy, the competition becomes more severe and the tactics more ruthless. There are counterexamples. Some individuals, companies, countries, and other entities care less than others about rising. But these entities are, through their quiescence, usually relegated to the fringes of power and conflict throughout bureaucracies, economies, and international systems. Over their lifespans, the sum total of which makes up history, they are marginalized, discarded, or destroyed by the hierarchy. The victors then write them out of history.[58]

Contrary to the overly distinct theoretical categories in international relations scholarship of realism, liberalism, and constructivism, this book demonstrates that all of the variables championed by these theories matter. Economic power, military power, ideological power, and institutional power (treated in and of itself as a subset of ideological power, because all institutions are based on ideas) all have powerful effects on one another, on the historical development of hierarchy in general, on the acceleration of power concentration, and on contemporary international hierarchy in particular.

What is inadequately addressed in liberalism, constructivism, institutionalism, and realism is that all, or nearly all, entities in the international system seek to rise in the international hierarchy, and leaders (as well as those who fail in the attempt) are selected for risk-acceptance. Those not rising typically do not have the power to do so, or are strategically waiting for others to weaken one another and leave an easily filled power vacuum.

There are, of course, degrees of striving. Many individuals would not lie or cheat to rise. Even fewer would kill. But nation-states are different, and those whose greed exceeds these normative bounds by definition accept a risky historical selection effect that, if it does not kill them, enhances their rise in hierarchical environments. For every hundred avaricious risk-takers that fail, one succeeds. The millions of non-avaricious non-risk-takers never even try. They, therefore, stand next to no chance at climbing the highest heights of the hierarchy, even though their absolute numbers are greater.

CHAPTER 4

Origins of Hierarchy

There is controversy over whether the human drive for power and position in hierarchies and a sense of entitlement to those positions acquired—all of which result in the constitution of hierarchies—are common in most people and societies. The trope of a primitive equality and original absence of evil is clutched by religionists and reformers alike, from the Bible, through Jean-Jacques Rousseau, Lewis Henry Morgan, Karl Marx, and Friedrich Engels. These optimists claim (in sometimes contradictory ways) that humans are inherently good and cooperative, and thus capable of achieving a future egalitarian utopia, world of democracies, or heavenly end.[59]

This progress toward a future state of goodness and perfection is essential to the optimism that people tend to follow in leaders. After all, why follow leaders who are pessimistic about where they lead their flocks (or revolutionists)? Few believe that realistic pessimism will lead to a better place than the unrealistic optimism that ends in disaster due to ignorance, often willful in nature. Saying so is not a form of pessimism or catastrophism, but rather the offering of a simple warning: be careful of the bias in favor of optimism, search for subtle forms of dominance and hierarchy where egalitarianism is claimed, and take a fresh look at the direction that history is taking if you aspire, against all odds and common sense, to alter its course.

Despite occasional acts of altruism outside the family, the more generalized drive for individual and family power, dominance, opportunism, and position is evident in societies that are, today, succeeding by these metrics, as well as those that so succeeded throughout history. The drive for dominance and power, and the fear of violence and death—all within the context of hierarchy and coalition-building—is found in our primate ancestors,[60] market democracies in North America and Europe, and authoritarian communist countries like the USSR after 1917 and China after 1949. Even as individuals circumvent societal norms through corruption, and societies transform themselves to converge upon Keynesian or communist modalities in the late twentieth century, avarice, fear, and dominance persists.

Keynes and communism have, after all, been successful because they rationalize and justify what leaders already seek: more power. The same is true of fascism and totalitarianism. Whoever wins the ensuing fights among democracy, fascism, and communism, power still concentrates among the elites of the state or commercial varieties. Even if democracy wins for a time, economic and ideological power concentration makes that democracy increasingly at risk of an adverse regime change toward fascism or communism at some point in the future.

The Self, the Family, and the Origin of Politics

The fight for dominance within the Hierarchy is invariably one of greed over property, the origin of which is arguably deeply personal—rooted in our primate ancestors—and due to a consciousness and volition connected to the body and the ability to reproduce the body. Such reproduction was linked to control—which is akin to ownership—of material and human resources, including food, shelter, and other human beings.

The aggregation of political power started slowly. Seventy-two million years ago, the first primates likely lived lonely lives gathering food, only coming together briefly to mate. Fifty-two million years ago, primates began living in small multi-male/multi-female aggregations. Such aggregations can be seen as cultures or social technologies, invented by the individuals who constituted them. They were fitness-enhancing because in groups, they could outcompete the individual primates who were still loners. Such cooperative inventions were retained until later larger social and political units were invented that outcompeted the original smaller political units. This process continued through a ratchet of cultural, economic, and political transmission until the national and global political units of today.[61]

History at that earlier time, fifty-two million years ago, moved very slowly if measured by the rate of political aggregation. Primate dominance hierarchies developed, based on the physical stature of the males and their non-exclusive ability to socialize. Six million years ago, primates that would become humans, and those that became chimpanzees and bonobos, split from their common ancestor. Three million years later, hominins finally stood on two feet, developed hypercognition relative to other primates, and used primitive tools (though chimpanzees have also been observed with yet more primitive tools). Specialized tools used as weapons were created approximately two million years ago. Higher levels of human cognition were fitness-enhancing because they improved the ability to produce tools, compete and socialize within the band based on opportunism, and allowed more effective cooperation, labor specialization, and the greater articulation of hierarchies through cultures of limits, goals, incentives, and disincentives that could only be perceived at higher levels of intelligence. The larger the group and the greater its goals, the larger the brain size required to succeed as an individual and contribute to group success in competitions with other groups.[62]

Intragroup behaviors included pro-social sharing and leveling coalitions against strong leaders, including by females in what must have been the first example of an egalitarian social movement. Widely available weapons could be used against unpopular leaders to level power within the band. But such activity beyond incenting a distribution of food necessary for the mere survival of individuals, or the removal of ineffective leaders, would not be selected at the band level, as it would disorganize the group and hamper its ability to coordinate against other bands in the competition for scarce resources. More often, lower-ranking individuals in the band, such as women, could be denied the use of weapons, creating the first subordinated group based on ascriptive characteristics; with male members of the band supporting the dominant male in order to deconflict and strengthen hierarchical organization within the band, thereby more effectively achieving broader goals such as hunting large game, defending the band from outside threats, and defeating or combining with neighboring groups.[63]

One million years ago, hominins gained control of fire, thereby becoming yet more social, and aggressive where necessary. Cooperative hunting and breeding in small bands under dominant males expanded, as did warfare between bands. This proceeded in parallel with the origin of language between 700,000 and one million years ago, and the emergence of our species approximately 160,000 to 200,000 years ago. Archaeological evidence of violence arises from approximately 36,000 years ago, in Italy, Czechoslovakia, and Egypt. Australian rock art from 10,000 years ago depicts armed combat, with the number of combatants increasing by 4,000 years ago.[64] Thus, between the first primate, who typically foraged alone, to large-scale warfare of groups approximately 4,000 years ago, we already see the accelerating trend in history toward larger hierarchies that has, since the seventeenth century, resulted in remarkably large empires, alliance blocs, and international organizations that span the globe.

How did it all start? Our primate ancestors must have had a consciousness of their bodies, and some sense of defending the body as their own. This was arguably the first form of property—a feeling of ownership over one's own body. This property in the self was extended to foraged food and small and medium-sized game kills, which were soon to become part of the body and thus could already be considered part of the self, and therefore as a form of property. The property that resulted from violence over game extended over the millennia and development into hominins to a sense of property that resulted from the violent conquest of, or purchase of, other humans, probably first in the context of procreation. Thus, the male "conquest" of female sexual partners would likely be the first important feeling of property in one human over another. If this conquest came through a steady provision of goods, like food, then the female partner might have had a similar feeling of property in this revenue stream and its source, her male partner. This mutual feeling of property, shading into some feeling of love, might be the first form of monogamy or marriage.

As cognition developed, the physically larger male partners could start to see not only the conquered female's sexuality, but the female's nonsexual labor power as his own property. This subordination of the female in the male mind could then be extended by the dominant male in the band to a broader principle of human subordination, through the conquest or persuasion of not only a single female, but multiple females and males, through their subordination in accepting incentives, or fearing disincentives. The dominant male could then turn the subordination of labor power and revenue streams it produced, through a feeling of dominance and entitlement, into a sense of property over other human beings. This was arguably the origin of slavery, wage labor, and other forms of exploitation; for example, a division of foraged and hunted foods in a manner that advantages those higher in the band's dominance hierarchy.

Antoine-Louis-Claude, Comte Destutt de Tracy, was an early nineteenth-century French philosopher who argued that the individual,

> clearly sees that this *ego* is the exclusive owner of the body which it animates, the organs which it sets in motion, all their capacities, all their forces, all the effects they produce, all their passions and actions; for all this ends and begins with this ego, exists only through it, is set in motion through its action; and no other person can make use of these same instruments or be affected in the same way by them … nature has endowed man with an inevitable and inalienable property, property in the form of his own individuality.[65]

Property in humans, which is one early form of hierarchy, therefore, arguably started with the self, and extended through violence, persuasion, and the creation and reification of early dominance hierarchies. The self is closely tied to the family and band, which ethnographic and archaeological evidence shows was typically patriarchal in structure in an unbroken line from our primate ancestors to the earliest known human remains that indicate family and band social structure. Ethnographies show that the patriarchal family is one of close relations between father, son, and brothers, which form its core. The father has the preponderance of self-perceived reason, wealth, and physical power within the young patriarchal core and so takes the leadership position in the family and makes it his property. The origin of property is thus tied into the father's assertion of property and control over the family, which is, after all, the means and expression of his own genes.

Even as sons and brothers grow into adulthood and exceed the father in reason, wealth, or physical strength, the father still sees the family as property and is largely accepted as the patriarch. Only through the liberation of the sons and brothers through revolt against the father, or marriage and the establishment of new households, does the father lose his property in his sons, though he may still call on them as necessary to defend the assets of the family.

The patriarchal family, then, is not only one early form of property, but the initial political unit in that it defends itself from all who are foreign to the family. But it is not only defensive—the core of the patriarchal family can go on the offense to expand family assets in land, women, children, and slaves. This is achieved through the core's imposition of violence and capture against neighboring families and bands, including the capture of women to serve as wives to the core of the family, and the capture of entire families to provide economic rents through their enslavement or enserfment.

Male territorial violence, slavery, polygyny, and ownership of the family thus become endemic to not only a theorized origin of property, but scales through leadership of a clan or tribe, often captured through violence or war, and a sense of ownership or sovereignty over those "primitive" political units. Like other forms of ownership, such leadership of human groups and their territories become hereditary, based on conquest, and held by male chiefs, shamans, and kings. Property in the family and primitive territoriality is thus scaled and transformed into sovereignty over a band, clan, village, or kingdom.[66]

In prehistory, hunting skills and weapons double as means for the family core to defeat neighboring families, bands, and clans that also utilize hunting and gathering as a means of survival. Males monopolize use of weapons and training for combat and bond through the exclusion of women from male-centered socializing (e.g., secret societies and men's houses). Anthropologists William Divale and Marvin Harris analyzed 561 local band and village groups from 112 societies. They write, "the combat effectiveness of males is enhanced through their participation in competitive sports such as wrestling, racing, dueling, and many forms of individual and mock combat. Women seldom participate in such sports and to the best of our knowledge, almost never compete with men."[67]

Divale and Harris theorize that, due to the frequency of war in prehistoric and ethnographic societies, families and clans in band and village groups are incentivized to commit what is frequently observed in ethnographic studies: female infanticide. This maximized the chances of family survival by rearing the greatest number of male warriors. "Given warfare, males rather than females are trained to be fierce and aggressive because in hand combat with muscle-powered weapons the average height and weight advantage of males is decisive for individual and group survival," they write. "If women are to be the reward for military bravery, women must be reared to be passive and to submit to the decisions concerning the allocation of their sexual, productive, and reproductive services." Subordinate socialization conditions women for patrilocal marriage and their domination within the household. "Polygyny is the objectification of much of this system of rewards," they write. "At the same time, polygyny intensifies the shortage of females created by the postpartum manipulation of the sex ratio, producing positive feedback with respect to male aggressivity and fierceness, and encouraging combat for the sake of wife capture."[68]

Socialization leads men to serve as religious and political leaders, making the major decisions in most human societies, including those of indigenous hunter-gatherers.[69] Even some of the most egalitarian tribes, for example the Shoshone in the western US, had "bosses" or "headmen" who regulated information, hunting, and gathering. While many ethnographic accounts of nomadic hunting and foraging bands highlight the quantity of sharing as remarkably egalitarian, because they are seen through a Euro-centric lens accustomed to more obvious European forms of hierarchy and materialism, property and other forms of power are, in fact, typically stratified in these ethnographic accounts. For example, ethnographic studies of nomadic hunters indicate that they cannot carry much, and lacking refrigeration, their big game kills would rot if they did not share them with the tribe. Europeans who are ideologically predisposed to socialism can mistake this sharing for a primitive form of communism. However, there are subtle forms of property and rules on the division of kills, the sharing of which benefits male hunters through the status they receive, and resulting reciprocal altruism. See, for example, the subtle but very real and sometimes violent forms of hierarchy and private property among the !Kung tribe of South Africa, including a rule against women touching weapons, subordinate members of a hunt who get less meat and are not allowed to fire the first arrow—which is significant for the division of the meat—and the killing of a man for his theft of honey from a tree that was owned by another.[70]

Community property and natural resources—in the prehistoric and ethnographic context of a greater physical stature and musculature of the male, along with more aggressive male hormones—mean a more frequent *de facto* male attempt to assert property as the risks and opportunity costs for females asserting such property were greater.[71] The same applied to an assertion of property over the family, including children, with marriages typically determined by male heads of families, patrilocal exogamy (the woman moves from her community to that of the man), and a bride price or bride service paid to the bride's kin group by the husband's kin group. Such payments could turn wives into little more than the slaves of the men of the group. Perhaps as a result of bride prices and wife capture, almost all indigenous societies had a gendered division of labor in which men hunt, and thereby have control of the weapons, and women forage or farm.[72]

"Women in band and village societies are usually burdened with drudge work, such as seed grinding and pounding, fetching water and firewood, and carrying infants and household possessions," according to Divale and Harris. "Hunting with weapons is a virtually universal male specialty."[73]

The stature of men, and their organization into hunting parties and fighting groups for war, thus provided them with power and institutions for the domination of women in prehistoric family structures.[74] As the means of production and war became more technical and efficient, and leaders imposed political arrangements that broadened in scope from the family and tribe, to the kingdom and city-state, male institutional control scaled from women in the family to entire villages, kingdoms, and finally to states and empires. The original political violence, persuasion, and culture of wife capture was preserved and transmitted in the suffering and social contracts of states and empires that submitted to the conqueror of later millennia.

War, Contract, and State Formation

Starting at least in the eighteenth century, historians started to discuss gender in the context of societal origins. Italian philosopher Giambattista Vico wrote in his *New Science* (1725) that the original inhabitants of Europe, "in their bestial wandering," used their "enormous strength" to "penetrate the world's great forest ... As they fled from wild beasts and pursued timid women." The largest and strongest men chose to locate their families on defensible mountainsides. "They chose lands in naturally strong sites, which became the world's first citadels, *arces* in Latin," he writes. "Later, military engineers systematically fortified them, which is why the Italian word for fortress, *rocca*, derives from the word for a steep, rugged mountain, *roccia*." Plebeians, servants, and those who tilled the soil for the Italian noble lived in the valleys and fields.[75]

Organized violence in hunter-gatherer periods was less frequent and developed than in agricultural societies, because when faced with conflict, hunter-gatherers could more easily flee toward other relatively abundant natural resources than fight. Nevertheless, hunter-gatherers do attack and eradicate neighboring bands and villages, just as do the chimpanzee groups that share 99 percent of human genes.[76]

As agricultural, fishing, and trading technologies improved, the community invested labor and resources in a particular location or trade route. Conflicts developed over agricultural land, river, and marine resources, and over the tools and objects of trade. Those conflicts, including attempts by hunter-gatherers to dominate agriculturalists,[77] as presaged by Vico, turned into wars. Winning wars required deeper exploitation of the economic and human resources of the community, including through conscription, enslavement, and the production of specialized weapons and fortifications. And, frequent war made defensible sites an additional resource over which to compete, leading to additional wars.

Organized violence is by no means a constant in the archaeological evidence of band and village level societies, but it is found widely at a rate that is typically not more than once every two years.[78] Some of the worst violence found by archaeologists is that in the *Linearbandkeramik* Culture (LBK) of early Neolithic Central Europe. The digs indicate labor specialization as herders and cultivators on hereditary lines, social differences linked to immigration patterns, and fractious borders, evidenced by different flint trading networks. Archaeologists found evidence that with the onset of agriculture came an increase in collective violence, defensive architecture, warfare for land with loess soil, and the massacre and torture of entire LBK communities of thirty to forty people (except for the young women, who were abducted).[79]

The LBK provides evidence for the hypothesis that climatic changes are a source of instability and organized human violence and, therefore, of hierarchy and state formation. War and climatic changes are both a subset of uncertainty and risk, which is arguably a key early source of hierarchies of voluntary contract. Individuals seek and find security in the social organization that makes the whole stronger than the sum of its parts, and a maximin payoff that ensures survival, if not plenty. According to archaeologists Christian Meyer et al.,

> … climatic changes, especially those leading to increasing unpredictability of or even significant decreases in agricultural production, have played major roles in the change and collapse of societies throughout human history. Ecological imbalance and perceived or actual resource stress were … some of the main reasons for massacres and warfare in general, and at the end of the LBK aggression might have been aggravated further by patrilineally determined social inequality, especially with regard to access to coveted, high-quality farmland, food, and possibly prestige goods.[80]

Thus, instability creates greater demand for resources, which heightens conflict, leading to heightened instability. Individuals flee into hierarchies and defensible territories during these periods of instability, from which they fight other hierarchies for scarce resources. Social hierarchies and defensible territories are thus the first military technologies subject to the security dilemma—developing technology for one's own security decreases the security of others and causes them to build their own security technologies, decreasing the security of all.

All of the necessaries of life were needed for warfare, including the scarce resource of water, which required sharing or rationing, potentially through making it the property of a single leader. Water sources are the site of early political organization, according to Vico. "Political thinkers had these perennial springs in mind when they wrote that the communal sharing of water was the occasion for the first families uniting," writes Vico. "Hence, the Greeks called their first communities *phratríai*, clans, from *phrear*, well, or *phreatía*, cistern. In Latin, an early village was called *pagus*, and the Doric Greeks called a spring *paga*."[81]

Historical hierarchy within the family—including, typically, male ownership of water sources, land, women, and slaves—has been accentuated over time due to the hierarchy's ratchet effect that utilizes its own power to further concentrate power and wealth. However, anti-slavery and women's liberation movements of the eighteenth to twentieth centuries advanced principles of free association of individuals in family and economic life—for those who could afford to choose their associates. While this ascriptive liberation has begun to affect political life globally, millions of years of hierarchical animal and household relationships at the band and village levels conditioned human genetic selection and composition, and thus ingrained a patriarchal form of hierarchy in human psychology such that the projection of that hierarchy to higher political levels of tribe, state, and beyond is accepted as male and "natural," and continues apace. Females who climb the hierarchy often adopt male symbology and behavior. Attempts to transform the hierarchy into female-led feminized or feminist forms by capturing its leadership positions, and making it more egalitarian, is still relatively uncommon.

Those who fail to comply with patriarchal notions of hierarchy tend to be selected out of the hierarchy, and the population. As much as contemporary academics like to deny evolution when it comes to social matters, those individuals in history who rejected all hierarchy perforce rejected coordinated family or band activity in emergencies, and thus would be rejected by such hierarchies as non-performers and non-contributors. This rejection would have made them social outsiders if not outcasts, and vulnerable to weather, exploitation, and violence. They would have had more difficulty in reproducing, and other, more hierarchically acceptant, neutral, or supportive, individuals would have succeeded and reproduced, including culturally, in their place. Thus, the history of individual liberation from hierarchy is as rare as it is celebrated. Noble acts of liberation do occur, but they are contrary to the general trends of broader and deeper hierarchy in society, and are typically used by surviving forms of hierarchy as self-justifications that facilitate their growth.

Thus, we can reject certain theories associated with utopianism, socialism, and communism that humans evolved from primate dominance hierarchies to egalitarian hunter-gatherers, or into societies with gender equality (gylany) where the historical record is conveniently scanty, and then back to male-dominated hierarchies on their way to a future liberation of workers and women. Given what is now a more detailed archaeological, ethnographic, and historical record, and evidence of not only political and ideological but increased economic concentration of power over time, these theories beg credulity.[82]

As the record shows, hierarchy and violence have almost always, if not always, powerfully affected animal and human relationships and societies. Violence has fundamentally affected family relationships, and war has played a central role in state formation in the Middle East, Europe, Africa, Polynesia, and the Americas.[83] History is the gradual and accelerating aggregation of smaller and more personalistic hierarchies, starting at the family level, into larger, less diverse, more sophisticated, more anonymous, and more personally articulated layers and forms of national and international hierarchy—albeit sometimes with greater rights for the individual imposed through the skimming of power from mediate levels of the hierarchy.

CHAPTER 5

Functions of Hierarchy

Hierarchy is often forced, but it develops more consensually and functionally where completion of a coordinated task is required for which there is insufficient time for group deliberation, or for which secrecy is required. The paramount such example is war, which Plutarch likens to a storm at sea for which a captain is needed to make split-second decisions. He discusses the campaign of Pelopidas and Epaminondas against Sparta in the fourth century BCE.

> He took many of the enemy's cities, and ravaged all their territory as far as the sea, leading an army of seventy thousand Greeks, of which the Thebans themselves were less than a twelfth part. But the reputation of the two men, without a general vote or decree, induced all the allies to follow their leadership without a murmur. For the first

and paramount law, as it would seem, namely, that of nature, subjects him who desires to be saved to the command of the man who can save him; just as sailors, when the weather is fair or they are lying off shore at anchor, treat their captains with bold insolence, but as soon as a storm arises and danger threatens, look to them for guidance and place their hopes in them. And so Argives, Eleans, and Arcadians, who in their joint assemblies contended and strove with the Thebans for the supremacy, when battles were actually to be fought and perils to be faced, of their own will obeyed the Theban generals and followed them.[84]

Hierarchy in these situations was apparently voluntarily adopted to extricate the group safely from an emergency.

Anthropologists have found that many in the communities that they study revere and value hierarchy for these and other reasons. "While individualism and egalitarianism are central to Western conceptions of justice and the good, many people in hierarchical societies see them [individualism and egalitarianism] as immoral and destructive, as eroding the relationships that make meaningful personhood possible," write anthropologists Naomi Haynes and Jason Hickel. They cite anthropological studies in which Zambians and South Africans resist the erosion of family and seniority hierarchies, for example.[85] Graeber states that case studies have found that hierarchy "is often considered a good thing, even a value in itself … Some resist power structures not in the name of opposition to power itself, but in order to restore more familiar forms of hierarchy or utopian hierarchical visions (whether set in the future or in the past)."[86]

Marx and Hegel should be included among these utopians for their belief in a future benign autocracy. But like Vico, Hegel saw an idyllic and pre-hierarchical "state of nature" with "natural rights" as a fiction. A political state of legality is not a restriction on liberty and natural rights, for Hegel, but an escape from the violence of nature. He writes, "the whole law and its every article are based on free personality alone—on self-determination or autonomy, which is the very contrary of determination by nature. The law of nature—strictly so called—is for that reason the predominance of the strong and the reign of force, and a state of nature a state of violence and wrong, of which nothing truer can be said than that one ought to depart from it. The social state, on the other hand, is the condition in which alone right has its actuality: what is to be restricted and sacrificed is just the wilfulness and violence of the state of nature."[87] This was surely not the perspective of many slaves in ancient societies, for example, or those suffering under contemporary forms of forced labor. But it might have been the perspective of many at medium levels of the hierarchy, and above.

Hierarchy does in fact serve some functions that serve those beyond just the elites, including coordination, specialization, deconfliction, communication, and security. Decision-making is less time-consuming when a single leader makes broad policy goals, delegates to a handful of lieutenants to implement, and the lieutenants delegate further to up to millions of laborers, soldiers, and others to actually execute policy. Attempting to involve all these millions in every decision could hamstring the organization, though contemporary information technology holds out some alluring possibilities for more decentralization.

Leaders resolve internal conflicts, engender specialized cells for particular tasks, sequence operations, establish chains of communication, specify and enforce rules for intraorganizational cooperation and competition, and capture control of other hierarchies to neutralize threats and realize economies of scale.[88]

Vico saw hierarchy as providing a means for society to evolve into societal forms of justice, from prior personalistic forms in which individual force asserted claims, rather than claims being decided by appeal to law. Duels and private wars, rather than law enforcement, "righted" private wrongs to gain restitution in the anarchic past. After the Middle Ages, "the ferocity of the age diminished, and judicial laws began to prohibit private acts of violence, so that all private forces were united in the public force called civil sovereignty."[89]

Civil sovereignty deconflicts factions within society and frees resources for greater economic differentiation. This social complexity expands more readily in large populations where such economies of scale can be realized. It lends itself to hierarchy, because political coordination (the ownership of property is originally and vestigially political) maximizes its gains. But, social complexity is not necessarily hierarchical. A diversified economy with skill specialization could, in theory, exist without hierarchy if concentration of wealth was not imposed by force in advance and did not thereafter emerge through market forces.

However, such lack of hierarchy in human societies is so rare, halting, and small scale as to have almost no effect on the unfolding of history. Where an effect from lack of hierarchy as hierarchy can be found, it is typically ideological and ephemeral in that non-hierarchies are outcompeted by hierarchies. Hierarchies have the advantage of enforced cooperation, which is critical in war and leads less-liberal hierarchies to outcompete liberal hierarchies. This dynamic holds great dangers for our current age.

Where piecemeal reforms are made to hierarchy—as in Robert Owen's experiments with socialistic industrial and village organization at the turn of the nineteenth century—there are, at the same time, new hierarchical forms that arise. Owen was paternalistic, a critic of democracy, and familial in his utopian political beliefs. He believed in a benevolent hierarchy in service to egalitarian principles. These beliefs spawned, and developed in the context of, his utilization of his property in a textile mill in Scotland. There he imposed his social engineering on workers and their families, forbidding children less than ten to work, and placing them instead into free company schools. These schools had a salutary effect on the children, including through a pedagogical emphasis on dance and music, but they were a new form of hierarchy imposed from above. In his factory, Owen furthermore instituted a public scoring system to increase the output of workers and shorten their working day. But this, too, was an imposition from above that did not really change the hierarchy of factory owner and factory workers. Nor did it adversely change Owen's profits, which rose due to his social reforms. Owen also provided free healthcare to his workers. Thus, the Owenite experiments—which are broadly seen as a model of reform even today—were facilitated by existing forms of hierarchy in the form of property, and constituted new hierarchies that improved the lives of workers and children, while continuing to control them through novel hierarchical forms. Even as progress was made, hierarchy evolved and retained control. Power did not deconcentrate.[90]

The functions of hierarchy detailed above are near timeless and apply in greater or lesser measure—and with positive and negative effects—to societies ranging from the Qin Dynasty that unified China in the third century BCE, to the EU of today. Democracies, too, are hierarchical— just less so, or in different ways—than autocracies. The conflict between democracy and autocracy is thus not necessarily one in which a win for democracy is a win against hierarchy; though, in some cases—for example, against fascist or communist dictators—it typically would be. Rather, a win for democracy would typically be a win for a different type of hierarchy that improves life for those at lower and middling levels in the hierarchy without necessarily diminishing the quality of life for those at high positions in the hierarchy. Democratization is a Pareto improvement for all levels in the hierarchy, including autocrats, as autocracy dehumanizes them through their dehumanization of others.

Hierarchies that lose in competitions with other hierarchies, sometimes because they are too decentralized in their decision-making, and those individuals within losing hierarchies, become subservient as subalterns or sub-hierarchies and pay the cost. Winning hierarchies are rewarded with further resources, which make them more likely to win in the future, and losing hierarchies lose resources, making it harder for them to climb out of subalternity. This constitutes path dependence or a feedback loop (both positive and negative) in the long-term determination of leaders and followers in hierarchies and meta-hierarchies (explained below).

For example, a national sports team that loses a championship can lose financial sponsors, air-time, and influence, as can individuals within those teams. Fewer sponsors mean less money to sign the best players in the next season. Winning and losing are path dependent and regularized, and lead to enduring winners at the top of the sporting hierarchy and enduring losers at the bottom. Losing teams can lose their financing, and star players, to winning teams.

The same logic applies to the concentration of intellectual power in leading universities, the concentration of economic power in leading investment firms, and the concentration of political power in the capitals of leading empires and alliance blocs. Success breeds success, and failure leads to a degradation of power, and the risk of enduring subordination.

An army that loses a battle against another army could be slaughtered to the man as were the Spartans who knew they had volunteered their own deaths when they volunteered to defend the pass at Thermopylae against a vastly more powerful Persian army in 480 BCE. Or, losers could be incorporated into the conquering army as were defeated foes of the expanding Roman Empire. So, even as hierarchy exploits individual members to the point of exhaustion or death, hierarchy can protect group members as a whole and incorporate, through conquest, those outside the hierarchy.

Japanese kamikaze flyers and British soldiers during World War II who volunteered for dangerous, near-suicidal missions did so for the hierarchies that they were members of, and for the broader interests, values, and expansion of the identities that their hierarchies claimed to represent and protect. Almost always, individuals who sacrifice for a hierarchy do so for their own hierarchy rather than the hierarchy of others, due to a sense of loyalty or identity with that particular hierarchy that stands for a particular identity or system of values. These ascriptions or near-ascriptive values are seen as functional beyond the hierarchy itself, providing identity and value to the individual or community that the hierarchy "serves."

Whether the winning hierarchy is authoritarian or democratic in its values, at this late point in the evolution of hierarchy, will have great effects on the future, as winning yields power, which helps win the next conflict. Winning, the institutionalization of power, and thus hierarchy are all path dependent. The closer the world gets to unipolarity, the fewer future wins, and the more consequential such wins become. This is the acceleration of history, in which later wins are more consequential for the rest of history than are early wins.

CHAPTER 6

Structure of Hierarchy

As the psychology of politics is historically patterned from the ancient patriarchal structure of family and clan, those hierarchies that more closely resemble familial and clan hierarchies through personal forms of leadership and *esprit de corps* are more successful, all else equal.[91] Where scarce resources are more concentrated, hierarchy develops to a greater degree through capture and then compacts meant to deconflict, or where those fail, through conflict itself.

Killing an enemy is the ultimate form of deconfliction. Those hierarchies more adept at killing, unfortunately, tend to have the ultimate disincentive at hand to more effectively structure future forms of hierarchy. Thus, the course of history has been a continual subordination of those less adept at, less interested in, or more against the use of violence.

In hierarchy, those at the top are expected to sacrifice as do those at the bottom, though such leaders usually benefit more and take less risk. Where identity of the hierarchy is unclear or fractured, leaders maximize their gain and the cohesion of their organizations by seeking to synchronize political values into one unitary value system. Alexander the Great's temporary unification of an empire stretching from Egypt to India illustrates these principles. He led his troops into battle on horseback and was wounded in the process. This bravery and self-sacrifice was utilized by himself and his followers to cement loyalty to Alexander as a symbol of the hierarchy to which he wanted them to belong, as opposed to the sometimes competing values found in the Greek state back home, and the newly conquered societies.

Alexander the Great was born in Macedonia, located between Athens and Persia. After conquering Persia, he sought a military and cultural synthesis between Greece and the conquered civilization in the east. His Greek generals did not. Indoctrination into the goodness of the Greek system, demonization of competing hierarchies, and an attempt to maintain privileges of the in-group against the out-group led to their individual sacrifice in conquering an empire for Alexander, but not the sharing of power once acquired. They excluded Alexander's Persian allies, and when he died, they divided the empire among themselves.[92]

Such exclusion of the conquered from a hierarchy is in the interests of elites who seek to increase their own power by controlling, rather than merging with, other hierarchies. They would prefer total control over their own independent hierarchy to serving in a sub-hierarchy of a greater whole for a greater, though likely more distant, purpose. This tension between dominant and subordinate units, for and against hierarchical consolidation, is common.

The British and French Empires faced a similar problem where the center sought to treat the indigenous populations more gently in the interests of unity or deconfliction, than did the European generals and farmers who lived in, imposed sub-hierarchies upon, and sought to exploit the conquered territories to the fullest extent. This often resulted in a cascade of revolts wherein European colonists sought greater independence from European capitals the more thoroughly to exploit their indigenous populations, which, in turn, revolted against them and the empire as a whole. Lack of colonial discipline at the ground level doomed entire empires.

Meta-Hierarchy

This chapter has thus far largely dealt with hierarchies as separate and competing, but, in fact, hierarchies are interlinked in what can be visualized as a single whole. We can think of the sum total of all interlinked hierarchies as *The Hierarchy*, which, to the extent it is not singular today, tends increasingly toward singularity: a unipolar world composed of an interlinked *meta-hierarchy* of competing global power centers.

When hierarchies compete they often seek to conquer one another or climb over one another in *meta-hierarchies*, defined here as hierarchies composed of other hierarchies. Individuals within a company compete with one another to lead the company, but the company sees these competitors as integral to the company's success. Companies launch hostile takeovers of one another with the help of capital from banks. But banks need the entire field of competing companies in order to pick the winners and maximize profit. Banks compete for political influence in their capital city, which sees all of the banks as important in growing the economy and maximizing tax collection.[93]

Nations compete to lead international organizations, which ostensibly see them all as necessary (though not necessarily in their current form) for achieving higher purposes such as diversity, democracy, global peace, public health, and efficient international trade. Hierarchies are not just competing with one another. They are self-organizing into meta-hierarchies in order to enhance their competitiveness against other hierarchies and meta-hierarchies. These meta-hierarchies are now global in scope, and their component parts at each level down are in a constant state of competition that sometimes devolves into a war against all.

Types of Hierarchy

Each form of power, and thus hierarchy, can be thought of on two axes, including their physicality and frequency of use. As shown in Table 1, force is the most physical of powers, but the least frequently used. Force can degrade economic and informational power through, for example, war, armed burglary, and anti-sedition laws, and killing those with whom the forceful individual disagrees. While this kind of force attracts journalistic and historical attention, it occurs relatively infrequently. The institutionalization of force through taxation is arguably the most frequent utilization of force, including through sales tax applied to daily purchases. The international corollary to taxation is the institutionalization of unequal conditions on a subordinate polity. For example, an imperial power can enforce payment of tribute, resource extraction, forced land transfers, usurious interest rates, privileges for an imperial elite, mercantile trade relations, or high customs duties against a conquered territory. This is done through not only the original military defeat of the territory, but the compromise of the territory's leaders through subsequent incentives and disincentives imposed by the conqueror or imperial power.

	Physicality	Frequency
Political-military	High	Low
Economic	Medium	Medium
Information	Low	High

Table 1: The physicality and frequency of power

The power of wealth is moderately physical in that, for example, a purse full of currency is possessed in the hand, and protected by the force of the hand and other means at the possessor's disposal. Possession is nine-tenths of the law, according to the saying, and that nine-tenths is physical. That physicality of wealth is transferred to banks as the wealth grows, and to digital currencies as the global economy undergoes the information revolution. The largest transactions are now done electronically, whether that be large bank transfers, frequent credit card use, or the increasing utilization of crypto- and other digital currencies. Over twelve months between 2019 and 2020, China experienced $50 billion in capital flight via crypto-currencies such as Bitcoin and Tether.[94] At the same time, it is the most prominent country to adopt its own state-backed digital currency, through which it seeks a first-mover advantage against all other countries, including Britain, which is likewise considering its own digital currency.[95] Wealth is ever more high frequency and granular in the part it plays in our increasingly small-scale but frequent purchases and reception of income.

But the transfer of information is more frequent still. Each individual with a smartphone—and they are proliferating in developing countries, too, especially due to smartphone use for financial payments where banks are scarce—is bombarded digitally with dozens, sometimes thousands, of micro-targeted electronic notifications daily through social media, emails, and apps that can track and store individual movement, buying, browsing, speech, and text in order to predict consumer preferences. The thoughts of each individual, at arguably every moment of the day and night, are subject to being channeled by this information stream that splinters into individualized digital *epistemes* to fit each category of user, based on that user's unique interaction of identities and behaviors.

Yet, for all its frequency, information is the least physical of the three forms of power. So there is some parity when averaging the two metrics for each form of power, with force hierarchies reinforced through physicality but infrequently, economic hierarchies reinforced through transaction relatively frequently, and informational hierarchies lacking physicality but reinforced almost constantly through digital delivery, thought, and speech processes. The consequences of each type of power are, therefore, on some theoretical level equal, because they are the interaction of negatively correlated physicality and frequency. The interactions of these types of power, at the personal, national, and international levels, can be considered a network theory of power, and a ranking of hierarchies and their interactions.

Force, wealth, and information hierarchies are interlinked and overlapping. The analytic division of power into three types that correspond with three types of hierarchy is arbitrary, with the number of categories dependent upon the epistemological purpose. Some like Hans J. Morgenthau, who sought to emphasize the importance of soft power to a military audience in 1963, divided power into just two kinds: military and non-military.[96] Others who engage in comprehensive military planning divide power into many more categories, such as the US Joint Forces Command groupings of political, military, economic, social, infrastructure, and information (PMESII).[97] There is theoretically an unlimited number of types into which power can be divided.

A division of power into just three forms, political, economic, and information, however, provides a good balance between simplifying abstraction and necessary specificity for the purposes of this theory.

While normally the political (including military) types of power are associated with people, including their economic and ideological activities, it is best to first examine that which is political in hierarchy as distinct from the economic and ideological elements of politics, addressed later. The power associated with politics as distinct from information and economics is a power associated with persons in their physical rather than economic or informational sense. Political power is, therefore, in its purest form, a power of physical force. When institutionalized, that force becomes a police or military power controlled by political (including military) leaders. Individuals with political power as distinct from economic or informational power are predominantly those associated with government, including legislators or high government officials, who exercise their power through laws or regulations that ultimately depend upon the threat of force. However, they can also be social movement leaders who threaten the government with physical overthrow, for example, or who do actually overthrow a government.

According to the sociologist Max Weber in his 1918 lecture "Politics as a Vocation," the state is defined as having a "monopoly" on the "legitimate" use of violence within a given territory.[98] In reality, there is never a monopoly on the legitimacy of violence, as that legitimacy is always contested, including almost always by the individual upon whom violence is imposed, and through micro-utilization of criminal and social movement forms of force and violence. Socrates, who willingly took the hemlock to his lips, was the exception to the rule, and was celebrated by rulers throughout the world.

Legitimacy is typically self-defined, as many within and outside a country's territory may disagree that a government's use of force—for example, to commit human rights abuse—is legitimate. Secondary forms of political hierarchy can be found within the boundaries of a "state," including in social movements or political parties that have the power to potentially take control of government through overthrow or election, and rebel or criminal networks that impose rules on those over whom they hold sway in a sub- or quasi-governmental manner. In practice, we normally equate the utilization of large-scale violence, such as the largest troop concentrations in an area, matched with international recognition of the often civilian leaders of those troops, as conferring state status. A "monopoly" of legitimate force is a convenient and simplifying myth that nation-states grant to one another in order to mutually exclude competitors for power within their geographies.

Political hierarchy is defined here as that hierarchy dependent upon force. Force in its most elemental form is the physical control of one person over another, and does not include informational (e.g., cultural) or economic forms of power.[99] Such force can also be thought of as the power to deprive individuals of security, and therefore the ability to incentivize them with the promise of security, or disincentivize them with the deprivation of security (for example, by imposing violence on an individual). The power of force aggregates through its institutionalization to become military power, police power, or on less-serious levels, the power of a sports team such as rugby or football of the American or Australian variety. Force can also be the power that a manager has over an employee to fire that individual and remove him or her bodily from their employment, or the physical power required to evict the tenant from his tenancy. These relatively familiar forms of force serve as a psychological or epistemological template for the national leader in addressing international hierarchy based on war rather than sports, control over a nation's population rather than control over employees or tenants, and a sense of ownership of national territory through sovereignty as patterned after ownership of assets, including land and slaves, through property.

The power of a manager over an employee or landlord over tenant is at the same time interlinked with the power of wealth. The employee would not typically work for the manager without a wage, and the tenant has a contract with the landlord that is ostensibly based on free choice in a free market. Such spatial forms of commercial hierarchy have an element of force, however, because they are backed by the security guard or police officer who implicitly threatens to eject employees from their workplace and tenants from their home. Identity hierarchies such as those based on the intersections of race, gender, or sexuality have been maintained by all three types of power. The intersections of commercial and physical force hierarchies are clear; for example, where territory is conquered and inhabitants made into slaves, as after the Danish conquest of England in 1016 CE,[100] or where, in antiquity, raiding parties would attack their neighbors to carry away women as the Romans did against the Sabines.[101]

In the case of slavery, we have a form of hierarchy that is simultaneously economic and intrinsically dependent upon force. Forcing or selling women into marriage has been a common historical practice, including among royals for economic and military purposes, and continues today among the global poor. It entails elements of political, economic, and knowledge power in that women might not only be sold against their will, but then be dependent upon the husbands for their livelihoods and fall in love, as reportedly in the case of the Sabine women and hostages taken during the 1973 Stockholm bank robbery. That Plutarch could describe the rape of the Sabines as not dishonorable shows the power of knowledge in the hierarchy imposed upon women, including into the future, as Plutarch was adopted into the canon of Western literature and philosophy.[102] On the international level, slavery and the imposition of spatial control through force and wealth is echoed in patriarchal, colonial, and imperial relations between countries and subject populations that are used by imperial centers for the purposes of expansion and economic exploitation.

Closely related to the power of force, in societies with paid employment, tenancy, and slavery, is the economic hierarchy dependent upon pure economic power, which is wealth. The power of wealth is the power that money, property, and other readily fungible assets possess to incentivize behavior that is to the advantage of the owner of that wealth, including the ability to incentivize individuals to surrender their agency to the holder of wealth in exchange for the promise of reward. While force can be used to steal wealth, the latter is more frequently used, on a daily basis, and can buy force in the form of security guards, and politicians who control police departments and armies. Powerful countries can influence the use of force by the UN, for example, through their ability to propose and veto such force on the UN Security Council (UNSC), but also through buying support among countries that vote on the UNSC as non-permanent members. Purchasing the votes of non-permanent developing country UNSC members can be done through international aid or bribing the national leaders of a country.

According to two government sources of mine, purchases of influence among heads of state and cabinet-level ministers of developing countries are routinely achieved by the Chinese government. Through buying itself into informational hierarchies, wealth can also condition beliefs in a way that compels willing consent to transactions and political hierarchies that would not otherwise be accepted.[103]

Informational hierarchy is dependent upon the power of knowledge, which is the most frequent of the three types of power in that it influences behavior on a constant basis and sometimes permanently through convincing the follower according to its component parts: theory and data. Informational hierarchy manifests in various forms, including through the perception of values, religious texts, hypotheses, news media, mathematical theory, and statistical analysis, all of which require the two component parts of theory and data to convince the audience. Information need not be true to have an effect, as the increasing awareness of fake news makes clear. Informational hierarchy is found in fiction and non-fiction writing, and institutionalized through, for example, media, academic, and religious organizational hierarchies that transcend international boundaries.

Wherever power of the political, economic, and informational types is institutionalized, those at the bottom of the hierarchy may feel a sense of loyalty, piety, or awe for those at the top. This loyalty is the result of the ideology that the hierarchy utilizes to obtain consent. The freed American slave Sojourner Truth explained in 1850 how some slaves adopted the perspective of the master (the ideology of slavery from the master's perspective) while others rejected it.

> Her [the slave named Isabel or Isabella's] ambition and desire to please were so great, that she often worked several nights in succession, sleeping only short snatches, as she sat in her chair; and some nights she would not allow herself to take any sleep, save what she could get resting herself against the wall, fearing that if she sat down, she would sleep too long. These extra exertions to please, and the praises consequent upon them, brought upon her head the envy of her fellow-slaves, and they taunted her with being the *white folks'* [racial epithet removed].' On the other hand, she received the larger share of the confidence of her master, and many small favors that were by them unattainable. I asked her if her master, Dumont, ever whipped her? She answered, 'Oh yes, he sometimes whipped me soundly, though never cruelly. And the most severe whipping he ever give me was because *I* was cruel to a cat.' ... She then firmly believed

that slavery was right and honorable. Yet she *now* sees very clearly
the false position they were all in, both masters and slaves; and she
looks back, with utter astonishment, at the absurdity of the claims so
arrogantly set up by the masters, over beings designed by God to be
as free as kings; and at the perfect stupidity of the slave, in admitting
for one moment the validity of these claims.[104]

The slave described here appears to love her master like a God,
when she believed in the hierarchy in which he was the apex. When her
belief wavered, so did her love, and the ideological basis of the hierarchy
vanished for her.[105]

Two elements of knowledge hierarchies rarely analyzed as such are
the power of love and the knowledge of hierarchy itself. The power of
platonic, familial, and romantic love—which has so much sway over
individuals—is a subset of the power of knowledge, because we cannot
feel in a religious, familial, or romantic sense without knowing. This
power of love is distinct from the transactional elements of marriage,
or of prostitution, though love can be a part of either arrangement, as
the transactional element does not necessarily obviate love, which can,
in part, be constituted by an exchange of two kinds of power. And, the
power of love can transcend that between two individuals to affect the
union of nations and royal houses. The love between Antony and Cleo-
patra makes clear the importance of love to international hierarchies in
the ancient world. With the transition of hierarchy from royal dynastic
lineages up to the nineteenth century, to democratically elected leaders
in the twentieth century, elite women have arguably lost a pathway to
power through royal family life even as other paths to power—including
universal female suffrage, women's participation in the workplace, and
election to national office—opened up to them. Given women's power
in royal families, democracy and universal suffrage did not necessarily
increase the political influence of women.

As with one element of love, the power of hierarchy separated
from force, wealth, and privileged access to information is a subset of
knowledge. Institutionalization of power requires *knowledge* of a hierarchical structure, which is an informational construction supported by
the power of force and wealth, admittedly, but not always dependent
on these elements as it is on elements of information like representa-

tion and symbology of hierarchical structure, religion, law, and rules. An organizational chart that depicts a hierarchy at the workplace is a form of information that then influences how individuals interact with one another in ways that institutionalize power and are quite distinct from the force and wealth that underlay a hierarchy. Value hierarchies, too, are forms of information, or, more specifically, moral philosophies, that do not always depend on force or wealth, yet have a strong influence on individual behavior.

Knowledge operates through influence, force is a matter of physics and operates through the application of that force, and wealth operates through transaction. Knowledge here signifies all things having to do with the mind that are not physical, including psychology. Force and knowledge can be commoditized for utilization in a transaction, but once the transaction is complete, their use reverts to their physical and influence forms. Force and wealth, too, can influence behavior but only through *knowledge* of that force and wealth; where force and wealth are used directly they impose their outcome through application of force and transaction, not influence. Where trespassers are physically removed from land, they are forced off, for example. Where trespassers decide to leave under their own power but due to the threat of removal, force is used to influence their will and actions. Strictly speaking, deterrence in international relations is likewise always achieved through knowledge, not application, of force. When actual use of force, rather than its threat, is required, deterrence has failed. Even the knowledge of actual use of force in prior or alternate situations is a knowledge of force, not the actual use of force in a present situation of a deterred individual. This influence in the case of force is the power of coercion or duress and operates indirectly through knowledge of the threat of force. Making such deterrence credible may require occasional or credible use of force. However, deterrence alone is based on the knowledge of that credibility. Where there is no knowledge of credibility, there is no deterrence.

All three types of power are multipliers of one another and institutionalized in interlinked hierarchies of force, wealth, and knowledge. Wealth supports knowledge hierarchies that, in turn, support economic and political hierarchy. In ancient Athens, religion was embedded in the *polis* through state decrees regarding religion and its finance.[106] The first universities—for example at Bologna and Oxford—were supported by the wealth of a city and pope in the case of Bologna, and king in the case of Oxford, and each university was expected, and did, to a certain degree serve the interests of the wealth that founded and supported them.

Subordination and Privilege

Most of the world's populations are marginal to power. They are nowhere near the global corporations, superpowers, elite universities, and international institutions that form the peaks of the global hierarchy. They instead find themselves subordinated within micro-hierarchies, as servants to poor families, or low-level menial employees, who produce a bare subsistence not only for themselves but for their bosses. One cannot understand the vast preponderance of hierarchy, then, without understanding the positions of these subalterns, including the hierarchies that they form in order to better themselves. These sub-hierarchies are found in marginalized economies, religions, social movements, ideologies, and identities.

Their loss of power in the hierarchy is particularly acute at its intersections, including, for example, poverty, refugee status, person of color, woman, and transgender. This is the insight of intersectional theory. The compounding extremes of subordination and privilege drive yet more subordination and privilege in an increasing concentration and institutionalization of power over time, as theorized above. Intersectional, race, gender, and third-world theorists such as Kimberlé Crenshaw, bell hooks, Chandra Talpade Mohanty, and others should therefore be read as a complement to this book, for a deeper understanding of these particular kinds of hierarchies, and how they intersect the leading informational, economic, and political-military hierarchies focused upon here.[107]

Conversely, the accentuation of power in the hierarchy is particularly strong at the intersections of privilege; for example, a wealthy white male jet-setter. Increasingly, wealthy East Asian and Middle Eastern jet-setters are also at the highest intersections of privilege. China's elites will resist this identification of their privilege, because they are still in the process of claiming themselves as a humiliated and underprivileged minority, with all the rights to redress they think that entails. They claim developing-country status, and "one-hundred years of humiliation," including from Britain and France's Opium Wars against the Qing Dynasty in the nineteenth century. We should expect CCP elites to work those claims for as long as they function to win privileges in international markets and politics. China's population is, on average, much poorer than its counterparts in East Asia. But it is the CCP and its privileged "princelings" who have most recently put the Chinese people into this subordinate status, and kept them there. It is also the CCP that self-servingly makes the most through its propaganda of the "one hundred years of humiliation."

We can think about both subordination and privilege at the intersections of various types and levels of hierarchy. Table 2 (below) is a theoretical framework of privilege in the hierarchy, locating nine causes of privilege and its increasing peakedness over time. Privileged identities at the intersections of hierarchical types and levels compound their advantages to power the hierarchy into accelerated growth of peaks and demotion of middle strata.

	Personal	National	International
Informational	Educated	Robust informational infrastructure	Global intelligence gathering
Economic	Wealthy	Robust economic infrastructure	Investment capital with access to global markets
Political-military	Organized and connected	Powerful and unified state	Powerful and unified alliance system

Table 2: Theoretical framework of privilege within the hierarchy

A theoretical framework of subordination within the hierarchy is presented in Table 3. It locates persistent subordination and its causes at the intersections of three types and three levels in the hierarchy. Due to the increasing peakedness of hierarchies, the proportion of individuals in subordinated identities at the lowest points in the hierarchy increases over time, all else equal. Subordinated identities at the intersections of hierarchical types and levels stay subordinated. Only rarely do individuals extract themselves from these lowest identities in the hierarchy.

	Personal	National	International
Informa-tional	Uneducated	Lacking informational infrastructure	Social movements without coordination (or the lack of social movements)
Economic	Poor	Lacking economic infrastructure	Social movements (or their absence) without economic resources
Political-military	Unorganized and disconnected	Lacking a unified state and alliances	Social movements (or their absence) without sufficient coordination

Table 3: Theoretical framework of subordination within the hierarchy

The twelve theories of hierarchy and hegemony can be applied as tools to the eighteen intersections of subordination and privilege identified in Tables 2 and 3. The examples of this below are non-comprehensive.

At the personal level, privilege is compounding through the concentration of informational and political power, and yields an output of an increasing concentration of wealth. Conversely, the poor are becoming increasingly poor relative to the wealthy, and politically unorganized due to the ability of the wealthy to mobilize their wealth to control media and political elites for their own purposes, and sow discord or repress social movements of the poor. This does not necessarily result in factionalism, partisanship, and infighting in democracies, beyond the initial struggles against loss of power by the lower rungs in the hierarchy. Once lost, the lower groups have no power left to fight back. It does result in increasingly unified and directed political initiatives by the wealthy in democracies, in potential coordination with the political leadership of autocracies.

Oscillation of power imbalances at the personal level of subordination encourages individual avarice and fear, leading to attempts to use such oscillations opportunistically to climb the hierarchy at the expense of others at similar intersections of subordination. Such climbing, however, is slow and ineffective because of the less avaricious and aggressive behavior of the subordinated, and because of their lack of organization.

Conversely, oscillation of power at privileged intersections leads to more rapid concentration, because the privileged have, through selection effects, sorted themselves into highly aggressive, avaricious, and strategic groups, leading organizations, or alliances, that are thereby more likely to rise in the hierarchy. This social and cultural evolutionary sorting of individuals within the hierarchy accelerates power imbalance in the entire hierarchy over time.

Subordinated identities provide one another with incentives and disincentives in the creation of micro-hierarchies that concentrate power over time. Such hierarchies are path dependent, with certain individuals rising at the expense of others and eventually exploiting those others through the power that they aggregate. At subordinated levels, this ratchet is looser because it is based on less power. Its operation is thereby more prone to slippage.

At privileged interpersonal levels, the ratchet is based on greater understanding of not only the ratchet itself, but the conditions in which power serves to aggregate. The pawl serves to stop losses to such aggregation. There is more economic and political power to pull the ratchet at these privileged levels, and less resistance through prior organization of the subordinated individuals subject to the ratchet's incentives and disincentives.

Subordinated individuals at the most powerless intersections find that whatever power they acquire is quickly disintegrated even with the slightest adverse conditions. Jobs are lost, homes and families evaporate, and substance addiction flattens the individual toward the most abject status. Such individuals become outcasts, regested and reaggregated by entrepreneurs if they are lucky, or relegated to semipermanent homelessness, hunger, or prison if they are not. They meet their end—either through death, exile, or failure to reproduce. Harsh disincentives and a selection effect at the subordinated end of hierarchy thereby produce a group that is largely quiescent and submissive to immediate superiors, but capable of passive forms of resistance.[108]

Another process of individual disintegration and regestion occurs at privileged levels, except that social mobility is such that the loss is typically just one or two rungs in the hierarchy rather than out of the hierarchy altogether. When privileged individuals cannot accept demotion, they can risk it all on bad bets, and are thus in these rare cases forced into abject poverty, exile, or death. But some of these bad bets may win. Thus, two types of individual tend to become leaders: the nonstrategic risk-loving and the strategic risk-acceptant. The nonstrategic risk-loving tend to rise and fall quickly, and spectacularly. Conversely, the strategic tend to rise gradually, punctuated with short-term minor setbacks. Those who are highly risk averse tend not to take the necessary risks to rise as leaders, and so are left in a position of mid-level stasis, outcompeted by the strategic and risk-acceptant (or risk-loving) upwardly mobile, but not falling to positions of total abjection.

Privileged individuals who lose position in the hierarchy and are strategic must rapidly and humbly readopt an attitude of submission to those above them in the hierarchy in order to survive in that new mediate position. They wait there, biding their time, for an opportunity to rise again. Over generations, the hierarchy thus causes a selection effect in which leaders of the most avaricious and aggressive type rise, as do the strategic and at least risk-acceptant, if not risk-loving. As they rise, their titles and the scope of their power increase.

At subordinated levels of the hierarchy, leaders siphon power from their subordinates, who have little to give but their persons, small quantities of property and information, and labor power. Where there are middle managers, leaders can innovate new social relations in order to skim that power and take it for themselves, or devolve that power to the lowest level of subaltern in the hierarchy to remove mid-level management and reaggregate those subalterns into direct reports or other more direct forms of subordination. As leaders rise, they delegate power to their direct reports, and thus free their resources for more climbing while simultaneously managing larger numbers of people. However, at the lowest levels of hierarchy there is as much, if not more, falling than rising, and so other than the rare individual lucky and skilled enough to rise, subordinated hierarchies remain prostrate and common. At middle levels of the hierarchy, too, there is more falling than rising, due to the increasing peakedness of hierarchy over time.

Factionalism at the Margins

At the national level, different hierarchies produce different marginalized groups, even as they mobilize other marginalized groups for their own purposes of defeating competitor hierarchies. Leftist political parties, for example, tend to marginalize the concerns of religious groups and nationalists, while conservative political parties tend to marginalize the groups that focus on economic, gender, racial, and sexual inequalities. Wealthy countries tend to marginalize the concerns of developing countries, and all tend to marginalize the concerns of the global poor. Even the global poor—in a process of internalized oppression that applies to almost all marginalized groups, and that is critical to the stability and reproduction of hierarchy—tend to marginalize their own identities, and any less fortunate than themselves.

Some groups are so marginal as to have little effect on the course of history. Where they do have an effect they are often used and discarded to help social movement entrepreneurs replace individuals within a hierarchy, or replace one hierarchy by another, rather than to change the hierarchy itself. Each tends toward a biased understanding of the hierarchy to the extent that individuals choose their identities, and then ally with overlapping organizational hierarchies of the left or right, academia or business, military or political, nationalist or internationalist.

As stated by Rufus Edward Miles, a relatively modest bureaucrat in the labor and welfare branch of the division of estimates of the US Bureau of the Budget in 1948, "Where you stand depends on where you sit." People tend to advocate for the identities and organizations that they identify with or join, or with which they ally. "Miles's Law" does not explain all variation in political, economic, and organizational beliefs, but the effect of ascription-based bias—including that resulting from being near the peaks of organizational affiliations—is too often forgotten by all sides in the rough and tumble of factional and partisan politics.[109]

Factionalism at the margins can affect conflicts based on race, gender, and class, including those involving the derogatorily labeled "basket of deplorables" who support right-wing politics.[110] Attention to their experiences—plus readings on other marginal factions, including labor unionists, anarchists, utopian communists, and libertarians—will reveal not only a generalized correlation between intersecting subordinated identities and institutionalized disempowerment, but a compounding effect that serves to accelerate history toward more extreme forms of hierarchy experienced at the margins.

The vast array of political theorists who set themselves against hierarchy should not be read uncritically. All have found part of the truth, and all are missing some of the strategy. Political utopians, including anarchists and communists, promise radical reforms that will flatten the hierarchy, but tend to ignore the most consequential realities of contestation between democratic and autocratic powers globally. Their proposed forms of non-hierarchical politics would cause a premature flattening that creates vulnerability, militarily and economically, as the Western and allied democracies they seek to flatten come under increasing military and economic threat from twenty-first-century authoritarian regimes like China and Russia.

Most such utopians appear to be unaware that these illiberal regimes' adoption of economic, industrial, and military technologies threatens to displace the power of democracy through, for example, China's acceleration in artificial intelligence (AI), hypersonic weapons, supercomputing, and the integration of industrial supply chains that in Shanghai, Beijing, Tianjin, Guangzhou, and Shenzhen are becoming more efficient than anything found in the world's most economically successful democracies.[111]

The industrialization of China at the expense of a deindustrializing West that was previously a global bulwark of democracy, albeit one subject to internal hypocrisies, does not appear to play a sufficient part in the utopian contestation of the West. Understanding this requires a step back from the domestic politics of the day, which can be imagined as an orb, around which is an equator. This equator is composed of a left-right spectrum that meets on the opposite side of the orb. From the perspective of a political moderate, the center of the equator lies between moderate leftists (sometimes of the liberal variety) and moderate conservatives (sometimes of the neoliberal variety). Most liberal and neoliberal moderates believe that international free trade is good economics because it decreases prices, and good politics because it decreases the chance of war. The median voter is right in the middle of these two groups. Whoever gets the median voter's vote wins the election.

Moderate leftists believe in just a bit more government intervention to achieve equality gains, while moderate conservatives believe in a bit less government to achieve gains for individual liberty and GDP growth. Both sides tend to believe that the minor reforms proposed by their opposites are a slippery slope in the direction of communism and fascism, respectively. This alarmism, combined with personal gains from victories of one's own party, makes even small differences in beliefs the basis of highly contentious politics, support for deplatforming of competitors, and a silence that amounts to complicity, on the violent excesses of the extreme wings of the left and right. This silence lends credence to worries about the other side's moderates, and their potential support for extremism.

On either side of the moderate positions are socialists and the radical right.

Socialists believe in radical economic redistribution through, for example, higher taxes on wealth, worker ownership of the means of production, rent control, and forgiveness of debt. They tend to support electoral tactics, but as they skew further to the left, they also consider tactics such as the general strike. Even further to the left are socialists who remain silent on the issue of social movement commitments to nonviolence, implying that their street protests and labor activism could, over time, develop into a violent revolution. Leftists of all types tend to ally with social movements against racism, sexism, and homophobia, leaving rightists of all types to react with social criticism, in what becomes a highly fraught culture war.

The radical right supports a defense against socialism and diversity that could veer into government repression, including McCarthy era–type investigations and imprisonment of socialists, communists, anarchists, and foreigners of adversary nations. The radical right tends to be nationalist and patriarchal in its orientation, meaning that it seeks to return to an ethnic and ideological state prior to demographic and political changes associated with feminism, socialism, immigration, and the removal of institutionalized racism. The extreme right in locations as diverse as the US, Europe, India, and Bangladesh tends to be nativist and anti-immigrant.

The radical right is typically male and of the dominant ethnicity, seeing new entrants into the job market—including women, minorities, and foreigners—as competitors for scarce jobs and positions of political power. The radical right is against affirmative action for minorities and against abortion rights. It tends to be allied with religious conservatives and, in the US, supports gun rights so that if the country becomes communist, or is invaded by foreign dictators, the right has the means to achieve a violent revolution or civil defense.

Further still from the moderate position are communists and fascists. Communists seek equality through government ownership of the means of production. Some are nonviolent, simply supporting the creation of utopian communities to model good behavior for the rest of society. Others, however—based on the writings of Marx, Engels, Lenin, and Mao—support violent revolution. Revolutionary violence is illegal, and so communist support for it is typically hidden. Communists have, at times, allied themselves with, and taken direction or gotten support from, foreign communist governments such as the former USSR and China. They tend to be supportive of communist revolutions in places like Cuba, Vietnam, Nicaragua, and Venezuela. Pure Marxists support violent revolution because they believe that societies cannot achieve socialism through nonviolent protests (voluntary socialist communities have failed throughout history) or electoral means (as the bourgeois controls electoral politics through corruption). They tend to ignore the failures of violent revolutions in improving the lives of citizens in the countries they take over, notably, Russia and China. They argue that socialism failed in these countries due to pressures imposed on them by capitalist countries.

Anarchists are similar to communists in that both stress egalitarianism, except that anarchists emphasize individualism and voluntarism rather than benign governance in their means and goals. They seek equality and freedom through the voluntary creation of egalitarian cooperatives, rather than through government action. They often ally with anti-racist, feminist, anti-fascist, refugee, homeless, and squatter movements. Some anarchists are pacifists, but others support violence for example, against fascist groups or the police. Anarchists have been implicated in terrorism; for example, against wealthy and political elites in the nineteenth century, and from the 1970s to the 1980s in the US, Europe, and South America. They have also participated in civil wars, including the Russian Civil War of 1917, and the Spanish Civil War of 1936 to 1939. The individualism and extreme forms of freedom that underpin anarchist philosophy have also been the source of a personal philosophy of fascist leaders. Max Stirner[112] and Friedrich Nietzsche,[113] for example, were influential thinkers for Mussolini, and Nietzsche influenced Adolf Hitler.[114]

When leftists such as communists, anarchists, socialists, or a combination amass sufficient levels of power to threaten the stability of market-based democracies, the wealthy typically mobilize nationalist and fascist social movements in reaction. All of these extremists, whether of the left or the right, put themselves and their thoughts above the whole, as did Stirner. He writes,

> As I find myself back of things, and that as mind, so I must later find myself also back of thoughts—namely, as their creator and owner. In the time of spirits thoughts grew until they overtopped my head, whose offspring they yet were; they hovered about me and convulsed me like fever-phantasies—an awful power. The thoughts had become corporeal on their own account, were ghosts, such as God, Emperor, Pope, Fatherland, etc. If I destroy their corporeity, then I take them back into mine, and they say: "I alone am corporeal." And now I take the world as what it is to me, as mine, as my property; I refer all to myself.[115]

Such philosophical solipsism easily leads to the egalitarian individualism of the anarchist, or the selfish individualism of the fascist leader. Individuals in these nationalist and fascist movements are often called "reactionaries." They are indeed often in reaction against communism and anarchism. They typically utilize violence against leftists, support governments that arrest or depose moderate leftists, stifle the free press, and seek to refocus domestic public opinion on foreign adversaries, territorial revanchism, or new conquests. Like communist revolutionaries, their violence in the beginning is typically extralegal, and so hidden.

Anarchists are located on the other side of the orb from the moderate position, next to libertarians on the right. Thus, the left-right spectrum meets on the opposite side from moderation. Like anarchists, pure libertarians seek total freedom from government, but prefer the individual liberty of markets, to the voluntary equality of collectivism.

Unlike anarchists, libertarians accept inequality as a necessary outcome of free individual choice.

Most, if not all, of these political factions justify some form of violence in support of their goals, whether it be the institutionalized violence of police enforcement of the law—supported by everyone except anarchists and libertarians—or the anarchist's propaganda by the deed. Each political identity tends to criticize the violence of other identities while ignoring their own. They are typically most averse to those factions on the opposite side of the spectrum that are most prone to use violence. Those prone to violence on their own side are indulged. Anarchism, communism, and the radical right, therefore, get the most criticism. Thus, all political factions (other than pacifists) criticize the violence of other factions and justify their own.

I here distinguish between "utopian communists" and "state communists." Utopian communism is an idealistic political philosophy, with large numbers of sympathizers among leftist students in market democracies. It is closer to advocacy of an ideal of "from each according to their capability, and to each according to their needs," along with democratic governance such as in Sweden or Germany, than to the dire conditions found in the former USSR or China. The same applies to "socialists," who, in market democracies today, generally seek to flatten economic hierarchies and retain democracy, rather than transition their governments to autocratic forms of state communism.

The subtleties of communist, socialist, and anarchist philosophies as they are held by citizens in market democracies do not stop those on the right from conflating such terms against the left, in order to tar it all with the atrocities of the USSR, or the CCP. Many contemporary communists in the West will argue that the former USSR, and China today, utilize market modalities. Therefore, they argue, China and the former USSR are not truly communist, and should instead be labeled "state capitalist."

I would argue that, by rejecting the terms *socialist* and *communist* for application to the USSR and China, respectively, western leftists cherry-pick only the least offensive outcomes of their ideology. They could instead work harder to explain the egalitarian economic policies that they support, as did Elizabeth Warren during the Democratic primaries for US president in 2020 when she, unlike Bernie Sanders, rejected the label "socialist."

Likewise, contemporary anarchists can object to use of the term *anarchy* to describe "chaos." I do not follow, for the same reasons. Anarchy, in common parlance, means chaos or terrorism, not the little-known and less-understood utopian goals of those who follow the philosophies of anarchism. Rather than enforce particular linguistic forms, anarchists of the pacifist variety could get more understanding by redoubling their efforts to explain and demonstrate their pacifist ideals, voluntarism, and utopian experiments. Sadly, this is typically not the case in the US, where the most public of anarchists gear up with plywood shields for street battles with better-armed fascists, exciting the far right in the process into even stronger forms of fascism.

Linguistic quibbles by factions are what marginalize and divide people in democracies, making them more vulnerable to takeover by foreign autocracies. Such quibbles are useful to leaders who seek to hive off their followers from larger groups, and thus head a micro-hierarchy of their own. Other than for the realization of group ideals, however, this is a self-defeating strategy. Radical social movements and radical language tend to be too violent for the average citizen, and thus incite the fear that leads to the very fascism and nationalism that they seek to oppose, just as fascism and nationalism incite their own nemesis in anarchism and communism. Radical politics of both the left and the right, therefore, tend toward the creation of violent and self-destructive factionalism on both sides in democracies.

Violence on the extremes of a political side are used by the opposite side to tar its moderates—even when less than 1 to 3 percent of protesters, which will include individuals from a broad swath on the left or the right, break the law, and even fewer engage in property damage or violence. Due to the bad reputation conferred on an entire movement by the violence and property damage of a small minority, most social movements in democracies have supporters of nonviolence who rightly seek to obtain nonviolence commitments from their entire organizations. However, as politics becomes more polarized in a democracy, there are, unfortunately, too few voices in support of written social movement commitments to the principles of nonviolence, nonviolence training in advance of protests, and nonviolence monitors at protests. This drives supporters of the movement who are explicitly nonviolent, out of the protests. Gandhi and Martin Luther King would immediately end protests that became too unruly or violent, rather than continue on their planned route. They understood the self-destructive effect such violence had on movement goals.[116]

There are an infinite number of other dimensions that could be mapped on our metaphorical orb of politics, using colors, elevations, etc., to indicate religious, national, and other political preferences. For example, we could place identity politics on the north-south axis, in which northern longitudes indicate preferences and reparations for past injustice to a particular ascription or identity, and southern latitudes indicate a politics that is color-blind, gender-neutral, and entirely accep-tant, but not otherwise advantageous to various ascriptive identities. A moderate position on this north-south axis would be at the equatorial middle: allowing for a modicum of affirmative action based on iden-tity, to achieve some level of symbolic ascriptive diversity in political, informational, and economic hierarchies, but without controversial reparations, or so much affirmative action that current elites lose their power. This moderate position on identity politics would be criticized as tokenism by the northern pole, and reverse racism by the southern pole.

Moderate positions in a democracy—including conservatives who compromise with progressives, rightists who compromise with leftists, and vice versa—have the advantage of being the location that has the best chance at unifying the country for the most popular domestic reforms, for defense against outside autocratic threats, and for the removal of inside extremist threats. Due to the dual and perilous dangers of interna-tional and domestic authoritarianism, we must be cognizant of the limits of factionalism in democracies, while at the same time seeking progress toward flattening the hierarchy and addressing the most subtle issues of power concentration. The comparative subtlety of race and gender hier-archies in the West—relative to global political-military, informational, and economic hierarchies—means that Western factional politics can be solipsistic and overstep into their own forms of bigotry on both left and right. Saying that one can put all or most conservatives into a "basket of deplorables," or that all progressives are evil, are forms of such excess.

The pursuit of liberty—if pushed to its furthest degree—can, and must, be on multiple fronts, including those identified by almost all of the world's many factions. Nearly all have some valid perspectives about hierarchy and the concentration of power, however extreme that may sound. People invariably want freedom, jobs, wealth, education, progress, security, and stability. Within our democracies, there is almost always more that unites us than divides us. Failure to grasp this fact makes us vulnerable to foreign autocratic threats at a critical time in history.

PART II

Competition Between Hierarchies

CHAPTER 7

Competition Introduction

At any rate, Pyrrhus used to say that more cities had been won for him by the eloquence of Cineas than by his own arms; and he continued to hold Cineas in especial honour and to demand his services. It was this Cineas, then, who, seeing that Pyrrhus was eagerly preparing an expedition at this time to Italy, and finding him at leisure for the moment, drew him into the following discourse. "The Romans, O Pyrrhus, are said to be good fighters, and to be rulers of many warlike nations; if, then, Heaven should permit us to conquer these men, how should we use our victory?" And Pyrrhus said: "Thy question, O Cineas, really needs no answer; the Romans once conquered, there is neither barbarian nor Greek city there which is a match for us, but we shall at once possess all Italy, the great size and richness and importance of which no man should know better than thyself." After a little pause, then, Cineas said: "And after taking Italy, O King, what are we to do?" And Pyrrhus, not yet perceiving his intention, replied: "Sicily is near, and holds out her hands to us, an island abounding in wealth and men, and very easy to capture, for all is faction there, her cities have no government, and demagogues are rampant now that Agathocles is gone." "What thou sayest," replied Cineas, "is probably true; but will our expedition stop with the taking of Sicily?"

"Heaven grant us," said Pyrrhus, "victory and success so far; and we will make these contests but the preliminaries of great enterprises. For who could keep his hands off Libya, or Carthage, when that city got within his reach, a city which Agathocles, slipping stealthily out of Syracuse and crossing the sea with a few ships, narrowly missed taking? And when we have become masters here, no one of the enemies who now treat us with scorn will offer further resistance; there is no need of saying that."

"None whatever," said Cineas, "for it is plain that with so great a power we shall be able to recover Macedonia and rule Greece securely. But when we have got everything subject to us, what are we going to do?" Then Pyrrhus smiled upon him and said: "We shall be much at ease, and we'll drink bumpers, my good man, every day, and we'll gladden one another's hearts with confidential talks." And now that Cineas had brought Pyrrhus to this point in the argument, he said: "Then what stands in our way now if we want to drink bumpers and while away the time with one another? Surely this privilege is ours already, and we have at hand, without taking any trouble, those things to which we hope to attain by bloodshed and great toils and perils, after doing much harm to others and suffering much ourselves."

—PLUTARCH[117]

Avarice, as demonstrated in the case of Pyrrhus above, is arguably the primary cause in humanity that leads individuals to compete with, and dominate, others and thus increase the concentration of power.[118] Military competition between individuals and nations produces—for the winners—more power, and—for the losers—less power, where there was previously a more egalitarian distribution. Winners are more frequently in, rather than outside of, hierarchies. Individuals are more effective in their attempts to acquire power and climb the hierarchy when they do so as part of a coordinated group with the same goals. Those individuals, corporations, and states with more power and organization are better able to defeat weaker entities, leading to the path-dependent rise of all in the group, and a generalized concentration of power that yields feedback loops that create future opportunities for further concentration.

However, avarice is checked by fear of harm to one's body, property, state, or position in the hierarchy. Reason serves as judge between avarice and fear in deciding the goals and strategies of individual and group action. Where avarice beats fear, reason can be used to choose an acceptable level of risk to expand the individual's or group's power, including through the expansion, or climbing, of a hierarchy. Where fear beats avarice, reason is used in the attempt to institutionalize or secure the power already gained, including through provision of service to those above in the hierarchy, or incentives to those below. But fear and avarice can, together, lead to aggression where another competing hierarchy threatens one's own. The more simultaneously brutal and reasoning is the individual or group, the more likely they are to defeat competitors and rise in the hierarchy. Prudence, based on fear, is the virtue of those who do not risk what is required to rise to the greatest heights of the hierarchy, but who might also endorse aggression to avoid takeover by a competing hierarchy. Avarice, fear, and reason are the three primary levers of human action that drive the ratchet toward greater concentration of power.[119]

Fear of disincentive maintains order in the hierarchy, along with avarice for incentives. The oldest informational hierarchy, religion, is based on fear, according to Vico.

> And piety originated in religion, which properly consists in the *fear of divinity*. The heroic origin of the word 'religion' was preserved among the Romans, according to the scholars who derive it from *religare*, to bind. For this verb refers to the chains which bound Tityus and Prometheus to mountain cliffs, where their heart and organs were devoured by an eagle, the symbol of the frightful

religion of Jupiter's auspices. This was the source of that invariable property of all nations, that piety is instilled in children by their fear of some divinity.[120]

This may be true, if religion is defined as a spiritual hierarchy, rather than spirituality itself. Spirituality, not religion, is based on love. Religion institutionalizes spiritual love, including through fear, in order to deploy its inordinate power. Sovereign power itself was based, in part, on the appeal to God, for Vico, as "no nation composed of fatalists, casualists, or atheists has ever existed in the world."[121]

Vico then claims that the first division of lands, boundaries of the field, and city walls were based on the fear of religion. They were inherently competitive and based on force, as one's division of the land was a division against another, who had to be repelled. Therefore, religion for Vico is bound up with secular power, and Roman forms of property were based on the spear as much as on religion.

> That commonwealths are based on the invariable principles of fiefs was sensed, if not fully understood, by the Romans. This is clear from their ancient legal formula for claiming property: 'I declare this ground mine by quiritary right', *Aio hunc fundum meum esse ex iure Quiritium*. This formula links the civil action of vindication to the ownership of the land, which belongs to the state and which proceeds from what I have called the central power. By this power, every Roman citizen is the recognized lord of his estate, which he owns *pro indiviso* ... and therefore by quiritary right, *ex iure Quiritium*. (The original Quirites were those Romans who, armed with spears in public assembly, were the only citizens.)[122]

Vico distinguishes his view of the origin of property from that of Hermogenianus, who "fancies that it was established by deliberate agreement, executed with complete justice, and observed in perfect faith."[123]

Vico traces government back to the aristocracy of Sparta in Greece, which was highly unequal. Any attempt to decrease this inequality was met by violence. King Agis was strangled because he attempted reform by cancelling all debts and legalizing inheritance outside the nobility.

Violence was also utilized to extend control of the city. The first provinces, according to Vico, were nearby conquered cities.[124] The function of the aristocracy was to uphold the power of the state. "During civil disturbances, anyone who strives to preserve the state is called an optimate, or aristocrat," according to Vico. "And 'states' are so called because it is their property to 'stand' firm and upright."[125]

But Vico describes an egalitarian morality in the city when he states, citing Thucydides, that cities had no walls by design: "for many centuries the heroic cities, composed of families, had no walls," he writes. "In the heroic aristocracies I have described, any violation of this rule was jealously punished as treason to the state. When the Roman consul Valerius Publicola built a house on high ground, he was suspected of attempting to create a tyranny." In response, he tore the house down and threw his symbols of power at the feet of the people.[126] Any technology held by a family or city by which it could achieve independence from the state was a threat to the state's sovereignty and immediately defeated as an incipient sovereign hierarchy. This disincentive deployed against potentially rebellious subunits maintained the sovereignty and power of the state. But the state or monarch could be repressive against not only rebellious leading families, but against those lower in the city's hierarchy.

Vico yearned for a benign monarchy that ruled by consent, equalized power between the classes, and secured the freedom of the masses. Presaging Hegel, Vico claims that such a monarchy is the best form of government based on its superior capability of reason. He believed in reasoned coordination above the wisdom of crowds.[127]

> In a free commonwealth, a powerful man can become monarch only when the people support his party. This is why monarchies must by nature be popularly governed through the following measures. First, monarchs use laws to establish the equality of all their subjects. Then, by a property of all monarchies, sovereigns humble the powerful in order to keep the masses free and secure from oppression. Next, by a similar property, they see that their subjects' needs are satisfied and their enjoyment of natural liberty assured.[128]

However, Vico and Hegel do not take seriously enough the aggregation of power that their support for monarchy enables, and how, over time, that aggregation of power can be used for not only the freeing of subalterns, but the reversion to less-benign causes and forms of governance in future.[129]

Vico's belief that religion prioritizes the utilization of fear—and religion's ability to establish property and city walls—is debatable, but to the extent that individuals do not respond to fear, or operate by the principles of avarice and reason, they are considered to be either saints, or crazy. These types are quickly displaced from their positions in the hierarchy, especially when they hold positions high in the hierarchy. This applies as much to Vico's time as our own.

As an AI researcher at Google said shortly before she was fired, apparently for taking a position against ascriptive bias at the tech giant, "Your life starts getting worse when you start advocating for underrepresented people. You start making the other leaders upset."[130]

The multitude of individuals—working simultaneously in a hierarchy geared toward avarice, fear, and reason—tend to respond to and utilize those elements to compete with and capture other such hierarchies (including their consumers, which constitute an essential part of their hierarchies) rather than for the liberation of subalterns, or for the liberation of those outside the hierarchy. Hierarchical relationships are the security that the individual withdraws into during times of danger, thus stopping the disaggregation of the hierarchy and deconcentration of power, when conditions are not ripe for its expansion.

Johann Gottfried von Herder, the late eighteenth-century German philosopher of history, saw expansion during war as the foundation of government in Europe.

> What has given Germany, what has given polished Europe its governments? War. Hordes of barbarians overran this quarter of the Globe; their leaders and nobles divided the land and the inhabitants among them. Hence sprung principalities and fiefs, hence the villanage of the subjugated people; the conquerors were in possession, and all the alterations that have taken place in this possession in the course of time have been determined by revolutions, by war, by mutual agreement between the powerful, and in every case therefore by the law of the stronger. History proceeds in this royal way, and

historical facts cannot be disputed. What brought the world under the sway of Rome? What made Greece and the East bow to the scepter of Alexander? What has founded all the monarchies that have existed since the time of Sesostris and the fabulous Semiramis, and again overturned them? War. Forcible conquest, therefore, has assumed the place of right, and has afterwards become law by course of years, or as our politicians phrase it, by a tacit compact; but the tacit compact in this case in nothing more than that the stronger takes what he will, and the weaker gives what he cannot preserve, or endures what he cannot avoid. Thus the right of hereditary government depends, like almost every other hereditary possession, on a chain of traditions the first link of which was forged by force or accident, and which has been drawn out occasionally it is true by wisdom and goodness, but for the most part either by fortune or force.[131]

After the democratic revolutions of the seventeenth to nineteenth centuries, monarchical power was disaggregated by nationalists and revolutionists to an assembly and elected head of state. Freedom of speech was established as a principle, and antitrust laws were put in place against the monopolization of industries. Intelligent design of political, informational, and economic hierarchy put checks and balances on royal, executive, and corporate power in Britain, France, and America, and sought to institutionalize a disaggregation of power to delay its reaggregation.[132]

But there have been other early pressures that disaggregated, or at least resisted the aggregation of, power in history; for example, the Magna Carta (1215), Martin Luther's Ninety-five Theses (1517), and the Treaty of Westphalia (1648). Such weak delaying mechanisms appear to be temporary impediments only—easily removed, amended, discounted, or ignored by other intelligent actors just as focused on utilizing the ratchet for their own aggregation and institutionalization of power over the long run.

More than the rights reserved to the individual citizen, consumer, or sovereign, the increasingly detailed loyalties that these must grant to higher levels of authority are the primary movement in history. For the individual, Hegel writes that "All the aims of society and the State are the private aim of the individuals," in the context of his discussion of the rights and duties of the individual within the hierarchy of the state. Individuals, according to Hegel, should adopt the aims of the state as their own.[133] Increasingly, and at progressively higher levels of state, empire, or international organization, that is exactly what we observe.

But, the avarice, fear, and reason of individuals that lead them to support successively more encompassing hierarchies operate on the leaders of hierarchies differently than they operate on individuals. Authoritarian leaders must stoke and satisfy the avarice of the public even when it puts them in danger, and, at the same time, can use control over information to moderate the public's artificially inflamed avarice, and steer the public away from fear even when danger is present. Democratic leaders, on the other hand, follow the public's normal preference for security over and above avarice. But when that security is threatened, they cannot moderate their fear and defense mechanisms through artificial means as can authoritarians.

Freedom in democracy does, however, maximize access of democratic leaders to the knowledge, reason, and wisdom of the populace, even when that reason is contrary to the individual incentives of the leader. Conversely, in autocracies, knowledge and reason from the bottom of the hierarchy to the top are biased to fit the leader's preferences, and thus lead to sometimes fatal information failures. So, the main causes and limits of individual action cannot entirely be mapped onto the causes of hierarchical action. Hierarchies are instead subject to the aggregation of power over time through the ratchet that utilizes incentives and disincentives to mold individual actions and sustain or expand the hierarchy. The operation of these factors on avarice and fear are thus important micro-level, but not always macro-level, causes of the concentration of power at higher levels in not only a hierarchy, but a meta-hierarchy. Avarice and fear at the hierarchical, rather than individual, level drive the concentration of power at a yet more accelerated pace because, at the hierarchical level, reason is transcended.

Avarice is the subject of the following example[134] on the hypothesized selection effect in autocracies for brutality and avarice, illustrated by Nero, the emperor of Rome (54–68 CE). Nero's murderous mother, Agrippina the Younger, handed him power at age 17, after which he executed his stepbrother Britannicus, along with his mother. Both were challengers to his power, despite being more pacifistic than he. Nero then killed two of his wives, Octavia and Poppea Sabina. The killings, especially of his rivals for power, cemented his political control and allowed him to amass wealth and construct an image of himself as powerful.[135]

Nero went beyond reason in killing his own family in the pursuit of power. He was not subject to the same elements of avarice, fear, and reason found in individuals at lower levels of the hierarchy. As emperor, he embodied the reason of the hierarchy, not the reason of an individual within the hierarchy, and that reason indulged a form of super-avarice not found in the average member of a hierarchy.

Nero also went beyond reason in his super-avarice for material goods. He only felt "like a human" when he had built an enormous palace in the center of Rome with a 120-foot colossus of himself in the courtyard. According to Suetonius, the palace, called *Domus Aurea* (Golden House), had a pool "like a sea," and parts of the house "were overlaid with gold and adorned with gems and mother-of-pearl. There were dining-rooms with fretted ceils of ivory, whose panels could turn and shower down flowers and were fitted with pipes for sprinkling the guests with perfumes. The main banquet hall was circular and constantly revolved day and night, like the heavens." When dedicating the palace, Nero signaled his approval by stating that he "was at last beginning to be housed like a human being."[136] Nero's lack of reason is shown here in that average human beings do not and cannot live like emperors.

Nero also sought to build a canal with slave labor all the way to Ostia. "For the execution of these projects he had given orders that the prisoners all over the empire should be transported to Italy, and that those who were convicted even of capital crimes should be punished in no other way than by sentence to this work."[137]

If to live "like a human being" one requires a canal built by slaves and a Golden House, what would be fit for an emperor? Nothing attainable in this world, it seems. Avarice at the peaks of the hierarchy is selected to tend toward the limits of megalomania.

Likewise, those who rise to the top in the highly competitive atmosphere of world politics today continue to be selected for their unquenchable avarice and *libido dominandi*, making conquest and corruption on a mass scale more likely as technology puts new forms of power into the hands of the world's leadership.[138]

Those who appear not to seek power may be advantaged in the court of public opinion, though even that is unclear. President Trump was clearly avaricious of power and material goods, which gained him the support of an electorate in 2016 that wants a strongman and a champion. Whether his avarice, or other elements of his policies and personality, lost him the election in 2020 is another question entirely. But it should be clear that those who truly care not about power typically do not get it. They may live more egalitarian, happy, and fulfilling lives, but they don't tend to make history when history is the story of the concentration and institutionalization of power in ever broader and more penetrating hierarchies. Many saintly acts never get noticed. Yet, criminal violence can lead to not only the wooden trumpet of infamy but the golden horn of glory.

Hierarchies are threatened not only by each other, but by the rebellion of subalterns beneath. In response, hierarchies repress and co-opt the rebellious. Social movement entrepreneurs also use calls to rebel, and claims about the utopia that will result from rebellion, to construct their own hierarchies with which to capture larger hierarchies.

The imprisonment of billionaire publisher Jimmy Lai—along with his two sons and four of his executives, on August 10, 2020, by Hong Kong authorities—is a recent illustration of rebellion and repression in the context of hierarchy. His newspaper, *Apple Daily*, and his personal social media have been unrelenting in support of democracy and opposition to the CCP, even after China's National Security Law of June 2020 extended China's takeover of Hong Kong's government to an extraterritorial restriction of freedom of speech anywhere in the world. After the National Security Law passed, mainland experts cited Lai's tweets as "evidence of subversion."[139] Authorities arrested Lai, and a China-backed newspaper advocated the closure of *Apple Daily*.[140]

Lai is no stranger to persecution. Beijing retaliated against his mainland clothing stores after he supported democracy protesters following the 1989 massacre at Tiananmen Square. He was forced to sell that business but remained unbowed.[141]

Just as power is imposed from above to reify hierarchy, as was attempted against Lai, power can be imposed from below to dissolve and reorganize hierarchy. The resulting rebellion, civil war, and protest are a contest for the determination of hierarchy; that is, for the institutionalization or reinstitutionalization of power. Where violent revolution succeeds, a new hierarchy is almost always imposed regardless of any egalitarian pretensions of the revolutionists. The new hierarchy may, for a time, be more egalitarian in some respects, but it is still a hierarchy, and it reverts over a few months or years to the general historical trend toward power concentration, often in a more concentrated form than the typically monarchical or dictatorial hierarchy that the revolution overturned.

This reinstitutionalization of power can be seen, for example, in the results of the Roman civil wars before and after the assassination of Julius Caesar, dictator of Rome, in 44 BCE; the English Civil War (1642–1651); the American Revolution (1775–1783); the French Revolution (1787–1799); the Russian Revolution (1917); and the Chinese Revolution (1949)—in all of which the contest facilitated the rise of a new hierarchy or a reconcentration of power in what was previously a sub-hierarchy. At the level of states and empires, there are always sub-hierarchies or competing hierarchies ready to replace the highest level of authority. Such replacement cannot be achieved without at least as much power as a competing hierarchy can provide.

CHAPTER 8

Competition Between Hierarchies

In his competition with the West, Mao hubristically pumped power from family farmers in China, including by aggregating them upward in the hierarchy toward massive and inefficient agricultural cooperatives and backyard steel production, more easily controlled by the state. Mao was following the lead of Stalin, who had committed genocide through starvation of Ukrainians in order to extract resources, weaken their secessionist elements, and better compete with the West through rapid growth of exports and utilization of the revenues for Soviet industrialization. As this hierarchical pumping by Mao and Stalin illustrates, state hierarchies can seek to compete not only with one another, but with subunits such as family hierarchies. The result was millions of deaths toward the bottom of the hierarchy. Even within states, there is reasonable rejection and sometimes armed resistance against these attempts by the center of a state to assert its sovereignty into the details of families and individual lives.

The sovereignty of the state over a given territory—as previously understood with the state defined as the monopoly of legitimate violence within a given territory[142]—then, is an abstract idea of law, self-justification, and peer-recognition, rather than a description of reality. Sovereignty has, therefore, wrongly been understood as *de facto* when its definition relies on a *de jure* abstraction. This is a logical contradiction in the definition of sovereignty and the state.

The state is better understood as the greatest concentration of legitimized force in a given territory. Sovereignty is the *de facto* ability of the state to project preponderant power of the informational and military types, with information following and used to legitimate the physical force of the state. That ability to project this power is continuous, as is the sovereignty of the state or the power of an empire. It does not necessarily stop at, or even extend to, the official borders of the state, which are differently defined by different actors in the international system. A state's sphere of influence beyond its official borders can extend into its noncontiguous territories; official colonies, unofficial colonies, and territories; official alliances; international organization memberships; and unofficial alliances and memberships. The state may also have an interest in, and therefore feel itself to have a property or protectorate over, territories and individuals that are ethnically or ideologically similar to the official ideology or population ruled over by the state. Thus, sovereignty is shifting, contested, divided, and pooled, but always based on ideological and military power.

Japan's empire, from the 1880s, was in reaction to the European empires and included conceptions of a "cordon of sovereignty" that encompassed those territories under formal occupation and vital to its survival, as well as a "cordon of advantage" that encompassed all of Japan's informal dominion, necessary for the protection of its inner line. This conception of rings of security—each of which required a more distant ring for its protection, along with Japanese social Darwinism and feelings of racial superiority—led to numerous foreign conquests and domestic problems, including over Korea in the 1870s, Manchuria-Mongolia in the 1920s, China in the 1930s, and Southeast Asia in the 1940s. The collapse of Japan's empire in 1945 might be attributed by some to overextension, which is a circular argument.[143] Actually, it was due to Japan's territorial aggression, matched with its lack of scientific and industrial strength relative to that of its resolved competitor. The aggression led to fear and a counterattack by the US, which, due to the latter's strong scientific and industrial foundation, was able to project power more effectively, with devastating results on Tokyo, Hiroshima, and Nagasaki.[144]

Competition between hierarchies is most dramatic at the international level, at which military conflicts over regional domination fill the pages of history. As power becomes more concentrated over time, regional power struggles aggregate power into alliances that wage global power struggles, as found in the age of empires, including both European and non-European colonialism, World War I, World War II, the Cold War between NATO and the Warsaw Pact, and current increased tensions between the US and authoritarian countries that ally with one another, like China, Russia, Iran, North Korea, and, most recently, due to a genocide in the 2010s and a coup in 2021, Myanmar (Burma).[145]

Victorious hierarchies defeat weaker or less-strategic hierarchies, which are then broken up and reabsorbed into newer, larger hierarchies over time. This process of breakup and regestion occurs at the military, economic, and informational levels. For example, traditional indigenous Lio religious hierarchies in Indonesia have been under pressure from Catholic hierarchies that first equalize individuals to break them from the indigenous hierarchy, render the traditional political-religious power of the Lio priest-leaders impotent through appropriating and belittling their most sacred rituals, and then impose the new hierarchy of the Church, which is unequal in other ways. According to anthropologist Signe Howell,

> Catholic priests introduce values derived from a Western human rights discourse that affect issues of both class and gender. In Lio value schema, women and children rank lower than men, male priest-leaders rank higher than male commoners, and children rank lower than adults. The priests are fully aware of this when they encourage commoners, girls, and women to participate publicly in Church affairs and thus challenge the *adat* hierarchy of values. On such occasions, Lio ritual practices are decontextualized and

introduced into Church events as sideshows. When schoolchildren
are dressed in the regalia of priest-leaders and perform traditional
adat dances inside the church, this can only be interpreted as a
direct attempt to undermine Lio cosmology and the priest-leaders'
authority. Powerless to prevent this, the priest-leaders grumble
among themselves.[146]

The Catholic Church was established in Indonesia by Dutch colo-
nialists. At the international economic or military level, such breakup of
a competitor prior to its regestion is deadly serious and all-too-common.
The fear of kill-or-be-killed is not a new idea, and, sadly, its banality fuels
the very wars of aggression that is its cause. World Wars I and II were
pushed by notions in the late-nineteenth century among diplomats and
military officials that being one of the top three or four powers in the
twentieth century required an expanded arms buildup. The alternative,
some thought, was loss of national sovereignty. The military buildups
that resulted were a self-fulfilling prophecy, in that they triggered arms
races that ended in war. Existential threats cause the wars and preemptive attacks that result from a security dilemma in which fear leads to
arms manufacture that increases the threat for all.[147]

Just as the US, EU, and China emerged in the twenty-first century
as the strongest and most successful of hierarchies toward a potential
end to history, there are relatively recent losers in history, such as the
British, Japanese, and Soviet empires. The French and German empires
have, to some extent, been sanitized, defanged, and reoriented as the
European project, which benefited from the breakup of the Soviet Union
and America's nuclear umbrella. The *Pax Americana* benefitted from the
addition of Western Europe, Japan, South Korea, and Australia as strong
allies.

China benefited from the failed American strategy of engagement
with it after 1972, in which the Asian country mobilized its large and
low-paid population to become the "world's factory," and the world
bought its products to gain it as an ally against the USSR. In retrospect, this was a strategic mistake on the part of the US and European
countries, as they were, in the process, deindustrialized for only marginal
price gains in their consumer products, and with little actual help from
China in defeating the USSR.

Chinese communists might, in the process, have been following the strategy of the bourgeoisie against the aristocracy as outlined by Marx and Engels, except with the wealthy democracies taking the place of the aristocracy:

> According to material history, it was the aristocracy that first put the gospel of worldly enjoyment in the place of the enjoyment of the gospel; it was at first for the aristocracy that the sober bourgeoisie applied itself to work and it very cunningly left to the aristocracy the enjoyment from which it was debarred by its own laws (whereby the power of the aristocracy passed in the form of money into the pockets of the bourgeoisie).[148]

The CCP, if members were reading their Marx (and they were), apparently followed this winning strategy against the world's wealthy democracies, even as other more utopian forms of Marxist economics failed them. The world's wealthy democracies thus created a powerful industrial and technologically advanced adversary that would, after the recession of 2008, threaten to destroy American, European, and allied economic and political systems based on diversity and freedom.

Within each of these competitions between superpowers or empires are diverse, overlapping, and competing hierarchies within societies— such as democracy versus oligarchy, communists versus nationalists, political party contests, and interest groups such as military factions, rival businesses, and adversarial identity groups—that fuel competing drives and coalitions to capture the seat of government, or secede, and thus determine the direction of their own government in its domestic and international relations.

Types of hierarchy also compete and attempt to influence or capture the other hierarchies' assets. For example, governments seek to tax wealth, wealth purchases knowledge, and knowledge seeks to influence government. Conversely, wealth seeks to bribe politicians, knowledge seeks to invent wealth for itself (thus increasing the relative economic power of knowledge at the expense of the wealthy), and government censors knowledge. Each form of hierarchy uses the tools at its disposal in competition with all other forms of hierarchy.

Imbalance among the elements of power leads to conflict and capital flight in the case of political dominance, civil unrest in the case of the dominance of wealth, and the risk of radical mistakes when intellect dominates and is heedless of real political or economic constraints. The concentration of wealth can lead to secession from a government, and to extreme forms of hunger among citizens, causing pressure for redistribution of power in the hierarchy either through subsidies to the secessionists, or redistributive revolution, including of the communist variety. Communist intellectuals then tend to impose overly radical solutions that incite fascism and capital flight.

Notably, the Bolshevik Revolution of 1917 was, in part, the result of hunger in Russia. The revolution caused the spread of revolutionary trade unionism throughout Europe and fear among industrialists and landowners. The wealthy, in turn, supported the rise of Italian fascism in the 1920s, and Nazi and Spanish fascism in the 1930s. Mussolini initially targeted trade unions in the name of farmers, and Hitler wooed German industrialist financial support by promising to suppress communism.[149]

In the context of poverty, unpopular imperial wars, church abuse, and decades of instability in Spain—including Carlist revolts due to a disputed royal succession, loss of the Spanish-American War and colonial possessions, anarchist general strikes and bombings at the turn of the century, Catalan secessionism, anarchist and socialist burning of as many as fifty churches and monasteries in 1931, and failed 1932 and 1934 leftist revolutions and general strikes—the first global empire was in disarray. General Francisco Franco led a military rebellion in 1936 that utilized German, Italian, and Catholic support to defeat a narrowly elected leftist government whose followers called it a "*dictadura del proletariado*" (dictatorship of the proletariat).[150]

Violent solutions to leftist and labor unrest throughout Europe after the Russian Revolution led to mob politics, demagoguery, and the fall of democratic and constitutional-monarchist institutions to fascism, war, and capital flight. Extremism of the communist, anarchist, royalist, and fascist varieties led to militaristic dictatorships and war that destroyed what broad-based political participation citizens already had in their countries.

As in Russia, Italy, Germany, and Spain between 1917 and 1939, the conflict that follows upon extremist imbalances can lead to disastrous regime change, in which a government dominated by one or two kinds of power is overthrown by those elites on the outside along with their supporters. These supporters may or may not include the dispossessed or subaltern groups in society that are used as tools in capital-city power struggles. Their leaders in the process almost always impose new hierarchies that concentrate power further.

Even in contemporary democracies, power is concentrating as wealth concentrates. That wealth can be moved or invested into democracies from abroad, severing ties of patriotism by the wealthy to their own countries, and making those countries yet less attractive as places to store wealth. For autocracies typically have greater restraints on the ability to export capital and profit, making them less attractive destinations for investment. All else equal, the more authoritarian a country, the more capital flight ensues, including that of indigenous elites and leaders. This is one advantage that the US, Europe, Japan, and India currently have over China and Russia.

Throughout history—and except in the case of crises like wars or depressions—micro-authoritarians, in the person of commercial leaders, do not like to be controlled by macro-authoritarians, in the person of kings and dictators. Micro-authoritarians much prefer the accessibility and corruptibility of legislators and presidents, who are smaller scale and on a shorter leash due to electoral and legal term limits. When they have the opportunity to secede due to their increasing wealth, either territorially or by carving out a space within the national polity in which they are nearly sovereign, they will do so. Mitigating the risk of such secession requires providing them with subsidies, or increasing the relative power of the military-political and ideological hierarchies. Similar tactics have been used against concentrations of military-political or ideological power centers. Stability occurs where there is a balanced division of power between the types in which all are kept at a relatively equal level.

CHAPTER 9

Division of Power

The power of melded hierarchies was clear in Spain in the early twentieth century, in that the church participated in prison, asylum, and other law-enforcement roles, and the state, at times, forbade alternative non-Catholic birth and death rights to the population. The interlinking of the church and state hierarchies was a major complaint of the socialists, anarchists, and republicans in their anticlerical campaigns of the 1930s.[151]

In some instances, however, the state decreased its linkage to religion by imposing rules or following customs that separated those hierarchies. Partial division of hierarchical types from one another are found in India and Saudi Arabia, for example. India's caste system includes a distinction between religious (knowledge) hierarchies and temporal (force) hierarchies, which are vested in government.[152] Similarly in Saudi

Arabia, the military power of force is held by royalty while the power of knowledge is held by clerics and, increasingly, universities imported from abroad. Royalty cedes to clerics in Saudi Arabia the enforcement of religious law only, including through officers called *mutaween* who, for example, police women's attire, and beat a British businessman in 2014 for haplessly queuing in the women's line at a supermarket.[153]

While Saudi military and religious leaders seek official separation, they are nevertheless mutually dependent upon and influence each other's decisions to cohere their respective power bases and stabilize their elite positions and authority over society as a whole. They are in a symbiotic relationship, as are American academic, business, and government interests that support one another through the exchange of compliant students as new employees, for corporate grants, and government tax money that goes to higher education. The academic, business, and government hierarchies are thus mutually and self-reinforcing.[154]

Democracies typically maintain a division of power between executive, legislative, and judicial branches of government, thus seeking to strengthen, check, and balance the power of any one sub-hierarchy. Checks and balances strengthen hierarchy by making it more trustworthy as a store of power for economic and intellectual elites.

However, democracies have not, and arguably almost never have, effectively separated the power of wealth from politics, leading autocracies to challenge the thoroughness of true democracy—that is, the ability to represent citizens rather than money—in ostensibly democratic nations. Autocracies argue that democracies are more plutocratic or oligarchic than truly democratic or republican in nature, which allows autocracies to ignore democracies' normative claims to legitimacy based on popular approval and the vote. This argument is an attempt by autocratic power to degrade the power of democracy through undermining its philosophical foundations, illustrating how different types of power and kinds of hierarchy are both divided, and in ideological competition. But democracy's critics, unfortunately, have a point that applies equally or more so to republics. Republics are not and should not be plutocratic by nature—in fact, the opposite, as they are etymologically "of the public" or "for the public" not "of the money" or "for the money."

Knowledge in the form of values and argument can determine how wealth and force, including police and military force, are utilized and

institutionalized as hierarchies. But force can silence those with knowledge and wealth, as is found where monarchs and autocrats execute,
imprison, or penalize those with whom they disagree, or those who use
their wealth against the authorities. Thus, the three types of power influence one another and the intermingled hierarchies of each in a highly
complex, progressive, and ratcheted construction and reconstruction of
hierarchy over time.

Symbiosis of hierarchy yields compromises and boundaries, agreed
upon where government limits taxation, wealth limits its own influence
on knowledge production, and knowledge self-censors where it might
displease the powerful. Laws limit bribery, progressive taxes limit the
power of wealth, and liberal governments constrain their power to censor
through the promulgation of individual rights.

CHAPTER 10

Conflict Between Freedom and Organization

While in Saudi society there is some distinction between the inter-linked types of power, totalitarian leaders go one step beyond typical authoritarians to seek the seamless fusion of power. Under totalitarianism, there is little limit on the ability of the ruler to determine the exact nature, interplay, and deconfliction of force, wealth, and knowledge hierarchies. This is a strength and weakness of totalitarian forms of government. The strength is that totalitarians can better coordinate the wealth and knowledge resources available to the state. Totalitarians, thereby, see themselves as bringing a beneficent order to political, economic, and intellectual chaos.

The weakness is that in the process, knowledge must be constrained to the official version, which clouds the totalitarian's power of perception and innovation. Without allowing knowledge to be free, the disincentive to transmit knowledge and the failure to transform intellectual labor into guidance or property remove the incentive to think productively, and civic engagement degrades. What knowledge is transmitted must cleave to the official version even when fatally inaccurate. This dynamic leads to information failures that cause wars, famines, and the stifling of scientific progress, along with the acceleration of ethical decay due to intellectual and moral lassitude.

With respect to domestic politics, totalitarianism is one extreme of the continuum between centralization and decentralization of power. The other extreme is anarchy. Anarchists and libertarians have an almost religious hope and faith that, without the state, society will develop into some form of utopian collectivism, or consensual market relations marked by egalitarianism. More often, if not always, a lack of government devolves into violent chaos, as found in the interstices of power during the European Middle Ages, the warring states period in ancient China, and failed states such as Somalia and Afghanistan. A lack of government transforms societies from one of laws that reify hierarchy to one of violence that establishes hierarchy, because most humans are not pacifistic anarchists but rather avaricious and fearful opportunists.

Democracy is found in the middle between anarchy and autocracy in that it institutionalizes protections—at the domestic level—for the freedom of individuals, political associations, and corporations from arbitrary control or victimization by state and criminal violence. Relatively powerless and unorganized individuals are thereby protected through laws and regulations that limit, but do not destroy, the economic power of business, the knowledge power of intellectuals, and the political power of government and the military. Democracy is inherently conservative and risk averse, because, unlike other forms of government, it requires deliberation and agreement for the state to take action. With deliberation comes a consideration of proposals from multiple perspectives, including by those who are against the proposal and sure to highlight its risks. However, it does allow for change and progress where most people believe that "progress" should take place.

Democracy is a stable political system, as is totalitarianism. Transition from democracy to anocracy, which is an only partially autocratic state, runs counter to public expectations of democracy and progress, and thus increases the likelihood of instability, civil war, and the overthrow of government. Statistical analysis of regime types and transitions, historically, provides support for this theory.[155]

The Dominican Republic in the early 1960s is an example. The country enjoyed established democratic institutions, but in 1961, President Trujillo was assassinated. A coup took place, and a power struggle ensued. At the end of 1963, counterrevolutionaries ousted the government and the country devolved toward civil war, which included an armed citizenry and constitutionalist military rebels who sought a return to democracy through revolution. The constitutionalists had occupied a rebel zone, but some radicals among them were getting support from Castro's Cuba. Their leader and the former president, Juan Bosch, was seen by the US as too weak and incompetent to resist this communist influence. US President Lyndon B. Johnson responded in 1965 by sending in a detachment of marines, who isolated the rebels and stabilized the country in favor of the autocratic government.[156]

The broader global contest between autocracy (today represented by China, and previously represented by the USSR) and democracy (represented by the US and its allies) trumped the narrower struggle for democracy in any one country if that so-called democratic struggle leaned politically toward communist dictators and their allies, and thus risked democracy on a global level.

In the context of its 1978 election, the Dominican Republic returned to democracy through pressure by US President Jimmy Carter and democratic politicians in Europe and Latin America. Supporters of the authoritarian in power, President Joaquín Balaguer, attempted to utilize fraud, intimidation, theft of ballot boxes, claims of election fraud, and rumors of a military demand for a "subsidiary election" to overturn the election he lost. But international pressure worked. The democratic socialist opposition candidate who won, subsequently freed political prisoners and eased press censorship.[157]

Each society arrives at its own temporary equilibrium, with adverse regime change into anocracy occupying the unstable space between autocracies and democracies, and tending to cause civil war and gravitation toward one of those two relatively stable poles. Transition in the other direction—from autocracy to anocracy—is seen by the population as a benign change, and therefore does not tend to cause civil war.

To understand why autocracies are stable, it helps to consider the position of citizens in China or North Korea. They cannot do much, unfortunately, to liberate their countries. Censorship, surveillance, targeted travel restrictions, and the banning of even small protest groups from meeting privately, much less publicly, make it nearly impossible for social movements to overthrow the government.

Conversely, the structure of voting in the US, where both candidates try to appeal to the median voter, yields a government in which, whoever wins, most moderates are relatively satisfied. Moderates are uninterested in overthrowing the government if their candidate does not win, and there are not enough extremists to do so, as evidenced by the small size of violent groups on the fringes of massive BLM protests, and the slightly larger relative size of the rioters at the Capitol insurrection on January 6, 2021. Of approximately 30,000 protesters at the legal Trump rally, approximately 10,000 got onto Capitol grounds, and only 800 made it into the Capitol Building itself.[158]

The 800 people who got into the building, and scattered violence by BLM and Antifa protesters, were insufficient to overturn an election, much less overthrow a democratic government such as the US. But they are enough for the opposite political side to tar their moderate political allies.

Despite occasional insurrections and revolutions, the entire system of polities evolves over time toward the centralization of power and is only arrested on that path when subunits congeal into institutions that deliberately seek to impede the concentration of power. Yet, such institutional attempts to impede concentration do not typically roll back concentration—in fact, they often fail, or, if successful, the institutions themselves become a means, and new locus, for the concentration of power.

For example, nationalism and patriotism can protect a relatively weak state's power and sovereignty from aggregation into an empire, sphere of influence, or international institution. Indian nationalists broke their country free of the British Empire in 1947, and are still independent. But nationalism can also lead a powerful state to impose its will on weaker citizens or foreign states. Hindu nationalism in India today is used to discriminate against Muslims. Thus, nationalism is necessary to deconcentration (or stasis) of power for a weak state in its defense against a powerful state, and for concentration of power by a powerful state if it is totalitarian and territorially aggressive, and the totalitarian leader buys public support through successful military campaigns abroad.

In China, Han nationalism succeeded in imposing rule from Beijing on East Turkistan (now Xinjiang) and Tibet in the early 1950s. A civil war ensued in Tibet, and Uyghurs in Xinjiang, perceived by the central government as disloyal, are currently enduring a genocide, according to UN and US legal definitions. These previously independent regions are now under virtual occupation by the People's Liberation Army (PLA), with dissent or even the display of ethnic or religious diversity harshly repressed. Nationalism can therefore be a force for independence or for domination.

There are many small countries that are highly patriotic, but not expansionist. And some behaviors that appear expansionist to some—for example, American military bases abroad during the Cold War—are not driven by American nationalism or imperialism, as its detractors allege, but by an ideological belief in defending democracy and the independence of others abroad, or because by supporting and creating allies, those allies might one day do the same for America.

Likewise, an international institution such as the UN can, according to its charter, protect the sovereignty of states in the international system and the human rights of citizens in repressive states. Or, it can be influenced by large powers, including repressive ones, to pull that sovereignty away from weak states and, through a process of hierarchical skimming and pumping, erode human rights and freedoms in the entire system. Nationalism and globalism are not good or evil in and of themselves, but tools used against, or for, freedom and democracy. Knowing the difference requires an understanding of the political context and motives of the powers behind a particular initiative.

CHAPTER 11

International Hierarchy

In ancient Greece, the Athenian League of democracies served both to defend against outside authoritarian powers like Persia and Sparta, and to force Greek city-states into compliance with the will of its leading member, Athens, including through regime change into democracy and through the supply of ships, sailors, armed men, and taxes to the center. The relatively disaggregated nature of Greek city-states still made them vulnerable to Persian influence. As Athens subjugated some of the recalcitrant, disloyal, and reluctant allies in the region, the league became more of an empire than an alliance system. The Athenian League thus indicates one way in which sovereign states can be coerced and persuaded, within the context of an alliance, into subordinating themselves to an emergent empire.

During the Cold War, NATO was a voluntary defensive alliance.

This was proven by the fact that some Western democracies within the geographic region of NATO—such as Austria, Switzerland, Sweden, and Ireland—chose not to join. But the Soviet Union's Warsaw Pact, also putatively an alliance, was forced on all Eastern European countries that had been occupied by Soviet forces during World War II. Any attempt at liberalization, such as in Czechoslovakia in 1968, was seen by Moscow as a threat. Attempting to leave the pact would have been even worse. Premier Leonid Brezhnev told the Czechs that year,

> Your country is in the region occupied by Soviet soldiers in World War II. We paid for this with great sacrifices and we will never leave. Your borders are our borders. You do not follow our suggestions, and we feel threatened ... we are completely justified in sending our soldiers to your country in order to be secure within our borders. It is a secondary matter whether or not there is an immediate threat from anyone.[159]

Brezhnev was in the process of consolidating his territorial control over Eastern Europe through asserting Soviet nationalism into distant lands. Xi Jinping is doing the same today into Taiwan, islands in the East and South China Seas, Xinjiang, Tibet, and parts of India and Myanmar, all under the supposed justification, more or less, of unity and justice for the Chinese people.

Nationalism and international organizations are therefore tools that can be used for the concentration, or the diffusion, of power. However, those nations and organizations on the side of history that seek to concentrate and expand power or, conversely, to consolidate and defend democratic polities, tend to be the only ones that, over the long term, succeed against other nations and organizations. They have to try to expand, consolidate, concentrate, or defend in order to survive. Those that do not try fall by the wayside when the opportunity for expansion, consolidation, concentration, or defense (not always at the same time) presents itself. If democracies do not consolidate and defend their gains and expand democracy globally when they have the chance, including through the democratization of authoritarian states, then when those authoritarian states have the chance to expand their autocratic power at the expense of democracies, the illiberal concentration of international power will proceed. Unfortunately, this creates a security dilemma in which both sides are distrustful of the other, which increases instability and the threat of war. This is currently the case between the US and China.[160]

The same holds true for voluntary organization into hierarchies. NATO is a form of self-organization of democratic states, yet it is still the creation of a hierarchy. It is more decentralized than that of the former USSR or contemporary China, to be sure. And, as such, its vulnerabilities are different. Decentralized hierarchies are more open, and so it is easier for outside influence, of the foreign or corporate variety, to access decision-makers. One might then think that democracies are more vulnerable from a force or wealth perspective to the hijacking of sub-hierarchies for use by outsiders, as indicated above in the case of the Athenian League. Therefore, centralized authoritarian hierarchies might appear to better withstand such outside influence. But this is not necessarily true where centralized hierarchies lack the power that comes with the free transmission of knowledge. The lack of knowledge transparency in centralized hierarchies facilitates the kind of opaque transactions, including bribery by foreign states (one form of elite capture), that divert leadership from its own national or corporate interests.

Democratic freedoms of speech and assembly tend to alert society to foreign attempts to influence a hierarchy in a manner unavailable to autocracies. Compare the United States and Vietnam between 2016 and 2021. The US, with its free press, had hundreds of articles printed in its major papers, investigating possible financial and political links between the Trump family, and Russian and Chinese interests. There were articles about the Biden family, too, though some of the Democrat-leaning papers were slow on the uptake. Vietnam is also vulnerable to such influence, according to a source of mine, but lacks a free press to make it public. As a result, foreign influence in Vietnam can act with greater impunity, and approximately 60 percent of political elites in the country were pro-Beijing in 2016, according to the source.

For authoritarian leaders who are unaccountable to public opinion because of a lack of free press, and see themselves and their families as incumbents for only a fixed number of years, there will be little constraining them from selling off the assets under their control at a steep discount. This dynamic of seeking personal gain at the expense of the corporate identity can include sacrificing future profitability when company executives violate the fiduciary responsibility placed in them by stockholders, for example. National government leaders can sacrifice the entire nation's security when they allow themselves to be bought off by foreign powers. By the time shareholders or citizens realize their betrayal, it can be too late.

A case in point are Western airline companies that provide technological know-how to China as the cost of gaining market share. In 2019, Boeing estimated China's commercial aviation market to be $2.9 trillion over the next twenty years.[161] China uses the technology it receives from airline companies to build its general aviation industry. Due to China's lower labor costs, the country will likely outcompete Western airline manufacturers in the future, and could very well put them out of business. Such technology transfers easily cross over to China's military aviation industry, as well. At some point, China's air force may well outcompete the U.S. Air Force. Major airline sales to China are therefore a national security threat to the US. But, they provide huge short-term revenues to airline companies and, therefore, big bonuses to airline executives. These airline executives are well-connected in Washington, DC, giving them top cover. The losses to long-term shareholder value and US national security do not sufficiently enter into the personal calculus of the CEOs, or the politicians they support, and rarely make it into the public discussion.[162]

Totalitarian hierarchies—such as found in fascist Italy, Nazi Germany, Stalin's Soviet Union, or the People's Republic of China (PRC) since Mao—unify the three primary elements of power: force, wealth, and knowledge, in that the state has not only a monopoly on the military and police, but immense influence over the means of production and speech of inhabitants. The totalitarian state also controls knowledge production, including academia and popular culture. This makes totalitarian governments stable and relatively impervious to overthrow, except by powerful outside armies or internal elites close to the seat of power. Political organizations—such as the CCP and the North Korean dynastic leadership—that utilize totalitarian tactics are unlikely to be overthrown by even the largest of social movements, if these movements have no support among domestic military leaders.

In any country, the military—through its option of a coup—and the population—through its option of revolution—are the final arbiters of political control. Foreign political leadership can be imposed from outside the country, if such leadership can utilize any of the three types of power to do so. But military power is the ultimate form of international and domestic power. If military power does not accept a settlement, there is no settlement. The same does not hold true for economic and ideological power, which, according to the network theory of power, are, in any case, equally as powerful because they are more frequently used.

Much of history can be seen as a conflict between individual freedom and group organization. Each side tends to choose words that demonize the other, such that parliaments will depict their struggle as one of the people versus rapacious kings, autocrats, and empires; Marxists will define a struggle of workers against capitalists and equality versus exploitation; libertarians and anarchists will define a conflict between freedom and coercion; and fascists may describe a conflict between chaos and order. Moderate democracies tend to find a medium between trade-offs of freedom and group organization, but during times of stress—such as economic downturns or war, the government tends to increase its control over the economy, and decrease civil liberties.

Strongmen who favor market economics and oppose a powerful foreign foe, when confronted by revolutionary communism or even just trade unionism or environmental movements that threaten to slow the economy and thus degrade military power, use these arguments to claim that temporary authoritarian government is the only effective antidote to domestic chaos and the international defeat that would result. The counterargument in a democracy is that following the authoritarian path risks permanently turning a country into what it opposes.

The US, EU, and China

The US, EU, and China are the world's three most powerful economies, and so are emerging as regional hegemons in partial competition with one another for the title of global hegemon. This competition, or something like it in the future, could be the final competition in the aggregation of political units that started fifty-two million years ago when our primate ancestors first coalesced into multi-male/multi-female aggregations that became families and clans. This is the acceleration of history, and fifty-two million years later, we could be on the threshold of its end.

China and the US are already consolidated as global superpowers, and the EU is moving in that direction with, for example, French President Emmanuel Macron's proposal for an EU army, and the July 2020 decision led by Germany and France to fund coronavirus pandemic relief by raising EU debt for the first time collectively rather than through individual countries.[163]

It is this consolidation of power—the gradual homogenization of culture in the EU, a gradual takeover of economic, foreign, and defense policy by Brussels, and the facilitation of migration from poor to wealthy countries within the EU—that led to Britain's exit (Brexit) in 2020. However, the EU lost only about 17 percent of its GDP due to Brexit, and is continuing its process of political integration.

One year prior, in 2019, China, the US, and the EU controlled approximately 48.9 percent of world GDP by purchasing power parity (PPP), and 28.4 percent of world population according to the World Bank. These comparisons are shown in Table 4. The substantial complement to those percentages shows that other countries matter, as well. In fact, the rest of the world's population is growing at a faster rate than these three powers, while the proportion of GDP held by the three is increasing. This is another illustration of the concentration of global power.

	GDP PPP (trillions, 2019)	Population (millions, 2019)
World	$136.7	7,674
China	$24.0	1,406
US	$21.4	328
EU	$21.4	448
Total of three powers	$66.9	2,182
Percentage of three powers	48.9%	28.4%

Table 4: Comparison of three meta-hierarchies. Figures for China include Hong Kong and Macau. Source: World Bank.

All three powers are courting the rest of the world's countries and entities to land them as allies through their own preferred mix of engagement, including international organizations, multilateral cooperation, and bilateral diplomacy. The US and EU have not been entirely successful in their democratic competition against China. For decades, they have largely ignored China's human rights abuses and territorial theft to maximize lucrative and increasing trade flows with the country. The US and EU rationalized this economic engagement as a means to bring China into the world as a responsible power. However, China is arguably changing democracies more than the reverse.

US Attorney General William P. Barr said in July 2020 that, "instead of America changing China, China is leveraging its economic power to change America."[164] Secretary of State Michael Pompeo said in August 2020 that one NATO ally with whom he spoke did not want to raise issues with China for fear of losing access to Chinese markets. Most likely, all NATO allies worry about losing market access in China if disputes with the country escalate, explaining why Pompeo followed with, "If the free world doesn't change ... communist China will surely change us."[165]

This concern about coming under China's influence is not new. In 1957, just eight years after the Chinese communist revolution, sociologist Stanley Spector said about Singapore that the "attempt to acculturate the Chinese may make the host culture more Chinese."[166] The idea that engagement with China could harm countries that attempt such engagement—including through ignoring and thus being complicit in China's human rights violations—has, since the 1950s, been systematically ignored in the US, UK, and elsewhere, in the interests of expanded commerce. China's negative influence is even more pronounced, and publicly underestimated, outside the world's top economies.

As strong as China's influence was even in the 1950s, the Soviet Union was, until the 1990s, the third peak of the world's economic hierarchy instead of China. Europe during that period had only partially proceeded in its post-1945 process of economic consolidation. But the PRC was rapidly expanding its power. In 1971, the PRC obtained enough votes in the UN General Assembly (UNGA) to oust Taiwan from its UN membership, including its permanent membership on the powerful UNSC. After Mao's death in 1976, Beijing started to join hundreds of international organizations. By 2000, it was a member of more than fifty intergovernmental organizations (IGOs), as well as 1,275 international nongovernmental organizations (INGOs).[167]

The most important of these economically was the World Trade Organization, which with US support, admitted China in 2001. Massive growth in the PRC's export-oriented industry followed. By 2017, China was stealing intellectual property from the US at the rate of approximately $225 billion to $600 billion per year, according to US government calculations.[168] Europe, Japan, and India probably received similar treatment, going a long way to explain China's manufacturing and new export growth rates. Since 1991, China's GDP growth rate vacillated between 8 percent and 14 percent yearly, according to the self-reported figures that the World Bank uses. China's nominal GDP increased by the phenomenal total of 3,725 percent over those same years.[169] With this economic growth came a concomitant increase in military spending and the erosion of relative US military power and political influence in Asia, including the Middle East. Other than imposing a lot of pain that will be a deterrent in the future, the US was unsuccessful in its Iraq and Afghanistan wars. Iran is drawing closer to China and Russia as the US imposes more economic sanctions. As American imports from Saudi Arabia dropped after 2004, the kingdom drew closer to Beijing. Technologically, China has taken the lead from the US in certain fields, such as AI, supercomputing, anti-ship missiles, and, most important for exports, industrial supply-chain integration.[170]

Many smaller countries throughout history realize they are not in the running for regional or global hegemon and so sit on the fence and watch rather than participate in dangerous superpower conflicts. As late as spring 2021, even the EU was vacillating between supporting the US in confronting China, and sitting out the conflict. As a diplomat from one of the Southeast Asian countries explained to me in 2015, "When the elephants fight, the grass gets trampled."

These smaller countries—the diplomats of which bridle at such a diminutive description as they tenaciously grip the sovereign basis of their "equality" with other nations—might seek to sit on the fence, form balancing coalitions such that no country becomes hegemonic, or bandwagon with the more powerful country in the hopes of being on the "right side of history." If bandwagoning becomes the norm, and China beats the US in Asia, they reason, they could profit from China's growing economy and avoid the disaster of fighting on the losing side of a war.

But they will thereby hasten the growing global concentration of power by adding their own power to that of China. I say "hasten" rather than "defeat" power concentration because even balancing is an ineffective means against the global concentration of power. While balancing could theoretically work indefinitely to stop a hegemon from emerging, just one moment of imbalance, or an unexpected event, could provide the opportunity for a major power to make huge strides in the international system's evolution toward hegemony. At this late stage in the process of evolution, the next step could be the last.

Whether or not the world arrives at hegemony could depend on whether the CCP is allowed to continue expanding its power and influence. If not, a diverse world of sovereign democracies has a chance. As Immanuel Kant theorized in *Perpetual Peace* (1795), and subsequent social science has proven through statistical analysis,[171] only democratic dyads (pairs of countries) are consistently peaceful. Autocracies are almost always involved in any given war, either against another autocracy or against a democracy.

The economist John Maynard Keynes expanded upon Kant in his *General Theory of Employment, Interest, and Money*. "Dictators and others such, to whom war offers, in expectation at least, a pleasurable excitement, find it easy to work on the natural bellicosity of their peoples," he wrote. "But, over and above this, facilitating their task of fanning the popular flame, are the economic causes of war, namely, the pressure of population and the competitive struggle for markets."[172]

Keynes could have been writing about China today. But not only are its population and exports growing competitively. Its economy is expanding at a faster rate than that of other superpowers. It seeks to complement that growth with territorial expansion at the expense of its neighbors, and control other countries and their economies through political influence at the international and national levels.[173]

As China is the world's most powerful autocracy by far, only it today has the force and ideological proclivity to transform the international system into one of global autocracy. Conversely, only the US and its allies have the military strength to stop the PLA and shore up the UN system as it was originally conceived: a support to global democracy and human rights. Abandoning the UN, as some conservative isolationists hope to do, is not a strategic option as China would then fill the power vacuum and use the UN against democracies to an even greater degree. The UN has tremendous popular appeal in Africa, Latin America, and Southeast Asia because it is where these countries are treated as equals. America and its allies cannot afford to be isolationist when it comes to the UN. Democracies and our allies must instead redirect, redefine, and lead the organization in a manner that supports global democracy, sovereignty, and diversity rather than abandon the organization for use against these principles.

The future development of the international system thus depends on whether China turns into a democracy and strengthens prospects for a world of diverse sovereign entities, which is unlikely, given the difficulty of civil society mobilization in China, or whether it continues on its current authoritarian path. That path is indistinguishable from one that seeks global hegemony, as should be clear from its taking of the South China Sea from the Philippines, Vietnam, Indonesia, Malaysia, and Brunei, not to mention its territory grabs against India and Burma in the 1960s that have been so normalized as to continue under Chinese occupation today with very infrequent comment.

That some of the countries from which China is taking territory are poorer than China, on a per capita and absolute basis, puts the lie to the country's claimed egalitarian values. The PRC, through its homogenization of regions such as Tibet and Xinjiang (East Turkistan),[174] along with the same process in Hong Kong imposed more gradually since 1949, provides an indicator of the kind of hegemony it seeks: one in which the Mandarin-speaking Han "race" rules those within the borders it imposes on peripheral populations. Even distant countries such as Britain are not entirely safe from the CCP's extraterritorial legislation, such as the Hong Kong National Security Law. China is the newest globally imperialist and neocolonial power. History has reversed itself as to the primary actors, but not as to the developing concentration of power. Decolonization was not a disaggregation of power, but part of the regestion of European and Japanese power into US and Chinese spheres of influence.

After thousands of years of political history, we are therefore already close to a single global hegemon. The major wars of the twentieth century—between the Allies and Axis during World War II, NATO and the Warsaw Pact during the Cold War, and the US and China in what is already being called a New Cold War—are attempts by democratic alliances to defend themselves against, and perhaps roll back, autocracies with global ambitions. A world of diverse and sovereign democracies would be able to coexist without a hegemon. Kant's democratic peace theory and later statistical literature prove that democracies almost never go to war against one another. But the same does not apply to autocracies—they will likely continue fighting as long as they have a chance at achieving hegemony.

It is in the autocrat's value system to fight for global dominance as long as he (most are male) has a chance. Unfortunately, the US and China therefore cannot coexist as hegemonic powers. As long as China is ruled by autocrats, it will likely always seek to defeat the US, and the US will likely always seek to democratize China. As a result, either the CCP or American independence will eventually be extinguished. America also has its value system: liberating people around the world through democratization. The CCP understands this and sees America as an existential threat, putting the two countries on a collision course. While the CCP claims that the US and China can coexist, this is only to buy time and continue its increase in relative power compared to the US.

In World War II, the Cold War, and now the New Cold War, large alliance systems compete for global dominance and the ability to determine the nature of the international system. In the 1990s, some in the US even claimed that the country had achieved global American hegemony or a *Pax Americana*. The 2008 financial crisis, followed by China ending its policy of biding time and hiding strength, disillusioned all involved. Fukuyama's optimistic *End of History* had not arrived, after all. But as I argue here, that end is not far off if one redefines the end pessimistically as global conquest by an illiberal and unipolar hegemon.[175]

With the rise of China in 2001, the US recession of 2008, Xi Jinping installed as "emperor for life" in 2018, and China's increasing political influence in governments and international organizations, the globe does appear to be getting closer to a point of decision. US and allied elites will either stall in order to avoid military conflict and maximize lucrative trade with China, or attempt to somehow stop China's rise and the reach of its influence. The US and allies will either allow China's continued economic and military ascendency and therefore likely future hegemony given the CCP's aggressive past, or will seek to contain or defeat the CCP.

This fundamental conflict between liberal democratic and authoritarian political systems—repeated thousands of times throughout history since the days of ancient Rome and Greece, if not millions of times when counting the leveling coalitions in primate groups against dominant males—is now upon the world again on the grandest of scales. As Xi Jinping threatened shortly after Joe Biden took office in 2021, in response to the latter's tepid attempt to contain China through an alliance of democracies, "Repeatedly, history and the reality reminded us that, if we walk down the path of confrontation—be it a cold war, a hot war, a trade war or a tech war—all countries are going to suffer in terms of their interests and their people's well-being." What Xi left out is that from the South China Sea to the Himalayas, from Hong Kong to Xinjiang (East Turkistan), and from intellectual property theft to cyber-espionage, the CCP has led the more trade-oriented democracies down the path of military confrontation. China took advantage of their acquiescence, which could abate too slowly to turn the tide.[176]

A military conflict between the two nuclear-armed superpowers was unimaginable to most during the Obama administration, which ended in 2016. However, the world came close to use of nuclear weapons during the Cold War with the USSR, and during the Korean War. And, the stakes are equally high in the developing Chinese Cold War. Whichever country or alliance wins could determine the type of social system under which humans on a global scale live for most of the rest of history. A Chinese military win against the US would be an acceleration of the global concentration of power that is unparalleled in world history. Such a win would almost certainly entail nuclear weapons. US nuclear weapons capabilities are currently degrading relative to China, which is rapidly modernizing and expanding its nuclear weapons systems.

Never before has a weapon of war existed that was not used by man against humans. Ignoring the possibility of a nuclear war given the stakes just makes a nuclear surprise more likely. While Fukuyama claims that history is the unfolding of the unexpected,[177] according to the theories presented here, the world should predict, and prepare, for future superpower conflict. If China does not win via the military route, which would be painful for not only Washington but Beijing, it could beat the US through subverting and corrupting American domestic institutions.

International Organizations and Alliances

In its rise, China is taking full advantage of the international meta-hierarchies that were built after World War II to facilitate global trade and prevent future wars. These meta-hierarchies are composed of nations within alliances and international organizations, corporations with global supply chains and distribution networks, and elite individuals who network in the world's most powerful economic capitals.

There are today multiple interlinked power centers at the top of the hierarchy in the world's most powerful cosmopolitan metropoles, including New York, Washington, Boston, London, Paris, Brussels, Berlin, Moscow, Beijing, Shanghai, Tokyo, Seoul, and New Delhi. Elite politicians, financiers, and academics mix in these cities, engage in national- and international-level politics, and together—under the influence of the US, EU, China, and major global corporations—lead the world in a direction not always consistent with democracy, freedom, and human rights.

The mix of international hierarchies is becoming culturally more singular, with the *lingua franca* having transformed from a mix of French and Italian in Europe during the Middle Ages, and Portuguese used in trading networks from Japan to Africa from the fifteenth to eighteenth centuries, to the gravitational pull of English today. The US, UK, and Europe—and therefore democracy—has that linguistic advantage, at least.

In global trade and political networks, English has been driven into prominence, first by the expansive British Empire in the nineteenth century, followed by the US-led world economy and international organizations after 1945, and finalized through the first-mover advantage of an English-language internet that, until the 1970s, was exclusive to the US and Britain, from which it spread globally.

Today, the language of choice in the EU is English despite Britain's Brexit from the institution. China's attempt to accelerate its linguistic influence in the international system, including through the proliferation of subsidized Mandarin-language education internationally, is, in the short term at least, failing. The promotion of Chinese has come late, utilizes difficult-to-learn logograms, and is now associated with the autocratic overstep of the Xi Jinping regime following his rise to General Secretary of the CCP in 2012. Even China's own Shanghai Cooperation Organization (SCO), whose official and working languages are Russian and Mandarin, is being pushed to add English given India and Pakistan's membership.[178]

Yet the value system that is currently proliferating among international elites in English is not as democratic and egalitarian as would be necessary to reverse the centralization of power in Beijing, and among interlinked global corporations that care less about human rights than they do about their own short-term profit margins. The promotion of international trade and profit by these powerful actors in the international system runs roughshod over liberal democratic principles, political institutions, and human rights that have, since the time of ancient Athens, struggled to take root in any meaningful way.

International trade is ongoing, for example, between the US and EU on one side, and China and Myanmar on the other. I include Myanmar not because it is a powerful state. It is not. I include it to illustrate that the system of international trade is almost entirely devoid of any principle other than profit. Myanmar's military imposed a China-supported coup in 2021, and three genocides are taking place in these countries, according to the UN definition of the term: in China against the Uyghurs and Falun Gong, and in Myanmar against the Rohingya. Even the recognition of genocide is largely political, rather than the result of ethical or definitional principles evenly applied on a global level, as should be clear by the failure to recognize genocide in the cases of the Falun Gong and Rohingya.

American and British conservatives, for example, may criticize China for its treatment of the Uyghurs. But as the evidence mounted, they have for years ignored the issue in order to prioritize trade with China. The Rohingya get even less attention, as Myanmar is seen as a small country and therefore no threat to the US and Europe. Myanmar's close relations with China—including reports of Chinese support to the 2021 coup, ethnic rebels in the country, and bribery of its military leadership—are largely ignored in the West. Yet if China advised Myanmar in its Rohingya genocide, it may be just as culpable as it is for the Uyghur and Falun Gong genocides.[179]

And, even the plight of the Uyghurs receive insufficient attention from non-Western governments that depend, to a much greater extent, on China's trade and investment than do the Western governments. Indeed, fifty developing and autocratic countries in 2019 supported China's position on the Uyghur issue, calling for noninterference in its sovereign affairs, compared with just twenty-two developed democracies (not including the US) that condemned what would later be recognized as genocide. Beijing had earlier put diplomatic pressure on UN members to abjure the critical letter, threatening by implication their "continued multilateral cooperation" with China.[180]

Such threats work. In February 2021, I had a call with an ambassador who knew I had a favor to ask of him. When I brought up the US designation of the genocide against the Uyghurs, I was told, "Please don't ask me for anything on the Uyghurs, because that is China. We can't do anything there. Rohingya we can do, because there is much discussion at the UN; there are debates. But Uyghurs, I cannot help you." The ambassador is from a Muslim country, yet preempted any request for assistance to his coreligionists. In international politics, China apparently matters more than religion.

While millions of Uyghurs and Rohingya are ground away at the margins of global hierarchy, others toward the top of these structures ignore their existence, and human rights violations at the genocidal level, the better to move laterally between hierarchies; for example, from a job as an embassy diplomat to a job as a UN diplomat, and then to a position as high government official, lobbyist, or, during years in which one's party is out of power, as a think-tank analyst. The same lateral moves occur among the largest of international businesses, by both American and international business leaders. Google, 3M, and PepsiCo are all US companies, for example, that have had non-US CEOs.

Political, military, and social hierarchies are enormously consequential in China, including for international firms that operate there. Dinner meetings, for example, include strict protocols for exactly where each diner sits, alternating on either side of the most senior individual, according to level in the hierarchy.[181] Large international shareholders, such as China's institutional investors, demand board seats, invariably for

CCP members, in foreign and domestic firms.[182] The Chinese government demands that a CCP cell be lodged not only in China's largest domestic corporations, but in foreign corporations operating in China. The world's largest corporations are vulnerable to such demands because, like small countries, they straddle the fence on superpower disputes, all the while making outsized profits facilitated by their Beijing connections.

The US and Europe, not making demands for greater support of democracy and the free market to their corporations, or the corporations of foreign powers, leave a power vacuum that Beijing fully exploits through this institutionalization of CCP power within supposedly free-market corporations. Such demands would not seem American, liberal, free market, or capitalist, and are therefore avoided by the US and EU for ideological and political reasons. The advantage to this Western laissez-faire approach is that corporations seek to keep their capital and governance headquartered in capital-friendly, free-market democracies.

But despite corporate statements on the values they hold, when push comes to shove corporations care about profit more than democracy or anything else. So, they are freed by US and EU moral lassitude to selectively acquiesce to Beijing's demands; for example, by treating Taiwan like a Chinese province, rather than an independent country. As these Chinese demands are normalized, China makes more such demands, expanding its ideological, economic, and political power at the expense of Washington and Brussels. Once Beijing's gravitational pull in the international system exceeds that of Washington and Brussels, it will be too late to pull Western corporations back into democratic orbits. At that point, Beijing will be entirely free to use Western corporations against the West in a much more comprehensive manner.

Universities are corporations, too, and their presidents and professors are also part of an emerging international elite, who can grease their rise in global hierarchies by ignoring democratic values and human rights abuses the better to acquire jobs in elite universities that depend upon autocratic countries and global corporations for grants, student tuition, and job opportunities for students after they graduate. Professors are often hired based on their ability to win grants that will fund their salaries and labs. Sometimes these grants involve universities like Harvard, MIT, and Cambridge, some of whose professors give a little too much sensitive technology to their Chinese counterparts, or fail to disclose these relationships, thereby putting themselves at legal risk. Dozens of other universities lower down in the academic hierarchy face similar legal troubles.[183]

Meta-hierarchies are, at their broadest, part of the international hierarchy. Professors with the greatest status in their university meta-hierarchies are linked to the university's biggest corporate and international donors. These are the professors who can be appointed president of a university, as they are the most likely to secure tens or hundreds of millions of dollars in donations. From university president, if successful, they might move laterally to other high leadership positions in business and government internationally. Such moves are facilitated by global conferences in which government, economic, and academic elites socialize and identify leaders who will not threaten the hierarchy upon which they all depend.

The goals of these international conferences and organizations are often laudable. They can include support for international peace, the environment, human rights, or democracy. They may be seeking to engage their more polluting and illiberal members to move toward better environmental stewardship. But as elite venues they are also biased toward the path of least resistance for wealth and trade, leaving any lasting commitment to the environment, human rights, and democracy, where they compete with profit maximization, as non-goals after attendees fly home first class.

With the reversal of political liberalization, the flouting of science regarding pandemics and global warming in some countries, and especially with the rise of Vladimir Putin in 1999 and Xi Jinping in 2012, the track record of corporate leaders at effectuating their ostensible social goals is lacking. What is not in question is that global elite networking is on the rise, having proliferated from Davos, Switzerland; to Aspen, Colorado; Hainan, China; and St. Petersburg, Russia. Countries of all ideological persuasions are increasingly competing to stake their claims to a globalizing and pliable elite mycelia. These elite networks demonstrate sophistication and pliability through intelligent promotion of globalized markets that advantage the world's biggest autocrats and corporations, regardless of the cost to human rights, and smaller nations, communities, businesses, and ecosystems.

China and Russia use their economic influence with these elites to, in turn, influence capital cities. These illiberal governments seek to advantage their exports in bilateral organizations and negotiations, and win support at the UN and other international organizations for their candidates and the policies that advantage their own countries. Illiberal regimes gain adherence to their preferences for international meta-hierarchy, including strong norms of sovereignty and noninterference internally, but only where it serves the big two: China and Russia. They want impunity to abuse their own populations, and the populations of nearby states, without interference. They want a relaxation of such norms where it does not advantage them; for example, China and Russia's attempted bribery of foreign leaders and occupation of their neighbors' territory.

Both countries seek to cohere and protect the rights and influence of Chinese national and Russian national populations abroad, for example. Sometimes they seek to advantage their own "race," which is an entirely illiberal and racist throwback to the nineteenth century. Russia uses the Russian-speaking populations in Ukraine and Georgia, for example, as justification for its conquests there, and China has an apartheid-like system at home that advantages the Han "race," while seeking to "defend" Chinese populations abroad, rather than human rights more generally.

Russia and China claim to prioritize economic development over the rights of their minority and indigenous populations, ignoring democratic and free speech norms to deepen their control internally and create the domestic conditions they require for further territorial conquest, technology theft, and political influence abroad. They seek to expand their own norms of autocracy and charismatic leadership, socializing elites in global power centers to destroy their moral authority, or buy acquiescence to China and Russia's future expansion.

Whereas through most of the 1950s the CCP took its lead from the USSR, it split from the Soviets starting in 1956, including in opposition to Soviet Premier Nikita Khrushchev's denunciation of Stalin, embrace of "peaceful coexistence" with the West, and refusal to transfer nuclear weapons technology to Beijing. The dispute resulted in a border war between the two nations in 1969, and the US opening to China in 1972. Over the following decades, Beijing adroitly used the opening to build its economy and global influence, while the USSR was under heavy economic sanctions. After the breakup of the Soviet Union in 1991, China became the more economically and militarily (except for aerospace and nuclear technologies) powerful of the two nations.[184]

Sanctions against Russia for its 2014 invasion of Ukraine forced it to seek China as a customer for its oil and gas exports. China leveraged this to become the undisputed senior member in a Sino-Russian partnership against NATO and allies. Now, Beijing leads what should be considered an emerging meta-hierarchy, with Russia and other junior members such as Iran, Syria, and North Korea in its sphere of influence. China and Russia also seek to extend the principle of noninterference when it advantages their allies with no harm to themselves; for example, their allies' "right" to abuse the human rights of their citizens.

An alliance is invariably a hierarchy of hierarchical governments, in that one alliance member at any given time usually has more power and options than the other members. Leading meta-hierarchies today include the United States federal government, which rules over state governments and leads NATO. Each government in NATO is itself a hierarchy with subunits such as provinces and states. NATO overlaps with the EU, which is another meta-hierarchy.

The CCP is a totalitarian meta-hierarchy, in that it controls nearly all government workers, military leaders, CEOs (of public and private companies), academics, and journalists within the country. The CCP has immense influence over a large group of international organizations, sovereign countries, and businesses globally that depend on China for markets, financing, and, as evidenced in some cases, outright bribes.[185]

Junior members in alliance systems, if relatively lacking in military capabilities, can be considered subalterns of lead alliance members. The word *subaltern* originates from British military organization, meaning an individual of lower rank relative to a superior. Applying the concept at the international level, subalterns can most easily be created by wealthy countries, from among the poorest countries. The PRC, for example, typically counts on countries from Africa, Latin America, and Southeast Asia to vote with the Chinese Permanent Representative to the UN in the UNGA. Many of these countries are organized into the Group of 77 (G77), which, according to a government source of mine, is essentially controlled by China.[186] Another source linked to the group described to me in about 2015 that it was called the "Group of 77 and China," because China, at the time, insisted on having the organization present itself in this way on official documents.[187] China has used similar forms with other groups; for example, the 16+1 group of Eastern and Central European countries, with the "+1" indicating China.

China seeks to set itself apart as a leader rather than an equal by adding itself as a "+1" to these country groupings that are relatively low in the international hierarchy. Yet in the Group of 20 countries (G20), which includes all of the world's biggest economies, China allows itself to be one of the twenty on an equal basis. That could change over time as China surpasses even the wealthiest economies, given its status as the world's largest economy by GDP on a PPP basis. If its own figures are to be believed, China surpassed the US in GDP PPP in 2014.[188]

Yet, China is excluded from the G7 group, which is limited to democracies. Admission of China in its current state to the G7 at some point in the future, if China is not required to undergo major democratic reforms, would indicate an important shift and acceleration of history toward China as a rising hegemon.

Rather than solely rely on other countries or the UN for global governance, China is opportunistically seeking to take the lead by utilizing existing international organizations, creating new ones, or, as opportunities arise, acting unilaterally. The country sees itself as exceptional and is in violation of international law for its genocide against the Uyghurs and Falun Gong, violation of the Sino-British Joint Declaration of 1984 on Hong Kong, threats against Taiwan and Japan's Senkaku Islands, and occupation and claim to the entirety of the South China Sea (minus approximately twelve nautical miles of territorial seas along other claimant countries' coasts). China declared its new South China Sea territory in a 2009 *note verbale*, distributed to every UN member country.[189]

In case international organizations distance themselves from China as a result of its aggressive "leadership," the country has a contingency plan that it is already executing by creating its own international law and institutions, including, for example, a yuan-denominated system of international settlement, the Cross-Border Interbank Payment System, to compete with the dollar-denominated trade of the SWIFT international banking system;[190] the Asia Infrastructure Investment Bank, to compete with the World Bank; the e-yuan to compete with digital currencies;[191] and the Hong Kong National Security Law (NSL) that applies extraterritorially to anyone, including foreigners, who advocate independence for Hong Kong or sanctions against the Chinese government.[192] In October 2020, China used the NSL to urge British authorities to act in Britain against protesters who burned the Chinese flag.[193]

China seeks to coerce countries into agreement through the threat or actuality of war, including against East Turkistan in 1949, Tibet in the 1950s, India and Russia in the 1960s, Vietnam in the 1970s and 1980s, British-administered Hong Kong in the 1980s, the Philippines in 2016, Taiwan throughout its entire history, and the US in 2021. To the extent that China can convince countries, companies, and individuals to agree to treaties under the threat of war, or to join its institutions and follow its extraterritorial laws, it makes new international law with Beijing as the center and final arbiter. The sovereignty of countries that increasingly submit to Beijing—notably, North Korea, Cambodia, Laos, and Myanmar, but increasingly other states that depend on China for trade—is now in question.[194]

UN organizations used to be an important tool of US and allied power when they were founded in 1945, and were actually used as umbrella organizations with which to fight a war against China and North Korea in 1950. Where Trump pulled back from the UN after his win in 2016, the PRC saw its opportunity to step into the power vacuum and attempt to increase its use of the UN as a valuable tool for its own purposes, including to legitimize and protect its own illiberal governance, and that of its allies. President Joe Biden, who took office in 2021, reversed Trump's policies of withdrawing from international organizations, but it is unclear at the time of writing, in summer 2021, whether he is following an effective strategy for decisively defeating the CCP, or if he simply hopes that it will somehow reform itself under the threat, but not actuality, of stronger American alliances. Germany and France have shown little interest in combining with the US, since Biden's inauguration, in a tougher alliance against China and Russia.[195]

The system of international organizations, or something similar to it that the PRC is in the process of creating out of whole cloth, is the ultimate meta-hierarchy if it becomes illiberal at the same time as being allowed to solidify its power through increased political globalization under the control of a single power. The UN system already encompasses the globe, so if fully institutionalized and domesticated by a country like China, it will have no competitors.

The UN is not a static organization, but over time is changing its constituent members and the values that it supports. The PRC replaced the Republic of China (Taiwan) at the UN in 1971. As the PRC grows its influence further, it seeks to move the UN away from its historic support for democracy and human rights, thereby transforming the values and reach of UN organizations. As China repurposes the UN, supporters of democracy will increasingly cast a wary eye on what they used to see as a UN that served global peace, democratization, sovereignty, and human rights. Under Chinese and Russian influence, the UN and other international organizations could eventually act at cross-purposes to these international norms, making the world more authoritarian and unstable. As with countries that move from democracy to anocracy, the global public would see this as adverse regime change on a global scale, which would increase violence and the likelihood of war.

The liberal establishment in elite universities and democratic governments typically sees international organizations as an unmitigatedly positive influence in an otherwise chaotic and violent world of nation-states. That view was a reasonable one before about 2008, when China accelerated its attempts to utilize the UN as a tool for fulfilling its own goals, which, judging by its actions, are indistinguishable from goals of an illiberal and global hegemon. Now, the UN system of international organizations has a more complicated set of global effects, including the normalization of dictatorship and genocide, which academics have failed to sufficiently incorporate into their analyses.

CHAPTER 12

Domestic Hierarchy

The PRC's drive for regional or global hegemony—along with other regional hegemons, great powers, and superpowers throughout history that have done the same—entails the encompassment, dissolution, and assimilation of smaller hierarchies that stand in the way. The cultural resistance of these smaller hierarchies, including tribes, city-states, kingdoms, and nation-states, can act as a bulwark against the potentially illiberal consolidation of regional and international systems. This cultural resistance can, at times, include nationalism and patriotism. At the same time, these defensively oriented units toward outside threats, may, toward their domestic subunits, and individuals within their boundaries, act as oppressive powers.

This section of the theory characterizes the institutionalization of power within a given hierarchy, taking a critical view of hierarchy at the intranational, social, and individual levels both as important in and of itself, and as a pattern adopted by higher levels of international hierarchy. Instead of thinking about domestic politics solely in terms of class, race, gender, sexuality, and other identity or ascriptive categories, however, this theory of domestic politics centers a collection of competing, overlapping, intersecting, and sometimes cooperating hierarchies. Class, race, gender, and sexual hierarchies exist, but so do other types of hierarchy composed of a diversity of classes, races, genders, and sexualities. These hierarchies include governmental, corporate, academic, social movement, and union hierarchies.

Consistent with the trend in international politics, there is an accelerating tendency for these pluralistic domestic hierarchies, over time, to intersect ever-more tightly, and to consolidate and concentrate power into institutions. Those networks, including a mix of diverse individuals within them, that are toward the top of these hierarchies are the winners. But those diverse and unnetworked individuals toward the bottom of domestic hierarchies are thereby subordinated. In the long term, and regardless of its diversity, the peakedness of domestic hierarchy evolves from a relatively flat half-dome (a platykurtic distribution of power), to a normal distribution of power, and finally to a sharply peaked (leptokurtic) distribution of power.

Liberal, far-right, and far-left ideologies are contributing to this peakedness of hierarchy by, in the first case, advocating for markets in a fundamentalist way that ignores associated economic concentrations of power; in the second case, ignoring how gendered, racial, and national hierarchies increase the concentration of power; and, in the third case, generally ignoring the growth of power in Beijing and advocating for more social services at home that are gradually removing the competitiveness and independence of American industry and the small business owner.

Political philosophies that support communism or even activist forms of governance in liberal democracy are often critical of, but insufficiently so, the role that hierarchy plays in the domestic manifestation of their ideals, including individualism, freedom, and equality. Their typically governmental solutions to class, race, gender, and sexual hierarchies may rearrange individuals within hierarchies based on ascriptive characteristics, but they, at the same time, empower and accelerate the trend toward more peaked hierarchies through a process of hierarchical skimming, and then pumping. Power is devolved to levels that are easier for the apex of hierarchy to absorb. The ratcheting nature of this trend makes it nearly impossible to break down or return these hierarchies to a less-peaked form at a later date. Ascriptive prescriptions are, therefore, readily adopted by hierarchies as an easy way to placate the left while justifying measures that empower hierarchies, and therefore those at the top of hierarchies.

The most important domestic hierarchies that benefit from a focus on the ascription of power-holders, rather than a focus on economic, political, and intellectual power *per se*, correspond to domestic institutionalizations of force, wealth, and information. Government is the institutionalization of force, the interlinked economy is the institutionalization of wealth, and the educational and media sectors are the institutionalization of informational power. These three primary hierarchies are interlinked through elite networking and employment laterals that serve as payment on *quid pro quos*.

Each primary hierarchy is checked by the others. The government can censor the media, which can also be censored through its purchase by wealth. The media and the wealthy, including through biased coverage and campaign donations, affect the selection of government leaders (in democracies). Government taxes wealth, and the sellers of information (such as Bloomberg and Reuters financial services) inform and thus are determinative of the decisions of wealth managers.

Three ideological systems are emerging that are internally philosophically consistent, and that compete for the allegiance of domestic publics and governments: communist authoritarianism (as in China and the former USSR), market authoritarianism (as in contemporary Russia and Saudi Arabia), and market democracy (as in the US and EU). Domestic social movements and political parties each tend to have their favorites not only among the market democracies, but between the two authoritarian systems. Thus, conservatives, nationalists, and nativists tend to be more pro-Russia than their liberal or socialist counterparts. Liberals and socialists, for their part, tend to be more pro-China than their conservative counterparts. As China and Russia are themselves competing, with China an emerging champion of free trade globally because of the tremendous advantages it derives from exports, the two countries tend to support opposite sides in democratic elections in the US and EU. Democratic politics in the West is thus threatened with becoming a proxy war between Russia and China. It is therefore important for civil society to think not just of the immediate philosophies, policies, and parties that they support, but how these might be biased, influenced, and exploited by illiberal foreign actors.

Communism

Ascriptive prescriptions of greater governance for domestic minorities in the West are often paired with socialist ideology that sometimes shades into communism. Yet, communist countries are typically more hierarchical than market democracies, in that the government determines, to a much greater extent, the content of knowledge hierarchies and the investment decisions of wealth managers. China, in particular, is one of the world's most hierarchical in terms of political power (General Secretary Xi Jinping amended China's constitution and was recognized as an emperor for life as early as 2017);[196] economic power (the CCP controls China's economy and keeps its corporations on a short leash, and the distribution of wealth in China has been more concentrated at times than in the US); and media and academic power (the CCP controls the media in China, censors social media to a greater degree than in almost any other country, and ensures only CCP members in good standing rise in academic, business, and government hierarchies). Women and ethnic minorities in China are treated worse than in the US and EU, in what for the Uyghurs, Tibetans, and Hui, for example, amount to systems of apartheid.

The reason for the extreme peakedness of hierarchies in communist countries flows from Marxist philosophy that lionizes a "dictatorship of the proletariat" in order to achieve its utopian goal of "higher communism" in which the state will supposedly "wither away." According to China's contemporary Marxism, higher communism will supposedly be eased by machines that do all the work while humans devote themselves to such pastimes as leisure, art, music, and philosophy. Like a religious leader, Marx offered a future utopia in exchange for the breakdown of existing state, economic, and religious hierarchies. This led to mass support for the unachieved idea of communism, along with revolt, chaos, and, when no utopia arose, the reimposition of control and organization through totalitarian communist and fascist governments. The policy proximity and historical alliances between the two types of supposedly adversarial governments are remarkable.

The greatest power of religious leaders comes when they can take control of economic resources through ideological persuasion. In purely religious cults, the homes and savings of adherents are often donated to cult leaders. In the former USSR and today's China, it is more totalitarian. There must be complete conformity. If not, political and religious dissidents can lose their jobs, freedom, organs,[197] and lives, and are subjected to strenuous forms of "reeducation" that have been likened to brainwashing by some scholars.[198] Once one joins a communist state, or becomes a citizen of a territory controlled by the state, there is no way out other than that defined by the state.

Communist and other far-left recruitment relies on a series of myths. Marx believed that the French revolutions of 1789 and 1848 made France into an advanced country relative to Germany.[199] The Marxist and anarchist theories that there is a "class war" in market democracies might have sometimes been true in the nineteenth century. In England at that time, reforms were repeatedly passed "only as concessions to extreme pressure from below, and as alternatives to riot," according to historian David Thomson.[200]

The idea of class war and its effectiveness in winning concessions is useful in far-left recruitment campaigns and thereby empowers left social movements and governmental hierarchies. But they are fatally inaccurate when applied to contemporary politics. Instead, economic conflicts in market democracies are generally mixed disputes between mixed and interlinked hierarchies within, and crossing, domestic boundaries. In dismissing "the beer-swilling Philistines who dream of a united Germany" in the *German Ideology* (written in 1845–6), Marx and Engels missed the trend of history toward larger political units, which would result in that very unification of Germany into the German Empire less than thirty years later in 1871.[201]

Likewise, the typical labor conflict is between particular unions and particular employers, rather than an imagined "working class" engaged in a class war. The great preponderance of the working class is instead left out of the struggle, and the benefits (or punishments) that result.

The working class might actually be hurt by a labor conflict if it results in wages and other benefits that are so expensive for management as to cause capital flight to other countries, or a slower rate of investment in an entire industry (like auto or steel manufacture) because it is easily unionized. General wages can thereby fall for workers, except for the small minority of unionized and therefore privileged workers who are lucky enough not to have closed their plant through worker capture of it's the preponderance of profit.

Some of the unemployed may cheer from the sidelines of such labor disputes, because of anarchist and socialist propaganda that has taught them "class consciousness." But the unemployed generally do not benefit from these struggles, which raise wages beyond market rates, thus disincentivizing employers to invest and hire new workers. Capital flight ensues to countries with lower labor and environmental standards. These countries can then build their economies and military forces, eventually threatening the country from which the capital took flight. If, on a broad enough scale, such deindustrialization and downward pressure on employment can harm a democratic economy to such an extent that government revenues and social service expenditures fall, decreased defense expenditures will make the nation vulnerable to conquest by illiberal foreign powers.

Only in countries where there have been communist revolutions, class-based general strikes, or at least regional peasant uprisings (still possible in some developing countries such as Brazil in the 1980s)[202] can we say that there were class wars, class uprisings, or class struggles. In some autocratic countries these might result in better conditions for workers or farmers, and a flattening of economic and political hierarchy. The threat of class war can cause economic elites to make preemptive concessions; for example, shorter working days and socialized medicine.

However, such outcomes can also be achieved through political parties and democratic participation. They are more often the result of GDP growth, than of conflictual strategies. And, they are rare in either autocratic or democratic countries, because wealth-based hierarchies in both are typically so powerful as to easily compromise or repress any such revolutionary activity. In the few places where class war, usually as part of a nationalist war, "succeeded"—such as Russia in 1917, China in

1949, Vietnam in a series of insurgencies against the Japanese, French, and the US (and allies) from 1941 to 1976, and Cuba from 1956 to 1959—these economies and their workers thereafter suffered from lack of productivity and decreased standards of living compared to near-peer countries.

When comparing the USSR to Western Europe, China to Taiwan, North Korea to South Korea, and East Germany to West Germany, it is clear that communist revolution almost always serves to hurt the lowest-skilled workers in a country. The worst performers in Southeast Asia by GDP per capita (Myanmar, Laos, Vietnam, and Cambodia) are all communist or socialist one-party states. The Philippines is something of an outlier as a low GDP per capita market democracy in Asia. Indonesia has not done much better. Thailand and Malaysia, both market democracies, have done significantly better than their southeast Asian counterparts. The highest GDP per capita countries in southeast Asia are both small market-based autocracies. Brunei benefits from oil and gas resources, and so has a relatively high GDP per capita. Singapore, which is a city-state, specializes in finance and shipping.

Compare standards of living, at a more detailed level, of workers in market democracies with workers in communist countries. The bottom 10 percent of US workers made about $1,952 per month in late 2020.[203] The US federal minimum wage of $7.25 per hour in 2021 yields about $1,160 per month for employees. The data on wealth distribution in China is not as detailed, but the country's minimum wage is between about $250 and $600 per month, depending on the region. This is not just a regional issue. Taiwan is a market democracy near China, and its minimum wage is about $1,730 per month. Both China and Taiwan's minimum wages have been corrected for purchasing power (cheaper prices in those countries than in the US), so the discrepancy is not due to cost-of-living differences. Market democracies outperform communist countries for workers on all metrics, economic and political.[204]

Another far-left ideology is anarchism. Anarchists, with their studied lack of organization, never even got close to state capture. Neither have they been able to defend their territorial gains—such as they were, in the Russian (1918 to 1920) and Spanish (1936 to 1939) Civil Wars—from more organized forms of royalist, fascist, or communist violence.[205] Their romanticization of terrorism as "propaganda of the deed" starting in the

1870s, and including violence by the Weathermen and 2 June Movement from the 1960s to the 1980s in the US and Germany, failed to have any significant effect other than to give anarchism a bad name.

Pacifist anarchism remains an unrealized ideal for its adherents, who are now, in their most enduring forms, found in intentional communities in the West—paying rent, mortgages, and taxes—like most everyone else. Some anarchist squatters avoid this but thereby marginalize themselves to such an extent that they are more like fringe religious followers than a political movement with any effect on domestic, much less international, politics. They feed the homeless through organizations like Food Not Bombs, and the more violent among them can still be found in large protests wearing black, sometimes sporting homemade shields, and throwing the occasional rock or Molotov cocktail in the name of protecting social movements from fascists or sparking a class war in a wealthy democracy. Yet, wealthy democracies are the least likely place for revolution, with the least justification. Anarchists are more often college students than long-term factory or service workers. Workers, thereby, suffer from not only their lowly position in economic hierarchies, but the misguided leadership of labor unions, and, on its fringes, anarchists and communists who purport to wage class war in their name. Social movement use of violence in democracies is the worst strategy for achieving egalitarian ends as it causes political polarization, disunity, confusion, repressive government responses, and opportunities for illiberal foreign regimes.

Marx himself advocated violence. "Clearly the weapon of criticism cannot replace the criticism of weapons, and material force must be overthrown by material force," he writes. Here he means that weapons themselves criticize the government through its physical overthrow. "But theory also becomes a material force once it has gripped the masses" through becoming "radical" and by grasping "the root" of matters. Marx was a polemicist and he wrote to "grip the masses" and turn them into a material force. "The criticism of religion ends with the doctrine that *for man the supreme being is man*, and thus with the *categorical imperative to overthrow all conditions* in which man is a debased, enslaved, neglected and contemptible being."[206]

Marx's support for violence was arguably fueled by his perception of the violence of capitalism. He claimed that with the "disintegration" of the feudal system, there was a great increase in vagabondage. "As early as the thirteenth century we find isolated epochs of this kind, but only at the end of the fifteenth and beginning of the sixteenth does this vagabondage make a general and permanent appearance," he writes. "These vagabonds, who were so numerous that, for instance, Henry VIII of England had 72,000 of them hanged, were only prevailed upon to work with the greatest difficulty and through the most extreme necessity, and then only after long resistance."[207]

The power of this rhetoric of fighting, willfully ignorant of second- and third-order effects, beats the more measured prescriptions for incremental changes in line with the scientific method that Karl Popper called "piecemeal social engineering."[208] But Popper's entirely reasonable prescription of incremental improvements does not have the same crowd appeal as "revolution."

Marx criticized the competitors of communism, such as religion, law, and politics in his native Germany, which he called "a system of government which lives by conserving all this wretchedness and is itself nothing but *wretchedness in government.*" He sought to replace these competitors, through their violent overthrow, with communism, writing,

> But *war* on conditions in Germany! By all means! They are *below the level of history*, they are *beneath all criticism*, but they remain an object of criticism, in the same way as the criminal who is beneath the level of humanity remains an object for the *executioner.* ... It is not a scalpel but a weapon. Its object is its *enemy*, which it aims not to refute but to *destroy.* ... The criticism which deals with these facts is involved in a *hand-to-hand fight*, and in such fights it does not matter what the opponent's rank is, or whether he is noble or *interesting*: what matters is to *hit* him. The important thing is not to permit the German a single moment of self-deception or resignation. The actual burden must be made even more burdensome by creating an awareness of it. The humiliation must be increased by making it public. Each sphere of German society must be depicted as the *partie honteuse* [shameful part] of that society and these petrified conditions must be made to dance by having their own tune sung to them! The people must be put in *terror* of themselves in order to give them *courage.*[209]

THE CONCENTRATION OF POWER

Marx's revolt was totalizing, against everything. And so it ended in disaster, alike where it "succeeded" or failed. He did not understand the stabilizing, ethical, esthetic, communitarian, and comforting elements of the tradition, politics, and religion that nineteenth-century Germany, England, and Belgium had, and the twentieth-century fascist counter-revolution that would result from Marx's all-encompassing assault on established relations and social organization. One cannot violently take away most of the property of the wealthy without most of these property-holders fighting back.

Theology competed with communism for the loyalty of the worker, and Marx and his state successors saw themselves in a violent war against religion that would ultimately result in genocides, including forced labor, against Ukrainians in the 1930s to 1940s, and in China, against the Falun Gong starting in 1999, and minority Muslim Uyghurs thereafter. "Religion is the sigh of the oppressed creature, the heart of a heartless world and the soul of soulless conditions," wrote Marx. "It is the *opium* of the people. The abolition of religion as the *illusory* happiness of the people is the demand for their *real* happiness." Liberating the worker from religion would allow the worker to liberate himself from the slavery of capitalism, according to Marx.[210]

The communist war against religion eradicated a competing hierarchy from national life, making the worker more vulnerable to the state. Religious persecution ultimately degraded the workers' plight, rather than liberating them. China, North Korea, Cuba, and Venezuela are among the least free countries in the world, along with some Middle Eastern and African autocracies. There is a strong quantitative correlation between economic control by the state and personal control by the state. Human freedom, market freedoms, and a robust social safety net dependent upon a high GDP per capita tend to go together.[211]

Communist governments such as the USSR and PRC concentrate police power at the top, have lower GDPs per capita, less tax revenue and therefore sparser social safety nets, and a worse distribution of wealth than many liberal democracies. Communist countries lack freedom of speech for all but the leading dictator, and, to some extent, his politburo. Some leftists deny that the USSR and PRC are truly communist, even though these countries, and the parties that lead them, call themselves as much. These leftists might appeal to pre-1917 literature about socialism and communism, claim that Marx meant "democracy" and transitional government when he wrote "dictatorship of the proletariat," and claim that, in fact, the USSR and especially the PRC are instead engaging in "state capitalism," which looks nothing like the utopian egalitarian communities, or the even-more-socialist-than-Sweden countries, that Western leftists have in mind as an alternative to capitalism for their own countries in North America and Europe. Marx called for a "dictatorship of the proletariat," Engels promoted terrorism, and Lenin actually established a dictatorship in Russia under the name of the proletariat. Leftists should take them all at their words and actions, and look elsewhere for inspiration.[212]

While Marx was enthusiastic about the Paris Commune and described it in democratic terms, we cannot be sure that, had an authoritarian taken control of Paris in 1871 in the name of the workers and sought to centralize the means of production, Marx would not have been just as sympathetic. Indeed, Marx largely refused to "write recipes for the restaurants of the future." Ascription of a politically democratic philosophy to Marx based on his journalistic description of the Paris Commune is faulty methodology.[213] And, even if we grant that Marx was democratic in his political philosophy, it is arguable that his ideology was so radical, revolutionary, and violent as to throw societies into immediate and destructive conflict over changes to the status quo, resulting in more state repression. In the case of a "successful" communist revolution, the radical-egalitarian demagoguery that followed was itself sufficiently unstable as to be brought under control only through a communist "dictatorship of the proletariat."

Marx's promotion of "dictatorship" and "centralization" was successful because it was in line with the general historical trend toward the concentration of power, not because of his reading of history or because it approximated a democratic and egalitarian distribution of economic and political power. However one interprets Marx, his promotion of violence, "dictatorship," and "centralization" is culpable because his lack of clarity on the issues, at the very least, allowed Stalinism and Maoism to rise in Marx's name. At worst, we can take him for his sometimes self-contradictory word in choosing these phrases.

Political scientist Mehmet Tabak argues that Lenin was not representing Marxist theory when he said in 1919 that "it is precisely in the interests of socialism that the masses unquestionably obey the single will of the leaders of the labor process."[214] Yet, obeying the single will of leaders (plural) sounds about as dictatorial as the dictatorship of the proletariat (plural). Marxists are bending over backward to exegetically save their intellectual father from his own monstrous progeny.

But capitalism is blamed for enough, not to also be blamed for the states that the ideology of communism produced. Just as capitalist states never achieve the heights that capitalist theory promises of them, communist states do not achieve the promises of communist theory. By calling the USSR and PRC "state capitalism," communists cleverly attempt to divert criticism of communism back against their enemy, capitalism.

These "communist" leftists are a minority in their own countries, clinging to hope for a utopian "higher communism" rather than reimagining, rewriting, and redefining a non-Marxist philosophy that will actually make their societies more egalitarian, and more effectively defend them ideologically and materially from illiberal foreign regimes seeking to impose a communist or fascist government that would import more hierarchy than ever previously experienced in the West.

The leading candidate for exporting authoritarian politics via a sugarcoated Marxism is China. The country's GDP per capita is self-reported—so likely inflated—but even so, it registered at just $10,300 in 2019.[215] The Chinese government is spending much of its surplus on military expansion, both in terms of technology and territory, thus hurting its economy and social expenditures, and causing other, often poorer, countries like Vietnam and the Philippines (they are poorer by GDP per capita as well) to harm their workers with increased military spending and loss of oil and gas extraction revenues in the South China Sea. Due to the China threat, and that from Russia, the US and Europe increased their military spending from 2015 to 2020.[216] Thus, the global ambitions of authoritarians like Stalin, Mao, and their successors made state communism the main cause of global militarism and defense spending since 1945. And, state communism would not have been possible without the ideology of communism.

Communist Revolution

Marx and Engels advocated for a violent "communist revolution" that would force a new understanding upon the proletariat of their "world-historical" centrality. The proletariat would then usher in the "communist society," which the authors promised would bring a new social relationship that transcended prior false struggles. They wrote that "all struggles within the state, the struggle between democracy, aristocracy, and monarchy, the struggle for the franchise [extending the vote to new groups such as the propertyless and women], etc., etc., are merely the illusory forms—altogether the general interest is the illusory form of common interests—in which the real struggles of the different classes are fought out among one another." In the place of such "illusory" struggles, Marx and Engels offered a utopian ideal of a simultaneous world revolution that would result in states without divisions of labor.[217]

Marx and Engels sold their dream of a proletariat that would first conquer political power, as they must for a revolution, and then "dominate" the other classes in the name of representing the whole. Marxism was thus a theory of class bigotry, in which one class was constructed and made to dominate the others.[218] Coal miners were no longer in community with mine owners and managers, but constructed as in a class war with those owners. Textile workers were no longer a single community with textile owners and managers, but in opposition with them in a fight for division of the profit. Chaos, violence, and, in countries like Russia and China, violent dictatorships resulted.

To create dissatisfaction among the lower classes, Marx and Engels constructed a feeling of alienation or estrangement of the individual from "his" own labor products, which, they argued, "enslaves him instead of being controlled by him." Such alienation, they argued, would be overthrown by a communist dissolution of the division of labor and an abolition of private property. "For as soon as the division of labour comes into being, each man has a particular, exclusive sphere of activity, which is forced upon him and from which he cannot escape," they write. "He is a hunter, a fisherman, a shepherd, or a critical critic, and must remain so if he does not want to lose his means of livelihood; whereas in communist society, where nobody has one exclusive sphere of activity but each can become accomplished in any branch he wishes, society regulates the general production and thus makes it possible for me to do one thing today and another tomorrow, to hunt in the morning, fish in the afternoon, rear cattle in the evening, criticise after dinner, just as I have a mind, without ever becoming [a] hunter, fisherman, shepherd or critic." The individual would then be liberated from national and local barriers.[219]

Actual communist revolution, in their Russian and Chinese forms, did not develop as promised on a theoretical level by Marx and Engels. Economic and political power concentrated in politburos under the *episteme*, or system of knowledge, that fully centralized planning produced better economic outcomes, and a meritocratic technocracy produced better political outcomes. Such theories are still being sold today, but by elite Western academics rather than some communist international publisher out of Moscow or Beijing.[220]

Marx and Engels observed the way in which the French Revolution created new elites in place of the old. But they chose to ignore this by theorizing a series of revolutions, each of which successively improves upon the representation of the people as a whole, until a classless communist society is supposedly reached at the end. They write,

> When the French bourgeoisie overthrew the rule of the aristocracy, it thereby made it possible for many proletarians to raise themselves above the proletariat, but only insofar as they became bourgeois. Every new class, therefore, achieves domination only on a broader basis than that of the class ruling previously; on the other hand the opposition of the non-ruling class to the new ruling class then develops all the more sharply and profoundly. Both these things determine the fact that the struggle to be waged against this new ruling class, in its turn, has as its aim a more decisive and more radical negation of the previous conditions of society than all previous classes which sought to rule could have.[221]

In fact, there were no successive communist revolutions in Russia— just the one in 1917, followed by China's revolution in 1949. The new communist elites tenaciously held onto power, while millions starved to death in both countries due, in part, to Marxian economics. To boost industrialization in the USSR, Stalin introduced agricultural policies that led to famines between 1932 and 1950, resulting in approximately one million to three million deaths from starvation. Early Soviet "agricultural policies" were basically the theft of grain from Ukrainian peasants for export—including to France, Germany, and Finland—which were, therefore, arguably complicit.[222]

After the atrocities of Stalin, the USSR got cold feet and increasingly accommodated the West until its breakup between 1989 and 1992. But the CPP was ideologically harder and more Stalinist in its orientation than was the late Soviet Union. Mao innovated on Stalin, however, by seeking true agricultural reform along communist principles, rather than just the theft of grain from conquered peasants far from the center of communist power.

From 1958 to 1962, Mao sponsored the Great Leap Forward agricultural collectivization. Along with poor weather, it caused grain output to drop 25 percent due to lack of individual incentives and the attempt to transform in a few years, an agricultural system that had developed over centuries. Approximately eighteen million to thirty million starved to death as a result, as much as doubling the death rate. There was an additional shortfall of approximately thirty-one million to thirty-three million births (as much as 50 percent). The rural areas in the north of China were disproportionately affected.[223]

On the back of this "success," Mao sought to take the leadership of a world communist movement from what he saw as a softening USSR. He would supposedly seek to remake that movement as socialism with Chinese characteristics. The cost would be enormous for the Chinese people, but in the process of transforming revolutionary China into the "world's factory" under authoritarian control after the 1970s, Beijing effectively concentrated power. That process of concentrating global power is continuing apace under Xi Jinping, through the ongoing deindustrialization of the US and Europe.

But the GDP PPP per capita of China and Russia underperformed into the early twenty-first century compared to democratic peers in Western Europe and East Asia, including Japan, South Korea, and Taiwan. Thus, communism failed the world's workers and, true to its violent and conflictual origins, is hurtling the world from one military crisis to the next.

Market Democracy

Communism not only diverted global spending from social services to defense spending but created factions in the West on domestic issues that are increasingly polarized and continue to be largely ignorant of foreign threats. The reaction against communism is so strong among the extreme right in North America and Europe, including among supporters of former President Trump (who were about 75 percent of the Republican Party in February 2021),[224] as to fade into revolting justifications among some, like the Proud Boys paramilitary group, for what amounts to fascist vigilante violence against BLM protesters, domestic communists, and anarchists.

There is some equally reprehensible violence directed in the reverse direction, as well; for example, against fascist and neo-Nazi speakers and protests in the US. However, and with the exception of Trump himself, both sides are too weak, small scale, and peripheral in mainstream Western politics to be a real threat to democratic governance. And, if the Proud Boys and anarchists are both against totalitarianism—albeit of different types—neither group seems particularly focused in their street scuffles on the current center of totalitarian power in Beijing.

The rise of fascism and racism on the fringes of conservative politics, as exemplified by the carrying of the Confederate flag into the Capitol Building on January 6, 2021, provides fertile ground for vigilante violence and racism in the US and Europe. Such violence is an indicator of a deeper malaise, a displacement of working-class anger onto domestic minorities and immigrants who compete for working-class jobs, a form of cultural nativism against change to existing communities, and a way to reduce the number of voters for socialist, labor, green, and democratic political parties that compete with conservative and rightist parties.

Exacerbated by China's aggressive policies related to territorial expansion, the coronavirus pandemic, and political influence abroad, anti-Chinese racism and violence was on the rise among the far right and nationalists from 2014 in Vietnam, and since early 2020 in Britain, Italy, the US, and Myanmar (Burma).[225] Where Beijing's defenders can find evidence of such racism, or the broader and related anti-Asian racism, they often use it to try and paint all who are critical of the CCP with the same racist brush.[226]

While communist countries are undeniably more extreme in terms of personal and economic oppression, market democracies have less freedom and equality than they like to admit. The racism detailed above is a case in point. But, the most serious form of inequality in market democracies is the concentration of wealth, and the use of that wealth to buy not only the wage labor of relatively poor workers (including those living abroad in authoritarian countries), but political and informational power. This is the argument that communists and anarchists most effectively use against market democracies, claiming they are not really democracies because their governments are "controlled" by the wealthy and therefore are actually "plutocracies." It is effective propaganda, because it is partially true. Voters do have a lot of power, but their votes are swayed by the wealthy, who fund political campaigns and own the media.

Rebuttals of anarchist, communist, and fascist arguments and ideologies would not have been needed a couple of decades ago when these movements were too peripheral to domestic politics anywhere to matter. But since the refugee crisis in Europe caused by the wars in Syria and North Africa, and after the polarizing hard-right politics of the Trump presidency in the US, dangerously extreme ideologies and vigilantism have been on the rise. The extremes of both left and right trigger and thrive upon each other, leading to domestic violence when all who are against totalitarianism should be focused, as (relatively) free nations, on defending what liberties we have from truly illiberal threats emanating from China and Russia. Yes, we should expand those liberties and equalities domestically where we can. But we should not become so focused on our domestic issues that we risk getting stabbed in the back from foreign adversaries.

But, this is exactly what is happening.

Elites in free nations can help by proactively working to increase liberty and equality for those lowest in domestic hierarchies, including workers, the homeless, people of color, LGBTQ+, and women—especially where those identities overlap. Elites should recognize that wealth is concentrating, including from offshoring, and that the trend that is to their short-term economic benefit cannot continue forever without causing civil disturbance among the impoverished and unemployed, and therefore a political instability and polarization that increases communist sentiment, and its reaction, which is fascism. This instability, and the rise of illiberal politics in the democracies, will increasingly debilitate the ability of democracies to defend themselves domestically and internationally.

Conversely, leftists should realize that norms and laws of private property maintain and perpetuate inequality, but also incentivize labor, innovation, and risk-taking that buoy the economy for all (albeit at differential rates) in a market democracy. Property, even in its concentrated form, produces alternative peaks in the hierarchy to that of the state. Those peaks provide alternative hierarchies in which can be found some freedom at times of concentration in other hierarchies. And, they can, over time, be leveled in a way that benefits the broader population through progressive taxation, including a wealth tax, that still leaves the wealthy with enough to incentivize continued labor, entrepreneurship, and risk-taking on their part. This moderate and gradualist approach to economic equity in democratic nations will, in the long term, lead to less debilitating conflict, and more equitable and prosperous societies, than will communism and class war.

That said, workers in market democracies are still at the bottom of an economic hierarchy that facilitates wealth concentration and the corruption of political, business, and academic elites. Wealth concentrates in market democracies because of the central roles that luck, monopoly, monopsony, greed, and corruption play in economic growth. This applies as much to developing as developed countries, though the relative poverty in developing countries makes the issue there more urgent, including in the context of counterinsurgencies.

Afghanistan, whose democratic government is crumbling as this is written, is an example. According to General John Allen, who led US and NATO forces in Afghanistan from 2011 to 2013, the war against corruption in that country was important but neglected. "In retrospect, I would have put more law enforcement capabilities into play, to give our forces the increased capacity to war against corruption and criminality at the same time we were fighting a counterinsurgency," he told me in 2021.[227]

Monopolies are not a form of corruption, necessarily, but they do have similarly powerful economic effects. Of the many social networks that emerged over the last thirty years, the founders of Twitter and Facebook appear to have hit upon a good mix of functions and constraints. The programming behind these networks was not, at first, difficult, but as Facebook's popularity started accelerating, it would have been difficult for newcomers to start their own social networks and compete with what is a natural monopoly, duopoly, or triopoly (including LinkedIn).

It must be admitted that a perception of censorship on these platforms will incentivize the creation of new platforms and thus the breakdown of the current triopoly. After "big tech" censored the Hunter Biden story in October 2020—followed by censorship of President Trump and the closing down of the right-leaning Parler social media network after the January 6 Capitol riot—Google, Apple, and Amazon removed Parler from their services. Since then, Parler acquired new cloud services, Apple will again allow it in their store, and the flood of Parler enthusiasts continues to join.[228]

Right-leaning social media consumers, however, continue to use Facebook and Twitter, because big tech, by definition, remains the center of gravity in total social media users. They remain, then, a duopoly in casual social networking, with LinkedIn being a natural monopoly in online professional networking. Instagram and WhatsApp, which challenged the Facebook-Twitter duopoly, prove the point in that they were both purchased by Facebook. The incredible wealth that was created by the new phenomenon of the internet and personal computers tended to go to just a few lucky founders, associates, and investors, which increased wealth inequality substantially.

Eight of the top ten global companies by market capitalization are competing in the information technology sector. They range from Apple, at a $2.3 trillion market capitalization in February 2021, to Taiwan Semiconductor Manufacturing Company (TSMC), at $590 billion. TSMC is a world leader in computer chip manufacturing, which China lacks. This gives China another incentive to invade Taiwan.

In between Apple and TSMC are six more household technology names in the US and China: Microsoft, Amazon, Google, Tencent, Facebook, and Alibaba. Saudi Aramco is near the top at a $2 trillion valuation, and Tesla is trending up at $773 billion.[229]

These companies, including Saudi Aramco, established with the Standard Oil Company of California in 1933, were based on the excellence and innovation of their founders and associates. But they were also all based on luck. The Saudis, helped by their American friends, struck oil. They were lucky to live where they did.

All of the big tech companies had competitors that could have done technology development just as well. They were simply lucky enough to be the first past the post in a rapidly expanding, and path-dependent, industry.

Prior wealth and knowledge concentrations also played a part in many of these companies. Microsoft's Bill Gates, for example, came from a wealthy background. His father and grandfather were entrepreneurs. That wealth and family entrepreneurial knowledge gave Gates a fortuitous head start. He was lucky to have been born into that family, which supported his own successful entrepreneurship.

Mark Zuckerberg was a sophomore in 2004 when he started Facebook exclusively for students at Harvard. The network was then extended to a few other elite universities. Its elite origin and perceived exclusivity gave it an edge that made students from other colleges join when it was gradually opened to successively broader groups of students, corporations, and, finally, the general public. Zuckerberg was lucky enough to have been admitted to Harvard, where he could launch such a project.

I was told that no PhD student in Harvard's Government Department had a greater than 50 percent chance of getting in. For everyone who got in, there was at least one other person who had applied, did not get in, but was just as good a candidate.[230] Millions more didn't apply who were doubtless just as qualified. In a world with natural technology monopolies, luck matters immensely in climbing the upper echelons of the hierarchy, and in the concentrated distribution of wealth.

The real value of social media companies is arguably not the labor or luck of a handful of founders, years ago when they were founded, but the daily labor of billions of users, who freely produce the content on these platforms that make them so popular. Facebook and Twitter, therefore, are not only natural monopolies, but public goods. As such, they should be owned by their users, who should receive payment commensurate to their popularity and labor. Outsized compensation to the founders for their luck does not incentivize labor and productivity as might a more decentralized ownership structure. The whole point of private property is to incentivize labor, ingenuity, and risk. The founders of big tech have been compensated more than enough. Some of that value should be returned to society, and popular users should be compensated for their labors rather than banned from the platforms for saying the wrong thing (with some exceptions—for example, the advocacy of violence in a democracy).

Greed obviously plays a part in the concentration of wealth. The truly generous give away a lot of their time and money, removing them from the competition to amass the kind of wealth that facilitates the further amassing of wealth. Wealth managers with the greatest assets under management do not achieve that status by giving it all away, though they might eventually plan to do so as has billionaire Warren Buffett.

A selection effect thus ensures that the wealthiest tend also to be the greediest. The most avaricious of the wealthy are not only amassing wealth, but using that wealth to amass political power as well. They can thereby create political conditions that further ease their own particular kind of wealth accumulation. The Koch family, the second wealthiest at $100 billion in 2020, amassed their wealth in hydrocarbons, paper, and chemicals.[231] They spent hundreds of millions of dollars on political activities, including financial support to libertarian activism against the kinds of environmental regulations that limited their companies' growth and profit. They were libertarians when it suited them, but not when it came to government subsidies of their own business. Since 1990, Koch Industries has received over $536 million in subsidies.[232] What they did politically was hypocritical, and includes what might be considered legal corruption.[233]

Former Vice President Mike Pence and Secretary of State Mike Pompeo, both in office during the Trump administration, had extensive financial and professional ties to the Koch brothers. The Trump administration, of which they were a part, has been particularly aggressive against environmental regulations in the US, justifying its attacks as streamlining the country in its economic competitiveness, including with respect to China. Yet, the Kochs did extensive business in China.[234]

While *one person, one vote* is established in democracies, wealth can finance election manipulation, the purchase of media (including advertising), sponsorship of think tanks and universities, and other forms of political influence. Some of this wealth comes from China-linked corporations and high-net-worth individuals, including politically-influential billionaires like Mike Bloomberg, Ronnie Chan, Tim Cook, Ray Dalio, Larry Fink, Elon Musk, Stephen Schwarzman, and Steve Wynn. Donations, advertising, and lavish events influence votes, and, in exchange, elected leaders treat wealth of all types, and its continuing influence on politics, gently. The wolves guarding the chicken coop are not about to bite the hand that feeds them.

China's influence in US politics has coincided with the industrialization of China, at the expense of a deindustrializing US. Global corporations, to which US politicians answer, fled high wages and environmental regulations in the US for low wages and lax environmental standards in China. Now, the US is paying the price and might not recover sufficiently to defend itself against China's growing military.

Yet, at least some of the wealth accrued globally in authoritarian regions tends to flow into the banks of market democracies. The wealthy in China and Russia know that democracies are safer places to store capital. They have, after all, been founded by wealthy merchants as early as the seventeenth century to be safe stores of value against their former heads of state, who held autocratic and royal power over state finances. The power of the original merchant founders of most democracies was maintained in later historical periods, in part, by financial links between later waves of the wealthy; for example, industrialists. These links between the wealthy and politics continues today with the rise of service and information economies. The composition of wealth changes over hundreds of years in democracies, but the control of politics through that wealth remains relatively constant.

This is a criticism and dynamic that Beijing uses against the US and Europe. But, China and Russia face a double-edged sword in the attractiveness and permeability of democratic politics to the power of wealth. Illiberal regimes benefit from the vulnerability that democracies have in campaign donations and political advertising, in that dictators, like other wealthy interests, can engage in a *quid pro quo* with US corporations that support weaker foreign policies. But, Chinese and Russian elites also transfer their gains to investments, including real estate, in financial capitals such as London and New York. Illiberal governments cannot be trusted not to take the wealth for themselves; for example, through the imposition of draconian capital controls that make profit repatriation impossible. Illiberal governments thereby lose from the close links between capital and politicians in democracies that make those democracies highly trusted places for the storage of wealth.

The greater government expenditures are in any given state, relative to GDP, the more those expenditures come from taxes on the wealthy, and corporations. Thus, capital flees not only from autocracies, but from socialist-leaning democracies, into tax havens such as the Bahamas, Bermuda, the British Virgin Islands, the Cayman Islands, the Island of Jersey, Lichtenstein, Monaco, and Panama.[235]

Beijing and some socialists in democracies are trying to staunch the flow of investments to tax havens through support of global tax harmonization policies, and stronger anti-corruption and extradition laws, that will help Beijing repatriate ostensibly corrupt individuals who flee China with hundreds of millions, or even billions of dollars, in earnings. Exceptions to these laws may apply to family members of China's elite politburo, who have benefited from billions of dollars in sales of former state-owned enterprises, investing their wealth in mainland China, but also in Hong Kong and the British Virgin Islands. Xi Jinping's own family has allegedly salted away millions of dollars, including in Hong Kong real estate. The wealth of China's political elite creates particular political sensitivities in an ostensibly communist country where wealth concentration has, in some years, exceeded that of neighboring market economies such as Taiwan and South Korea.[236]

Geopolitical competition for investments leads to weak anti-corruption and money-laundering measures, including in market democracies like Canada.[237] Recipient countries have little incentive to comply with them. But some countries, like Switzerland and Luxembourg, have reformed their financial systems toward greater levels of transparency. This has sent wealth to other, more compliant, tax havens. The issue takes on political importance, as the money still tends to flee authoritarian countries for democratic countries, relatively weakening the former and empowering the latter.

Competition between hierarchies is a central theme of history, and one that leads, over time, to the centralization of power toward domestic totalitarianism, and global hegemony. This trend is only arrested through institutions that reserve power for individuals and sub-hierarchies. These alternative hierarchies include small states and corporations, but also poor families who subsist on social services. As power concentrates, all of these lesser entities will be at risk to the whims of autocratic leaders and their own particularistic conceptions of the good, including when that good is entirely personal.

The central and recurring conflict in history is then apparent between those attempting to impose order on chaos through the expansion of their own hierarchies, and those attempting to preserve freedom from outside control. The competition is not always idealistic, in that competitors can opportunistically choose sides depending upon their relative strength and the conditions of the moment. But this competition is nevertheless ongoing and, in present times, manifests as the competition between overlapping systems of democracy and autocracy, sovereignty and empire, and independent states and international organization.

Alliance systems, international organizations, and liberal norms such as free trade are sometimes a tool in this fight, and sometimes a battlefield. They are used by both sides to defend or destroy political diversity. Yet democracies have an advantage in forming broad alliances and networks because autocracies—whose ambitions are typically boundless, though their means are not—can never trust one another not to lead alliances and trade networks for their own benefit, and in a way that will eventually empower one autocracy over another in a process of state or empire consolidation toward hegemony. Democracies, on the other hand—because they do not typically seek to take one another's territory or repress diversity within their own boundaries to the point of genocide (though they do sometimes steal market share from one another)—are more trusted by one another in their democratic alliance systems.

Given the trend of history, however, it is not at all clear that the advantages democracy has over autocracy are leading to its victory. Even if democracy is victorious, it may be victorious in the name of a particular state only, as in a *Pax Americana* or *Pax Europa*, which is not necessarily equivalent to a victory for political diversity. All democracies, including a theoretical global democracy of the future, could be subject to adverse regime change such as a coup or the election of a fascist leader. Thus, not only democracy but a decentralized community of diverse sovereign states should be the goal if we are to maximize freedom and human rights in the future.

CONCLUSION

The Deconcentration of Power

I compare fortune to one of those violent rivers which, when they are enraged, flood the plains, tear down trees and buildings, wash soil from one place to deposit it in another. Everyone flees before them, everybody yields to their impetus, there is no possibility of resistance. Yet although such is their nature, it does not follow that when they are flowing quietly one cannot take precautions, constructing dykes and embankments so that when the river is in flood it runs into a canal or else its impetus is less wild and dangerous.

—Niccolò Machiavelli, The Prince (XXV)[238]

Machiavelli's strategies with respect to his raging river of Fortune applies equally to channeling, diffusing, and defeating—where necessary—the development of hierarchy and concentration of power. Similar to Machiavelli's violent river, hierarchy is a difficult force to control, especially when it is in motion, as in war or other emergencies. Democratic constraints domestically, and utilization of diplomatic, economic, and military force internationally, have all been important dykes and canals to channel, diffuse, and defeat the energetic growth of hierarchy, and its necessary outcome, the concentration of power.

But the river metaphor only goes so far. Strategies to defeat hierarchy also lead to their own hierarchies. Unlike overflowing water, hierarchy can be fought with hierarchy. Sometimes hierarchy is a forest fire rather than a river, and placing a line of fire between it and a biologically diverse forest in its path is the best strategy even as that line of fire destroys some liberties, equalities, and diversity in the process.

In this short conclusion, I broach the subject of strategies that have successfully been used in the past to defeat the worst excesses of hierarchy, thus protecting the diversity of human politics, increasing egalitarianism where it can be found, and thereby making space for individual liberty—at least for a time.

Channeling, Diffusing, and Defeating Hierarchy

Strategies to channel hierarchy will include attempts at the domestic level to decrease inequality and constraints on individual liberty. They will entail protection of institutions of democratic deliberation, including against would-be dictators, and the corrupting influence of money, wielded politically by billionaires, corporations, and foreign governments.

In the protection and global advancement of democracy as against more peaked forms of hierarchy, factionalism and partisanship should be avoided. Despite what progressives and conservatives may claim, equality and liberty need not always be in opposition. Channeling hierarchy for such positive purposes can be done from within a hierarchy—for example, as a government official—or from the outside, demonstrating through protest, the limits that governments and corporations can go in amassing power before meeting popular resistance.

The Hong Kong protests of 2019 to 2020 were an attempt to stall the spread of Beijing's hierarchy to that city. By treaty, Beijing had agreed to leave the city as a relatively independent entity until 2047. Beijing violated the treaty, Britain did little to stop it, and approximately 1.7

million people in Hong Kong protested.[239] They were effective at internationally publicizing the plight of Hong Kongers, and demonstrating the mendacity of the Chinese government with respect to their broken treaty and the CCP's territorially aggressive strategies.

In the US, UK, and Europe, the militant tactics of Hong Kong street protesters, plus the pressure of pandemic lockdowns, inspired similar tactics on the part of both left and right. Bottles, Molotov cocktails, and brawling were seen in Paris, London, and New York. But outside the context of an expanding dictatorship, these tactics elicited more opprobrium than admiration. Nonviolence is the best strategy when promoting domestic reforms to flatten hierarchies in democracies. In the context of democratic governance, social movement violence only hurts the social movement and its message. It also increases political polarization that can be utilized by foreign autocracies for their own purposes. When a social movement refuses to explicitly and publicly commit to nonviolent means, including through nonviolence training for all participants and cancellation of protests that become violent, they are likely open to the utilization of violence and should be avoided.

Diffusion of hierarchy occurs where individuals and organizations choose to invest in nondominant forms of organization and activity. This produces sub-hierarchies or even small independent hierarchies (a non-hierarchy of one can even be imagined), including civil society organizations and balancing alliances that problematize the path to greater power for a dominant hierarchy or hierarchies. Religious movements, social movements, independent political parties, labor unions, disruptive economic innovations, and democratic alliances that balance against emerging hegemons are all examples of the diffusion of hierarchy to smaller competing hierarchies. None of them are perfect; all still involve hierarchy and some concentration of power, but they do tend to diffuse power away from its highest peaks.

Defeating hierarchy occurs where one hierarchy defeats another, more concentrated, form of hierarchy. This could be a social movement that institutionalizes the power of its members temporarily to defeat a more concentrated, and illiberal, autocracy. Movements for the suffrage and rights of non-property owners, women, migrants, minorities, and people of color are examples of defeating racist hierarchies, and putting in their place more democratic forms of representative government. These are, at the same time, examples of the diffusion of hierarchy, away from a narrow class of elites in a peaked hierarchy and into flatter forms of social organization. But in the process, the new class of leaders must take on the tough responsibilities not only of ensuring greater equality at home, but of protecting that home from foreign domination. Liberal, democratic, labor, green, and socialist political parties in democracies must take their national security and defense responsibilities more seriously and proactively to protect the world from illiberal autocracies.

Defeating hierarchy includes instances when a relatively liberal form of hierarchy—that supports equality, diversity, and individual freedom— uses the tools of hierarchy to defeat another, more illiberal, form of hierarchy. Alliances of democracies and like-minded individuals, who defeated and then democratized Nazi Germany, and the Soviet Union, are examples. That Russia has now slipped back into autocracy demonstrates the fragility of such gains in the context of a general trend toward broader and deeper (illiberal) hierarchies. The ratchet effect is, unfortunately, in process today just as it has been for thousands of years.

As some form of hierarchy is inevitable, and hierarchy is growing in geographic space even as individuals' actions are increasingly determined and constrained by hierarchy, there is some urgency to joining campaigns against, and defeating, the worst forms of hierarchy. Hierarchies have new tools to suppress dissent and defeat flat organizations, including monopolization of social media, biometrics, AI-powered surveillance, microtargeted propaganda and advertising, and social credit scores that influence individual behavior through micro-incentives and disincentives.

We must accept that a strong defense against illiberal autocracies, both domestically and internationally, may require the building of new hierarchies on liberal principles. These new hierarchies will come with a cost. The European Union is a new hierarchy meant to protect against war in Europe.[240] But, at the same time, it is homogenizing a previously more diverse cultural, economic, and political landscape. The alternative of a weak, disunited, and potentially violent Europe, and one in which some states could turn fascist because they have no unifying commitment to democracy, is a worse outcome. The EU, if it can resist undue influence from Beijing and Moscow, is channeling the trend toward hierarchy in a direction that is far less damaging to diversity than the alternative. And, a strong EU will be an important partner to the US and other allies in defeating the world's most powerful autocracies.

At this late stage in the historical development of humankind, all politics are now global. Social movements in North America and Europe will affect the competitiveness of these regions against China. And, vice versa. Social movements in China, including in Hong Kong, have affected the competitiveness of the CCP. Citizens in Taiwan viewed the destruction of individual rights in Hong Kong, and the ongoing erasure of cultural diversity in Xinjiang and Tibet, with growing concern in the 2010s and early 2020s. Political parties in Taiwan that previously supported unification with the mainland no longer do. Younger generations increasingly see themselves as Taiwanese first, and as independent from Beijing. Unification with the mainland is going out of style.

The Hong Kong protests made Beijing's attempt to unify with Taiwan all the less likely. Many Hong Kongers sacrificed themselves for this democratic cause that was greater than themselves or their city. The US, Europe, and other Asian allies have also been watching and are now putting the brakes on economic and political engagement with China, starting, most obviously, by turning down the spigot of technology transfers.

Elites in the West, in order to compete effectively with China, will need to actively look for opportunities to make their societies more diverse, more egalitarian, more respectful of individual liberty, and less vulnerable to the influence of wealthy individuals and powerful corporations, both domestic and foreign. They will need to utilize strategies of channeling and diffusion to guide power away from Beijing and toward their own economies, and the economies of their allies. International organizations, where Beijing is concentrating its power, need to be reinvented and reformed in order to remove an increasingly determinative autocratic influence. Not doing so allows for additional bandwagoning with Beijing on the part of corporations, elites, and entire nations that want the immediate economic benefits of engaging China and believe that their individual actions will not have much effect on historical outcomes. Many such actions of selling out democracy by many lacking in loyalty to principle, however, will empower, and are empowering, the worst autocracies. This is a collective action problem that the US, EU, and allies like India and Japan must solve through forceful leadership and unified response.

Time is short. In fact, it may even be too late. Only concerted and independent actions in Washington, Brussels, London, Paris, Tokyo, New Delhi, Brasilia, Seoul, Ottawa, Canberra, and other allied capitals will force individuals and corporations to withhold their power from the developing economic centrality of Beijing, its corrupting global influence, and its rapid concentration of military power.

While confirming the need for greater diversity, equality, and liberty domestically, social movements in the US, Europe, and allied countries must, therefore, be mindful of the risk that domestic factionalism can disempower democracies in their international conflicts with autocracies. As President Joe Biden said in April 2021, "we can't be so busy competing with one another that we forget the competition that we have with the rest of the world to win the 21st century."[241] He was speaking about America, but the same could be said about America and its allies, or democracy generally.

We, in our various countries, might be able to resist the trend toward greater domestic hierarchy, notably that of economic concentration of wealth, by promoting progressive taxation, including on wealth and estates, and more diversity of representation in politics. Down that path is the building of a better society at home. But if we cannot, at the same time, unite to defend that society and what we have already achieved from outside illiberality—by ensuring democratic power and international diversity increase relative to outside threats—such short-term acts of perfection will mean nothing but failure in the long term.

Where too much domestic reform in terms of equality, diversity, and liberty means lack of national competitiveness abroad for a democracy, such reforms are penny-wise and pound-foolish. They could eventually lead to the global defeat of democracy, and should be postponed. All politics are global, and those who support equality, diversity, and liberty must be strategic in their sequencing and placement of democratic reform. The priority today should be democratizing the world's most powerful illiberal regimes, before they get too strong to defeat.

Success in the Hierarchy

While this volume has focused on meta-hierarchies, rather than the position of the individual within hierarchy, it bears noting that for individuals who seek positive societal change to be successful, they must not only sacrifice, but pay some attention to their own climbing of the hierarchy in order to make change from within. Such change will be helped through individual success and the support of other individuals who similarly seek to do good within a hierarchical context.

Such success and status are conveniently and self-referentially defined by the hierarchy as belonging to those who possess power and are in the process of effectively climbing the hierarchy. Individuals are "successful" when they go to "good" universities (those attended by elites and reproducing elite culture) and acquire a "good" job (that leads to a position high in the hierarchy and that institutionalizes individual power).

The "successful" are in the process of ascending by loyally making their own immediate boss look good, sometimes regardless of the broader goals of the organization to which they have both pledged their loyalty. A major in the army who is promoted to lieutenant colonel regardless of whether his actions contributed to organizational progress is a "success," while a colonel demoted to lieutenant colonel for standing on higher principles of the organization is a (sometimes respected) failure. One is experiencing the concentration of power; the other, its dispersion. Yet, both hold the same position in the hierarchy.

An individual's rise in the hierarchy, and then gradually stepping down the hierarchy as their faculties degrade, is nearly unheard of. Pride and the self-conception of progress toward personal concentration of power do not allow downward movement because the loss in status would be too costly for the organization to compensate. So, the downwardly mobile are instead shunted out of the hierarchy altogether into retirement. In a process of "up or out," the most successful banks on Wall Street invest power in those employees who are ascending, and cut loose those who stall, to see their power gradually wither off the vine. Younger, cheaper, hungrier, and more promising individuals are rising to take their place. Only those who sit at the top of a hierarchy cannot be removed, and so retain their position, and ever more sclerotic decision-making processes, until disability or death. Only then does their concentration of power disperse. But the hierarchy that got them there remains, sold to or inherited by others who go through the same process.

Except for the very few, we assume in labeling the individual as a success or failure that the individual seeks to ascend into positions with higher concentrations of power. We assume that seeking to ascend is the only legitimate life goal. Rarely is individual success defined as some philosophers have done: happiness, tranquility, virtue, honesty, self-restraint, or justice. The hierarchy touches all individuals and their self-conception of value, and almost all see the world and their place in it, only confinedly, and through lenses supplied by the hierarchy.

Escaping Hierarchy

Individuals within their hierarchies sometimes choose to hit the eject button. They parachute to earth, losing power in the process. This may be an attempt to escape the hierarchy entirely, either by moving to another hierarchy that they see as preferable, or by landing outside the hierarchy altogether. The latter choice of freedom from the hierarchy usually means a diminution of individual power and wealth, but can, at the same time, be personally liberating or even societally transformative if the escapees utilize their freedom to transform the hierarchy from the outside.

When sufficient numbers follow that path and thus deflate the hierarchy, or the hierarchy in response reforms itself as a form of accommodation, hierarchies can thereby be channeled, diffused, or defeated. However, mass escape from a hierarchy—if it is a hierarchy of greater relative freedom and equality—can lead to its weakening, conquest, and subordination to a foreign hierarchy with an even greater concentration of power. It is sometimes because of a society's freedom and equality that society loses control over its citizens, and is thereby defeated by a less liberal hierarchy abroad.

On the individual level, people have, for centuries, escaped hierarchy through accepting or even celebrating non-materialism, given that materialism is a powerful means of control within the hierarchy. Non-materialism also enables a sense of sacrifice and risk-acceptance that is critical for individuals who seek to problematize the hierarchy.

Not seeking material goods, formal education, or access to force has the typical consequence of a personal decrease in wealth and power. On a purely individual level, those willing to live an austere life in order to gain more freedom for themselves or others escape the sometimes numbing hierarchies in which most people place themselves in order to climb. The ability to abjure power leads to a better quality of life—if one does not mind the freedom of nothingness.

Diogenes of Sinope, a philosopher in ancient Greece, lived a life of voluntary poverty in a barrel at the market. He eventually discarded even his single possession (other than the barrel), a wooden bowl, and begged for his food with only his hands to receive. Diogenes is famous for having met Alexander the Great when the latter traveled through Corinth in 336 BCE. While likely an apocryphal story, the conqueror supposedly asked Diogenes if he could do anything for him, to which the philosopher requested simply that Alexander step aside so as to stop blocking the sun.[242]

Perhaps this was a metaphor for the critique of hierarchy, at which Alexander was then at an apex. Diogenes's disinterest in power, and near-total freedom from materialism, allowed him to ignore Alexander, tear down his elevated status through a benign insolence, and help found one of the main strands of Greek philosophy, that of cynicism.

As Kant later noted, for true intellectual maturity, all that is required is freedom.[243] The cynics' haughty rejection of democracy and freedom, however, was their downfall. They were impractical because they did not understand the ineluctability of hierarchy, the operation of a ratchet that concentrates power throughout history, and therefore the need to guide the best forms of hierarchy, and defeat the worst. One cannot just stand against all hierarchy and expect to survive.

Kant clearly saw the utility of using some hierarchies against others through the widespread adoption of democracy in the attainment of international peace. Unbiased by hierarchy, but part of a deliberative and egalitarian community, the individual and collective can more closely approach decentralized forms of power, including truth, and use that truth to achieve liberty and equality domestically, while defending the wonderful diversity of societies and individuals internationally.

Acknowledgements

The ideas for this book developed over several years, including as an undergraduate thesis at Yale in 2001, a PhD dissertation at Harvard in 2008, and a complete rewrite and expansion of scope for this book. The dissertation was based upon work supported under a National Science Foundation Graduate Research Fellowship.[244]

The author has surveyed and is indebted to a methodologically and philosophically diverse set of theorists in the fields of hierarchy, world-historical evolution, and political order, including Alberto Alesina,[245] Perry Anderson,[246] Robert Boyd,[247] Bear Braumoeller,[248] Robert Carneiro,[249] Lars-Erik Cederman,[250] Jared Diamond,[251] Benoît Dubreuil,[252] Francis Fukuyama,[253] John H. Herz,[254] Michael Hiscox,[255] Samuel Huntington,[256] Immanuel Kant,[257] Paul Kennedy,[258] David Lake,[259] Michael Mann,[260] Louis Marano,[261] Peter Richerson,[262] Enrico Spolaore,[263] Hendrik Spruyt,[264] Joseph Strayer,[265] Charles Tilly,[266] Max Weber,[267] and Alexander Wendt.[268] The book is cognizant but critical of the historical theories of Giambattista Vico,[269] G.W.F. Hegel, and Karl Marx.[270] On the evolution of hierarchies' effects on the individual, the intersection of ascriptive hierarchies, and the power left to the individual even within highly hierarchical societies, it draws from the theoretical work of James Scott,[271] Michel Foucault,[272] and Kimberlé Crenshaw.[273]

For assistance, ideas, data, encouragement, and suggestions, I thank Alberto Alesina, John Allen, Graham Allison, David Apter, John Batty-Sylvan, Dean Baxendale, Thomas Beale, Elena Bernini, Bear Braumoeller, Pavel Brusilovskiy, Bruce Bueno de Mesquita, Anna Davidson, Thomas Davis, Alexis Diamond, Corin Royal Drummond, Ben Edelman, Tanisha Fazal, Mohshin Habib, Yoram Haftel, Bertie Harrison-Broninski, Myroslava Hartmond, Judith Hurley, Kosuke Imai, Iain Johnston, Gary King, Yevgeniy Kirpichevsky, Andrew Kydd, Olivia Lau, Phillip Lipscy, Kay Mansfield, Lisa Martin, Craig McIntosh, Carole McPherson, Andrew Moravcsik, Edward Moreno, Margaret Mullins, Robert Murphy, Keith Neal, Tuan Nguyen, Joseph Nye, John Patty, Maggie Penn, James Perry, Robert Powell, Stephen Rosen, Bruce Russett, Matthew Schwartz, James Scott, Jasjeet Sekhon, Kenneth Shepsle, Jeremy Shonick, Alastair Smith, Alvaro Smith, Brooke Smith, Enrico Spolaore, Allan Stam, James Stone, Kevin Sweeney, Charles Tilly, Arthur Waldron, Thom Wall, Janice Weaver, Ruth Wedgwood, Alexander Wendt, Donald Wittman, Daniel Ziblatt, and participants in the Research Workshop in International Relations at Harvard University, the 2005 American Political Science Association panel, "The Size of States,"[274] and the Graduate Student Political Economy Workshop at Harvard University. All shortcomings that remain are, of course, my own.

Bibliography

Achebe, Chinua. *Things Fall Apart*. Oxford: Heinemann, 2003.

Ackerly, Brooke, and Jacqui True. "An Intersectional Analysis of International Relations: Recasting the Discipline." *Politics & Gender* 4, no. 01 (March 2008): 156–73. https://doi.org/10.1017/S1743923X08000081.

Alesina, Alberto, and Enrico Spolaore. "Conflict, Defense Spending, and the Number of Nations." *European Economic Review* 50 (2006): 91–120.

———. "On the Number and Size of Nations." *Quarterly Journal of Economics* 112, no. 4 (November 1, 1997): 1027–56. https://doi.org/10.1162/003355300555411.

———. *The Size of Nations*. Cambridge, MA: MIT Press, 2003.

———. "War, Peace, and the Size of Countries." *Journal of Public Economics* 89 (2005): 1333–54.

Al-Osaimi, Najah. "Taming Riyadh's Religious Police." *World Today (Chatham House)* 72, no. 3 (June 2016): 34–35.

Anderson, Benedict R. *Imagined Communities: Reflections on the Origin and Spread of Nationalism*. Revised edition. London and New York: Verso, 2016.

Anderson, Perry. *Lineages of the Absolutist State*. London: NLB, 1974.

———. *Passages from Antiquity to Feudalism*. London: NLB, 1974.

Andrieu, Claire. "Managing Memory: National and Personal Identity at

Stake in the Mitterrand Affair." *French Politics and Society* 14, no. 2 (1996): 17–32.

Angle, Stephen C., Kwame Anthony Appiah, and Julian Baggini. "In Defence of Hierarchy." *Aeon*, March 22, 2017. https://aeon.co/essays/hierarchies-have-a-place-even-in-societies-built-on-equality.

Åse, Cecelia. "Crisis Narratives and Masculinist Protection: Gendering the Original Stockholm Syndrome." *International Feminist Journal of Politics* 17, no. 4 (2015): 595–610.

Ashe, Laura, and Emily Joan Ward. *Conquests in Eleventh-Century England: 1016, 1066*. Suffolk, UK: Boydell Press, 2020.

Ashton, Basil, Kenneth Hill, Alan Piazza, and Robin Zeitz. "Famine in China, 1958–61." *Population and Development Review* 10, no. 4 (1984): 613–45. https://doi.org/10.2307/1973284.

Asselin, Pierre. "The Algerian Revolution and the Communist Bloc." Wilson Center. Accessed February 26, 2021. https://www.wilsoncenter.org/publication/the-algerian-revolution-and-the-communist-bloc.

Augustine, Aurelius. *The Works of Aurelius Augustine, Bishop of Hippo.* Edited by Marcus Dods. Edinburgh, UK: T. & T. Clark, 1871.

Avrich, Paul. "Russian Anarchists and the Civil War." *Russian Review* 27, no. 3 (1968): 296–306. https://doi.org/10.2307/127258.

Ballhaus, Rebecca, and Beth Reinhard. "Trump to Group of Law-Enforcement Officers: 'Please Don't Be Too Nice.'" *Wall Street Journal*, July 28, 2017. https://www.wsj.com/articles/trump-to-group-of-law-enforcement-officers-please-dont-be-too-nice-1501273200.

Barboza, David. "The New Influencers." *Wire China*, April 18, 2021. https://www.thewirechina.com/2021/04/18/the-new-influencers/.

Barboza, David, Christopher Drew, and Steve Lohr. "G.E. to Share Jet Technology with China in New Joint Venture." *New York Times*, January 17, 2011. https://www.nytimes.com/2011/01/18/business/global/18plane.html.

Barr, William. "Transcript of Attorney General Barr's Remarks on China Policy at the Gerald R. Ford Presidential Museum," July 17, 2020. https://www.justice.gov/opa/speech/transcript-attorney-general-barr-s-remarks-china-policy-gerald-r-ford-presidential-museum.

Bazelon, Emily. "Should Prostitution Be a Crime?" *New York Times*, May

5, 2016. https://www.nytimes.com/2016/05/08/magazine/should-prostitution-be-a-crime.html.

BBC. "Coronavirus: Men Wanted over Racist Oxford Street Attack on Student." *BBC News*, March 4, 2020. https://www.bbc.com/news/uk-england-london-51736755.

Beauvoir, Simone de. *Memoirs of a Dutiful Daughter*. Harmondsworth, UK: Penguin, 1984.

Bell, Daniel. *The China Model: Political Meritocracy and the Limits of Democracy*. Princeton, NJ: Princeton University Press, 2015.

Bell, Daniel A., and Pei Wang. *Just Hierarchy: Why Social Hierarchies Matter in China and the Rest of the World*. Princeton, NJ: Princeton University Press, 2020.

Bentley, R. Alexander. "Mobility and the Diversity of Early Neolithic Lives: Isotopic Evidence from Skeletons." *Journal of Anthropological Archaeology* 32, no. 3 (September 1, 2013): 303–12. https://doi.org/10.1016/j.jaa.2012.01.009.

Biden, Joe. "Biden's Speech to Congress: Full Transcript." *New York Times*, April 29, 2021. https://www.nytimes.com/2021/04/29/us/politics/joe-biden-speech-transcript.html.

Blow, Charles M. "About the 'Basket of Deplorables.'" *New York Times*, September 12, 2016. https://www.nytimes.com/2016/09/12/opinion/about-the-basket-of-deplorables.html.

Borja, Horacio Sevilla. "Development of an International Legally Binding Instrument under UNCLOS on the Conservation and Sustainable Use of Marine Biological Diversity of Areas beyond National Jurisdiction." Group of 77, 2017. http://www.g77.org/statement/getstatement.php?id=170710.

Bouie, Jamelle. "If There Was a Republican Civil War, It Appears to Be Over." *New York Times*, February 17, 2021. https://www.nytimes.com/2021/02/17/opinion/trump-mconnell-republicans.html.

Braumoeller, Bear. *The Great Powers and the International System: Systemic Theory in Empirical Perspective*. Cambridge, UK: Cambridge University Press, 2012.

———. "The Great Powers in General (Dis-)Equilibrium." Mershon Center at the Ohio State University, May 20, 2005.

Breen, Richard. *Social Mobility in Europe*. Oxford: Oxford University Press, 2004.

Bregman, Rutger. *Humankind: A Hopeful History*. London: Bloomsbury, 2020.

Brennan, Timothy. *Borrowed Light: Vico, Hegel, and the Colonies: 1*. Illustrated edition. Stanford, CA: Stanford University Press, 2014.

Broadwater, Luke. "Militia Groups Want to 'Blow Up the Capitol,' a Police Chief Testifies." *New York Times*, February 25, 2021. https://www.nytimes.com/2021/02/25/us/politics/capitol-attack-state-of-the-union.html.

Brown, George W. "The Origins of Abolition in Santo Domingo." *Journal of Negro History* 7, no. 4 (1922): 365–76. https://doi.org/10.2307/2713719.

Brown, Wendy. "Neoliberalized Knowledge." *History of the Present* 1, no. 1 (Summer 2011): 113–29.

Buckley, Chris, Doan Chau, and Thomas Fuller. "China Targeted by Vietnamese in Fiery Riots." *New York Times*, May 14, 2014. https://www.nytimes.com/2014/05/15/world/asia/foreign-factories-in-vietnam-weigh-damage-in-anti-china-riots.html.

Bump, Philip. "A Pillow Salesman Apparently Has Some Ideas about Declaring Martial Law." *Washington Post*, January 15, 2021. https://www.washingtonpost.com/politics/2021/01/15/pillow-salesman-apparently-has-some-ideas-about-declaring-martial-law/.

Burstein, Ellen M., and Camille G. Caldera. "Harvard Took In $1.1 Billion from 63 Nations from 2013–2019, per Department of Education." *Harvard Crimson*, February 13, 2020. https://www.thecrimson.com/article/2020/2/13/harvard-billion-foreign-funds/.

Butler, Judith. *Gender Trouble: Feminism and the Subversion of Identity*. Routledge Classics. New York: Routledge, 2006.

Carneiro, Robert L. "Political Expansion as an Expression of the Principle of Competitive Exclusion." In *Origins of the State: The Anthropology of Political Competitive Exclusion*, 205–24. Philadelphia: Institute for the Study of Human Issues, 1978.

———. "A Theory of the Origin of the State." *Science* 169, no. 3947 (August 21, 1970): 733–38.

Cassius Dio. *Roman History*. Translated by Earnest Cary. Cambridge, MA: Harvard University Press, 1914.

Cederman, Lars-Erik. *Emergent Actors in World Politics: How States and Nations Develop and Dissolve*. Princeton, NJ: Princeton University Press, 1997.

———. "Generating State-Size Distributions: A Geopolitical Model." Center for Comparative and International Studies, 2003.

———. "Modeling the Size of Wars: From Billiard Balls to Sandpiles." *American Political Science Review* 97, no. 1 (February 2003): 135–50.

Chaudhury, Dipanjan Roy. "India Nudges Shanghai Cooperation Organisation to Adopt English as Working Language." *Economic Times*, August 26, 2020. https://economictimes.indiatimes.com/news/politics-and-nation/india-nudges-sco-to-adopt-english-as-working-language/articleshow/77749069.cms.

Cheng, Leng, Yan Zhang, and Ryan Woo. "Chinese Banks Urged to Switch Away from SWIFT as U.S. Sanctions Loom." *Reuters*, July 29, 2020. https://www.reuters.com/article/us-china-banks-usa-sanctions-idUSKCN24U0SN.

Cheung, Tony. "Beijing Urges Swift British Response to Burning of Chinese Flag, Hong Kong Pro-Independence Chants Outside Its London Embassy." *South China Morning Post*, October 2, 2020. https://www.scmp.com/news/hong-kong/politics/article/3103934/beijing-urges-swift-british-response-burning-chinese-flag.

Ciurtin, Horia. "The '16+1' Becomes the '17+1': Greece Joins China's Dwindling Cooperation Framework in Central and Eastern Europe." *China Brief* 19, no. 10 (May 29, 2019). https://jamestown.org/program/the-161-becomes-the-171-greece-joins-chinas-dwindling-cooperation-framework-in-central-and-eastern-europe/.

Claeys, Gregory. "Paternalism and Democracy in the Politics of Robert Owen." *International Review of Social History* 27, no. 2 (1982): 161–207.

Cleaver, Eldridge, and Ishmael Reed. *Soul on Ice*. Repr. A Delta Book. New York: Dell Publishing, 1999.

Cohen, Gerald A. *Karl Marx's Theory of History: A Defence*. Oxford, UK: Oxford University Press, 1978.

Colonial Office Information Department. "Singapore Police Capture Chinese Propaganda Press Then Issue Own Edition of Communist 'Freedom News,'" August 30, 1951. Fabian Colonial Bureau. MSS British Empire s365, Box 156/1, 35. Oxford University Library.

THE CONCENTRATION OF POWER

Commission on the Theft of American Intellectual Property. "Update to the IP Commission Report: The Theft of American Intellectual Property: Reassessments of the Challenge and United States Policy." National Bureau of Asian Research, 2017. http://ipcommission.org/report/IP_Commission_Report_Update_2017.pdf.

Cooper, Sam. *Wilful Blindness: How a Criminal Network of Narcos, Tycoons, and CCP Agents Infiltrated the West.* Toronto: Optimum Publishing International, 2021.

Corr, Anders. "American Primacy and Offensive Posture: A Reply to Stephen Walt." Harvard Kennedy School of Government, 2002. https://www.belfercenter.org/sites/default/files/legacy/files/corr_watl_response.pdf.

———. "China's Moneybag Friends at Harvard University." *Asia Sentinel,* August 18, 2017. https://www.asiasentinel.com/p/china-money-bag-friends-harvard-university.

———. *No Trespassing! Squatting, Rent Strikes, and Land Struggles Worldwide.* 1st ed. Cambridge, MA: South End Press, 1999.

———. "War, Technology, and Change: The Ratchet Effect and System Unification." Harvard University, 2008.

Crenshaw, Kimberlé. "Demarginalizing the Intersection of Race and Sex: A Black Feminist Critique of Antidiscrimination Doctrine, Feminist Theory and Antiracist Politics." *University of Chicago Legal Forum* 1, no. 8 (1989): 1–31.

De Waal, Frans B.M. "The Integration of Dominance and Social Bonding in Primates." *Quarterly Review of Biology* 61, no. 4 (December 1986): 459–79.

Dezan Shira & Associates. "Minimum Wages in China 2020: A Complete Guide." China Briefing News, April 29, 2020. https://www.china-briefing.com/news/minimum-wages-china-2020/.

Diamond, Jared M. *Guns, Germs, and Steel: The Fates of Human Societies.* New York: W.W. Norton & Co., 1997.

Diogenes, Laërtius, Robert Drew Hicks, and Robert Aitken. *Lives of the Eminent Philosophers.* Kindle, 2014.

Divale, William Tulio, and Marvin Harris. "Population, Warfare, and the Male Supremacist Complex." *American Anthropologist* 78, no. 3 (September 1976): 521–38. https://doi.org/10.1525/aa.1976.78.3.02a00020.

Doshi, Rush. *The Long Game: China's Grand Strategy to Displace American Order*. New York: Oxford University Press, 2021.

Dubreuil, Benoît. *Human Evolution and the Origins of Hierarchies: The State of Nature*. Cambridge, UK: Cambridge University Press, 2010.

Dumont, Louis. "On Value: The Radcliffe-Brown Lecture in Social Anthropology, 1980." *HAU: Journal of Ethnographic Theory* 3, no. 1 (March 2013): 287–315. https://doi.org/10.14318/hau3.1.028.

Dunbar, R., and S. Shultz. "Evolution in the Social Brain." *Science* 317 (2007): 13v–47.

Durkheim, Émile. *The Division of Labor in Society*. Glencoe, IL: Free Press, 1960.

Engels, Friedrich. *The Origin of the Family, Private Property and the State*. London: Penguin, 2010.

Evans, Danny. *Revolution and the State: Anarchism in the Spanish Civil War, 1936–1939*. London: Routledge, 2018.

Fanell, James, US Navy Captain (ret.). "China's Global Naval Strategy and Expanding Force Structure: Pathway to Hegemony." Testimony presented at the House Permanent Select Committee on Intelligence, Washington, DC, May 17, 2018. https://docs.house.gov/meetings/IG/IG00/20180517/108298/HHRG-115-IG00-Wstate-FanellJ-20180517.pdf.

Farré, Juan Avilés. "Los socialistas y la insurrección de octubre de 1934." *Espacio Tiempo y Forma. Serie V, Historia Contemporánea* 20 (2008). https://doi.org/10.5944/etfv.20.2008.1506.

Fawcett, Peter. "'When I Squeeze You with Eisphorai': Taxes and Tax Policy in Classical Athens." *Hesperia* 85, no. 1 (January 2016): 153–99.

Ferguson, R. Brian. "Violence and War in Prehistory." In *Troubled Times: Violence and Warfare in the Past*, by Debra L. Martin and David W. Frayer, 321–56. Amsterdam: Gordon and Breach Publishers, 2014.

Ferguson, Yale H. "The Dominican Intervention of 1965: Recent Interpretations." *International Organization* 27, no. 4 (1973): 517–48.

Fogel, Joshua A. "The Debates over the Asiatic Mode of Production in Soviet Russia, China, and Japan." *American Historical Review* 93, no. 1 (1988): 56–79. https://doi.org/10.2307/1865689.

Forbes. "#2 Koch Family," December 16, 2020. https://www.forbes.com/profile/koch/.

Forsythe, Michael. "As China's Leader Fights Graft, His Relatives Shed Assets." *New York Times*, June 17, 2014. https://www.nytimes.com/2014/06/18/world/asia/chinas-president-xi-jinping-investments.html.

———. "Panama Papers Tie More of China's Elite to Secret Accounts." *New York Times*, April 6, 2016. https://www.nytimes.com/2016/04/07/world/asia/china-panama-papers.html.

Foucault, Michel. *Discipline and Punish: The Birth of the Prison*. Reprint. London: Penguin Books, 1991.

———. *The History of Sexuality*. Vol. 1. London: Penguin Books, 1990.

———. *The History of Sexuality*. Vol. 2. London: Penguin Books, 1992.

———. *Madness and Civilization: A History of Insanity in the Age of Reason*. Translated by Richard Howard. Routledge Classics. London: Routledge, 2007.

Freeman, Jacob. "The Socioecology of Territory Size and a 'Work-Around' Hypothesis for the Adoption of Farming." *PLoS ONE* 11, no. 7 (July 8, 2016): e0158743. https://doi.org/10.1371/journal.pone.0158743.

Freire, Paulo. *Pedagogy of the Oppressed*. New rev. ed. Penguin Books. London: Penguin Books, 1996.

Fukuyama, Francis. *The End of History and the Last Man*. New York: Simon and Schuster, 2006.

———. *The Origins of Political Order: From Prehuman Times to the French Revolution*. New York: Farrar, Straus and Giroux, 2011.

———. *Political Order and Political Decay: From the French Revolution to the Present: From the Industrial Revolution to the Globalisation of Democracy*. New York: Farrar, Straus and Giroux, 2014.

Gandhi, Mohandas K., and Mahadev H. Desai. *Autobiography: The Story of My Experiments with Truth*. Dover ed. New York: Dover, 1983.

Gillenwater, Sharon. "Today's Immigrant CEOs: Bringing a Global Sensibility to American Business." *Salesforce Blog*, June 16, 2017. https://web.archive.org/web/20200611184309/https://www.salesforce.com/blog/2017/06/immigrant-ceos-global-sensibility-business.html.

Gintis, Herbert, Carel van Schaik, and Christopher Boehm. "*Zoon Politikon*: The Evolutionary Origins of Human Political Systems." *Current Anthropology* 56, no. 3 (June 2015): 327–53. https://doi.org/10.1086/681217.

Glasser, Susan B. "Mike Pompeo, the Secretary of Trump." *New Yorker*, August 19, 2019. https://www.newyorker.com/magazine/2019/08/26/mike-pompeo-the-secretary-of-trump.

Goldman, Adam. "Officer Attacked in Capitol Riot Died of Multiple Strokes, Medical Examiner Rules." *New York Times*, April 19, 2021. https://www.nytimes.com/2021/04/19/us/politics/brian-sicknick-death.html.

Goldstein, Melvyn C. *A History of Modern Tibet, 1913–1951: The Demise of the Lamaist State*. Berkeley: University of California Press, 1991.

———. *The Snow Lion and the Dragon: China, Tibet, and the Dalai Lama*. Berkeley: University of California Press, 1997.

Goodall, Jane. *The Chimpanzees of Gombe: Patterns of Behavior*. Cambridge, MA: Harvard University Press, 1986.

Graeber, David. "The Rise of Hierarchy." In *Hierarchy and Value: Comparative Perspectives on Moral Order*, 3335–3681. New York: Berghahn Books, 2018.

Gupta, Anubhav. "How Can Biden Strengthen Ties with India?" *Diplomat*, February 1, 2021. https://thediplomat.com/2021/02/how-can-biden-strengthen-ties-with-india/.

Habib, Mohshin, Christine Jubb, Salahuddin Ahmad, Masudur Rahman, and Henri Pallard. "Forced Migration of Rohingya: An Untold Experience." SSRN Scholarly Paper. Rochester, NY: Social Science Research Network, September 1, 2018. https://doi.org/10.2139/ssrn.3242696.

Hamilton, Clive, and Mareike Ohlberg. *Hidden Hand: Exposing How the Chinese Communist Party Is Reshaping the World*. London: Oneworld Publications, 2020.

Harari, Yuval Noah. *Sapiens: A Brief History of Humankind*. Translated by John Purcell and Haim Watzman. London: Vintage Books, 2015.

Hasenstab, Michael. "China's Digital Currency Is a Threat to Dollar Dominance." *Financial Times*, April 14, 2021. https://www.ft.com/content/3fe905e7-8b9b-4782-bf2d-fc4f45496915.

Haynes, Naomi, and Jason Hickel. "Hierarchy, Value, and the Value of Hierarchy." *Social Analysis* 60, no. 4 (Winter 2016): 1–20.

Hegel, G.W.F. *Elements of the Philosophy of Right.* Edited by Allen W. Wood. Translated by H.B. Nisbet. Cambridge, UK: Cambridge University Press, 2003.

———. *The Phenomenology of Spirit.* Translated by Terry Pinkard. Cambridge, UK: Cambridge University Press, 2018.

———. *The Philosophy of History.* Translated by J. Sibree. Kitchener, ON: Batoche Books, 2001.

———. *Philosophy of Mind.* Translated by William Wallace. London and Oxford, UK: Oxford University Press, 1894.

Herder, Johann Gottfried von. *Outlines of a Philosophy of the History of Man.* Translated by T. Churchill and David G. Payne. N.p.: Random Shack, 2016.

Hermanussen, Michael. "Stature of Early Europeans." *Hormones (Athens, Greece)* 2, no. 3 (September 2003): 175–78. https://doi.org/10.14310/horm.2002.1199.

Hernández, Javier C. "Harsh Penalties, Vaguely Defined Crimes: Hong Kong's Security Law Explained." *New York Times*, July 1, 2020. https://www.nytimes.com/2020/06/30/world/asia/hong-kong-security-law-explain.html.

Herz, John H. "Idealist Internationalism and the Security Dilemma." *World Politics* 2, no. 2 (January 1950): 157–80. https://doi.org/10.2307/2009187.

———. "Rise and Demise of the Territorial State." *World Politics* 9, no. 4 (1957): 473–93. https://doi.org/10.2307/2009421.

———. "The Territorial State Revisited: Reflections on the Future of the Nation-State." *Polity* 1, no. 1 (1968): 11–34. https://doi.org/10.2307/3233974.

Hickel, Jason, and Naomi Haynes, eds. *Hierarchy and Value: Comparative Perspectives on Moral Order.* New York: Berghahn Books, 2018.

Hill, Evan, David Botti, Dmitriy Khavin, Drew Jordan, and Malachy Browne. "Officer Brian Sicknick Died after the Capitol Riot. New Videos Show How He Was Attacked." *New York Times*, March 24, 2021. https://www.nytimes.com/interactive/2021/03/24/us/officer-sicknick-capitol-riot.html.

Hiscox, Michael J., and David A. Lake. "Democracy, Federalism, and the Size of States." Harvard University and University of California, San Diego, January 2002.

hooks, bell. *Talking Back: Thinking Feminist, Thinking Black*. New edition. New York: Routledge, 2014.

Howell, Signe. "Battle of Cosmologies: The Catholic Church, Adat, and 'Inculturation' among Northern Lio, Indonesia." In *Hierarchy and Value: Comparative Perspectives on Moral Order*, by Jason Hickel and Naomi Haynes, Kindle 658–1094. New York: Berghahn Books, 2018.

Hsu, Tiffany, and Katie Robertson. "Covering Pro-Trump Mobs, the News Media Became a Target." *New York Times*, January 7, 2021. https://www.nytimes.com/2021/01/06/business/media/media-murder-capitol-building.html.

Human Rights Watch. "Covid-19 Fueling Anti-Asian Racism and Xenophobia Worldwide," May 12, 2020. https://www.hrw.org/news/2020/05/12/covid-19-fueling-anti-asian-racism-and-xeno-phobia-worldwide.

Huntington, Samuel. *Political Order in Changing Societies*. New Haven, CT: Yale University Press, 2006.

———. *The Third Wave: Democratization in the Late Twentieth Century*. Norman, OK: University of Oklahoma Press, 1991.

Hutchinson, Lincoln. "Roman and Anglo-Saxon Agrarian Conditions." *Quarterly Journal of Economics* 7, no. 2 (1893): 205–10. https://doi.org/10.2307/1883048.

Ibrahim, Azeem. *The Rohingyas: Inside Myanmar's Genocide*. London: Hurst & Company, 2018.

Iodice, Emilio. "Lessons from History: The Startling Rise to Power of Benito Mussolini." *Journal of Values-Based Leadership* 11, no. 2 (15 July 2018): 1–32. https://doi.org/10.22543/0733.62.1241.

Jian, Chen. "The Tibetan Rebellion of 1959 and China's Changing Relations with India and the Soviet Union." *Journal of Cold War Studies* 8, no. 3 (July 1, 2006): 54–101. https://doi.org/10.1162/jcws.2006.8.3.54.

Johnson, A. Ross. "The Warsaw Pact: Soviet Military Policy in Eastern Europe." *Rand Paper Series*, July 1981, 1–55.

Jordan, William Chester. "Anti-Corruption Campaigns in Thirteenth-Century Europe." *Journal of Medieval History* 35, no. 2 (June 1, 2009): 204–19. https://doi.org/10.1016/j.jmedhist.2009.03.004.

Kant, Immanuel. *To Perpetual Peace: A Philosophical Sketch.* Indianapolis, IN: Hackett Publishing, 2003.

———. "What Is Enlightenment?" Translated by Mary C. Smith, 1784. http://www.columbia.edu/acis/ets/CCREAD/etscc/kant.html.

Karlsson Sjögren, Åsa. "Voting Women before Women's Suffrage in Sweden 1720–1870." In *Suffrage, Gender and Citizenship: International Perspectives on Parliamentary Reforms*, edited by Irma Sulkunen, Seija-Leena Nevala-Nurmi, and Pirjo Markkola, 56–82. Newcastle, UK: Cambridge Scholars Publishing, 2009. http://urn. kb.se/resolve?urn=urn:nbn:se:umu:diva-22097.

Kellermann, A. L., and J. A. Mercy. "Men, Women, and Murder: Gender-Specific Differences in Rates of Fatal Violence and Victimization." *Journal of Trauma* 33, no. 1 (July 1992): 1–5.

Kendell, Ashley. "The Crow Creek Massacre: The Role of Sex in Native American Scalping Practices." In *Archaeological Perspectives on Warfare on the Great Plains*. Boulder: University Press of Colorado, 2018.

Kenneally, Shannon M., Gina E. Bruck, Elaine M. Frank, and Lily Nalty. "Language Intervention after Thirty Years of Isolation: A Case Study of a Feral Child." *Education and Training in Mental Retardation and Developmental Disabilities* 33, no. 1 (1998): 13–23.

Kennedy, Paul. *The Rise and Fall of the Great Powers: Economic Change and Military Conflict from 1500 to 2000.* London: Unwin Hyman, 1988.

———. *The Rise and Fall of the Great Powers: Economic Change and Military Conflict from 1500–2000.* New edition. London: William Collins, 2017.

Kent, Ann. "China's Participation in International Organisations." In *Power and Responsibility in Chinese Foreign Policy*, edited by Yongjin Zhang and Greg Austin, 132–66. Australian National University Press, 2013. https://www.jstor.org/stable/j.ctt5vj73b.11.

Kent, Sherman. *Strategic Intelligence for American World Policy.* 3rd Edition, 1951. Princeton, NJ: Princeton University Press, 1949.

Keynes, John Maynard. *The General Theory of Employment, Interest and Money*. Cambridge, UK: Cambridge University Press, 2012.

Kryzanek, Michael J. "The 1978 Election in the Dominican Republic: Opposition Politics, Intervention and the Carter Administration." *Caribbean Studies* 19, no. 1/2 (1979): 51–73.

Kuleshnyk, Irka. "The Stockholm Syndrome: Toward an Understanding." *Social Action & the Law* 10, no. 2 (1984): 37–42.

Kupchan, Charles A. "The Normative Foundations of Hegemony and the Coming Challenge to Pax Americana." *Security Studies* 23, no. 2 (April 3, 2014): 219–57. https://doi.org/10.1080/09636412.2014.874205.

Kuromiya, Hiroaki. "Ukraine and Russia in the 1930s." *Harvard Ukrainian Studies* 18, no. 3/4 (1994): 327–41.

Kynge, James, and Sun Yu. "Virtual Control: The Agenda behind China's New Digital Currency," February 17, 2021. https://www.ft.com/content/7511809e-827e-4526-81ad-ae83f405f623.

Lake, David A. "Escape from the State of Nature: Authority and Hierarchy in World Politics." *International Security* 32, no. 1 (Summer 2007): 47–79.

Lake, David A., and Angela O'Mahony. "The Incredible Shrinking State: Explaining Change in the Territorial Size of Countries." *Journal of Conflict Resolution* 48, no. 5 (October 2004): 699–722.

Lau, Stuart. "Xi Warns Biden and EU Not to Reignite Cold War." *Politico*, January 25, 2021. https://www.politico.eu/article/xi-warns-biden-and-eu-not-to-reignite-cold-war/.

Layne, Christopher. "This Time It's Real: The End of Unipolarity and the Pax Americana." *International Studies Quarterly* 56, no. 1 (March 1, 2012): 203–13. https://doi.org/10.1111/j.1468-2478.2011.00704.x.

Legon, Ronald P. "Samos in the Delian League." *Historia: Zeitschrift Für Alte Geschichte* 21, no. 2 (1972): 145–58.

Leising, Matthew. "Crypto Assets of $50 Billion Moved from China in the Past Year." *Bloomberg*, August 20, 2020. https://www.bloomberg.com/news/articles/2020-08-20/crypto-assets-of-50-billion-moved-from-china-in-the-past-year.

Levy, Rachael, Ted Mann, and Andrew Restuccia. "Pro-Trump Mob Force Way Into Capitol; D.C. Orders Curfew." *Wall Street Journal*, January 6, 2021. https://www.wsj.com/articles/as-rioters-again-dispute-trumps-defeat-d-c-police-make-arrests-11609945368.

Liebert, Hugh. "Alexander the Great and the History of Globalization." *Review of Politics* 73, no. 4 (Fall 2011): 533–60. https://doi.org/10.1017/S0034670511003639.

Louis, Dumont. *Homo Hierarchicus: The Caste System and Its Implications.* Chicago: University of Chicago Press, 1980.

Lukács, Georg. "Legality and Illegality." In *History and Class Consciousness.* Merlin Press, 1967. https://www.marxists.org/archive/lukacs/works/history/.

Lüthi, Lorenz M. *The Sino-Soviet Split: Cold War in the Communist World.* Princeton, NJ: Princeton University Press, 2008.

Lutz, Helma. "Intersectionality as Method." *DiGeSt. Journal of Diversity and Gender Studies* 2, no. 1–2 (2015): 39–44. https://doi.org/10.11116/jdivegendstud.2.1-2.0039.

Machiavelli, Niccolò. *The Prince.* Translated by George Bull. Harmondsworth, UK: Penguin Books, 1961.

Man Hoi Yan, Lu Xi, and Mudie Luisetta. "China-Backed Hong Kong Paper Calls for 'Ban' on Pro-Democracy Apple Daily." *Radio Free Asia.* Accessed April 18, 2021. https://www.rfa.org/english/news/china/hongkong-appledaily-04162021084518.html.

Mann, Michael. *Sources of Social Power.* Vol. 1–4. Cambridge, UK: Cambridge University Press, 2013.

Marano, Louis A. "A Macrohistorical Trend toward World Government." *Behavior Science Notes* 8 (1973): 35–40.

Markle, Minor M. "Macedonian Arms and Tactics under Alexander the Great." *Studies in the History of Art* 10 (1982): 86–111.

Marshall, Lorna. "Sharing, Talking, and Giving: Relief of Social Tensions among !Kung Bushmen." *Africa: Journal of the International African Institute* 31, no. 3 (1961): 231–49. https://doi.org/10.2307/1157263.

Marx, Karl. *The Civil War in France.* Kindle, n.d.

———. *A Contribution to the Critique of Political Economy.* Translated by N.I. Stone. Chicago: Charles H. Kerr & Company, 1904.

———. "Critique of the Gotha Program." In *Essential Writings of Karl Marx*, edited by Friedrich Engels. St. Petersburg, FL: Red and Black Publishers, 2010.

———. *Essential Writings of Karl Marx*. Edited by Lenny Flank. St. Petersburg, FL: Red and Black Publishers, 2010.

———. *Karl Marx: Early Writings*. Translated by Rodney Livingstone and Gregor Benton. London: Penguin Books, 1992.

Marx, Karl, and Friedrich Engels. *The German Ideology: Including Theses on Feuerbach and Introduction to the Critique of Political Economy*. Great Books in Philosophy. Amherst, NY: Prometheus Books, 1998.

Masko, John. "CIA Operations in Tibet and the Intelligence-Policy Relationship." *American Intelligence Journal* 31, no. 2 (2013): 127–32.

Mayer, Jane. "The Danger of President Pence." *New Yorker*, October 16, 2017. https://www.newyorker.com/magazine/2017/10/23/the-danger-of-president-pence.

———. *Dark Money: The Hidden History of the Billionaires behind the Rise of the Radical Right*. New York: Anchor Books, 2017.

McDougall, Sara. "The Opposite of the Double Standard: Gender, Marriage, and Adultery Prosecution in Late Medieval France." *Journal of the History of Sexuality* 23 (May 1, 2014): 206–25. https://doi.org/10.7560/JHS23203.

McGranahan, Carole. *Arrested Histories: Tibet, the CIA, and Memories of a Forgotten War*. Durham, NC: Duke University Press, 2010.

Metz, Cade. "Who Is Making Sure the A.I. Machines Aren't Racist?" *New York Times*, March 15, 2021. https://www.nytimes.com/2021/03/15/technology/artificial-intelligence-google-bias.html.

Meyer, Christian, Christian Lohr, Detlef Gronenborn, and Kurt W. Alt. "The Massacre Mass Grave of Schöneck-Kilianstädten Reveals New Insights into Collective Violence in Early Neolithic Central Europe." *Proceedings of the National Academy of Sciences of the United States of America* 112, no. 36 (2015): 11217–22.

Miles, Rufus E. "The Origin and Meaning of Miles' Law." *Public Administration Review* 38, no. 5 (1978): 399–403. https://doi.org/10.2307/975497.

Mohanty, Chandra Talpade, Ann Russo, and Lourdes Torres, eds. *Third World Women and the Politics of Feminism*. Bloomington: Indiana University Press, 1991.

Montenaro, Domenico. "Timeline: How One of the Darkest Days in American History Unfolded." NPR.org. Accessed February 10, 2021. https://www.npr.org/2021/01/07/954384999/timeline-how-one-of-the-darkest-days-in-american-history-unfolded.

Morgan, Lewis Henry. *Ancient Society: Or, Researches in the Lines of Human Progress from Savagery through Barbarism to Civilization.* London: Routledge, 1998.

Morgenthau, Hans J. "The Nature and Use of Power and Its Influence upon State Goals and Strategies: A Lecture Delivered at the Naval War College on 25 September 1963." *Naval War College Review* 16, no. 6 (February 1964): 18–30.

Namnyak, M. et. al. "'Stockholm Syndrome': Psychiatric Diagnosis or Urban Myth?" *Acta Psychiatrica Scandinavica* 117, no. 1 (January 2008): 4–11.

NATO. "Member Countries." NATO. Accessed February 17, 2021. http://www.nato.int/cps/en/natohq/topics_52044.htm.

New York Times. "Church Asks Spain to Pay Big Damages: Papal Nuncio Demands Indemnity for Fifty Buildings Burned in 1931 Riots." *New York Times*, June 10, 1932. https://www.nytimes.com/1932/06/10/archives/church-asks-spain-to-pay-big-damages-papal-nuncio-demands-indemnity.html.

Nicas, Jack, and Davey Alba. "Amazon, Apple and Google Cut Off Parler, an App That Drew Trump Supporters." *New York Times*, January 10, 2021. https://www.nytimes.com/2021/01/09/technology/apple-google-parler.html.

Nice, Geoffrey. "The Independent Tribunal into Forced Organ Harvesting from Prisoners of Conscience in China." China Tribunal, March 1, 2020. https://chinatribunal.com/wp-content/uploads/2020/03/ChinaTribunal_JUDGMENT_1stMarch_2020.pdf.

Nietzsche, Friedrich Wilhelm. *Beyond Good and Evil: On the Genealogy of Morality.* Vol. 8. *The Complete Works of Friedrich Nietzsche.* Stanford, CA: Stanford University Press, 2014.

———. *Ecce Homo: How One Becomes What One Is.* London: Penguin Books, 1992.

———. *The Will to Power: An Attempted Transvaluation of All Values.* London: The Big Nest, 2019.

Norbu, Dawa. "The 1959 Tibetan Rebellion: An Interpretation." *China*

Quarterly, no. 77 (1979): 74–93.

Oppenheimer, Franz. *The State*. New York: Free Life Editions, 1975.

Paden, Roger. "Marx's Critique of the Utopian Socialists." *Utopian Studies* 13, no. 2 (2002): 67–91.

Pape, Robert A., and Keven Ruby. "The Capitol Rioters Aren't Like Other Extremists." *Atlantic*, February 2, 2021. https://www.theatlantic.com/ideas/archive/2021/02/the-capitol-rioters-arent-like-other-extremists/617895/.

Payne, Stanley G. *Fascism in Spain, 1923–1977*. Madison: University of Wisconsin Press, 1999.

Peattie, Mark R., and Ramon H. Myers, eds. *The Japanese Colonial Empire, 1895–1945*. Princeton, NJ: Princeton University Press, 1984.

Permanent Mission of the People's Republic of China to the United Nations. "CML/18/2009," 1–2. New York: United Nations, 2009. https://www.un.org/Depts/los/clcs_new/submissions_files/vnm37_09/chn_2009re_vnm.pdf.

Pew Research Center. "Despite Global Concerns about Democracy, More than Half of Countries Are Democratic," May 14, 2019. https://www.pewresearch.org/fact-tank/2019/05/14/more-than-half-of-countries-are-democratic/.

Piketty, Thomas. *Capital in the Twenty-First Century*. Cambridge, MA: Harvard University Press, 2017.

Pinker, Steven. *The Better Angels of Our Nature: Why Violence Has Declined*. New York: Penguin Books, 2011.

Plato. *The Republic, Charmides, Meno, Gorgias, Parmenides, Symposium, Euthyphro, Apology, Crito, Phaedo*. Translated by Benjamin Jowett. London: Arcturus Publishing Ltd., 2020.

Plutarch. *The Parallel Lives*. Translated by Bernadotte Perrin. Cambridge, MA: Harvard University Press, 1916. https://penelope.uchicago.edu/Thayer/E/Roman/Texts/Plutarch/Lives/Pericles*.html.

Pompeo, Mike. "Communist China and the Free World's Future." Speech transcript, July 23, 2020. https://2017-2021.state.gov/communist-china-and-the-free-worlds-future-2/index.html.

Popper, K.R. *The Open Society and Its Enemies*. London: George Routledge & Sons, 1947.

Popper, Stephen W. *China's Propensity for Innovation in the 21st Century: Identifying Indicators of Future Outcomes.* Santa Monica, CA: RAND Corporation, 2020. https://doi.org/10.7249/RRA208-1.

Post, Che, Jan G. Brouwer, and Michel Vols. "Regulation of Prostitution in the Netherlands: Liberal Dream or Growing Repression?" *European Journal on Criminal Policy and Research* 25, no. 2 (June 1, 2019): 99–118. https://doi.org/10.1007/s10610-018-9371-8.

Preston, Paul. "Spain's October Revolution and the Rightist Grasp for Power." *Journal of Contemporary History* 10, no. 4 (1975): 555–78.

Price, David H. "Wittfogel's Neglected Hydraulic/Hydroagricultural Distinction." *Journal of Anthropological Research* 50, no. 2 (Summer 1994): 187–204.

Radchenko, Sergey. "The Sino-Soviet Split." In *Cambridge History of the Cold War: Crises and Détente*, edited by Melvyn P. Leffler and Odd Arne Westad, 349–72. Cambridge University Press, 2010. https://pure.aber.ac.uk/portal/en/publications/the-sinosoviet-split(5efb136f-b2da-4441-ad62-453007b9a5ee).html.

Ramzy, Austin, and Tiffany May. "Hong Kong Arrests Jimmy Lai, Media Mogul, Under National Security Law." *New York Times,* August 10, 2020. https://www.nytimes.com/2020/08/09/world/asia/hong-kong-arrests-lai-national-security-law.html.

Ramzy, Austin, and Raymond Zhong. "Hong Kong Protesters Defy Police Ban in Show of Strength after Tumult." *New York Times,* August 18, 2019. https://www.nytimes.com/2019/08/18/world/asia/hong-kong-protest.html.

Reed, John, and Edward White. "Myanmar Protesters Accuse China of Backing Coup Plotters." *Financial Times,* February 17, 2021. https://www.ft.com/content/43e6ecfe-081a-4390-aa18-154ec87ff764.

Regan, Patrick M., and Sam R. Bell. "Changing Lanes or Stuck in the Middle: Why Are Anocracies More Prone to Civil Wars?" *Political Research Quarterly* 63, no. 4 (2010): 747–59.

Reid, David. "Boeing Values China's Aircraft Business at Almost $3 Trillion over the next Two Decades." CNBC, September 17, 2019. https://www.cnbc.com/2019/09/17/boeing-says-china-needs-to-spend-almost-3-trillion-on-new-planes.html.

Richerson, Peter J., and Robert Boyd. "Complex Societies: The Evolutionary Origins of a Crude Superorganism." *Human Nature* 10, no. 3 (September 1, 1999): 253–89. https://doi.org/10.1007/s12110-999-1004-y.

Richerson, Peter J., and Robert Boyd. "Institutional Evolution in the Holocene: The Rise of Complex Societies," 1–34, 2000. http://www.des.ucdavis.edu/faculty/Richerson/evolutioninstitutions.pdf.

Rousseau, Jean-Jacques. *Discourse on the Origin of Inequality.* Oxford, UK: Oxford University Press, 1999.

Russett, Bruce. *Grasping the Democratic Peace: Principles for a Post-Cold War World.* Princeton, NJ: Princeton University Press, 1994.

Sapolsky, R.M. "A Natural History of Peace." *Foreign Affairs* 85 (2006): 104–21.

Sautman, Barry. "'Demographic Annihilation' and Tibet." In *Contemporary Tibet: Politics, Development, and Society in a Disputed Region*, edited by Barry Sautman and June Teufel Dreyer, 230–57. London: Routledge, 2005.

Sautman, Barry, and June Teufel Dreyer, eds. *Contemporary Tibet: Politics, Development, and Society in a Disputed Region.* London: Routledge, 2005.

Scott, James C. *Domination and the Arts of Resistance: Hidden Transcripts.* New Haven, CT: Yale University Press, 1990.

———. *Seeing Like a State: How Certain Schemes to Improve the Human Condition Have Failed.* New Haven, CT: Yale University Press, 1998.

———. *Weapons of the Weak: Everyday Forms of Peasant Resistance.* New Haven, CT: Yale University Press, 1985.

Sellin, Thorsten. "Two Myths in the History of Capital Punishment." *Journal of Criminal Law, Criminology, and Police Science* 50, no. 2 (July–August 1959): 114. https://doi.org/10.2307/1140683.

Shepard, Todd. *The Invention of Decolonization: The Algerian War and the Remaking of France.* Ithaca, NY: Cornell University Press, 2006.

Sherratt, Yvonne. *Hitler's Philosophers.* New Haven, CT: Yale University Press, 2013.

Shirer, William L. *The Rise and Fall of the Third Reich: A History of Nazi Germany.* London: Secker & Warburg, 1960.

Shuqing, Guo. "Rejuvenation of China Is Unstoppable." Speech transcript presented at the Tsinghua PBCSF Global Finance Forum,
Beijing, June 27, 2019. https://www.bis.org/review/r190627m.htm.

Sorokin, Pitirim Aleksandrovich. *A Long Journey*. New Haven, CT:
College and University Press, 1963.

———. *Social Mobility*. London: Routledge, 1998.

Spector, Stanley. "Transcript of Discussion." In *Colloquium on Overseas
Chinese*, edited by Morton Fried, 73. New York: Institute of Pacific
Relations, 1958.

Spruyt, Hendrik. "The Origins, Development, and Possible Decline of
the Modern State." *Annual Review of Political Science* 5 (June 2002):
127–49.

———. *The Sovereign State and Its Competitors: An Analysis of Systems
Change*. Princeton, NJ: Princeton University Press, 1994.

Stanton, Elizabeth Cady. "Declaration of Sentiments and Resolu-
tions, Seneca Falls Convention," 1848. https://tildesites.bowdoin.
edu/~smcmahon/courses/hist246/readingguide/files/stanton_
declaration_resolutions.pdf.

St. Denny, Emily. "The Gender Equality Potential of New Anti-Pros-
titution Policy: A Critical Juncture for Concrete Reform." *French
Politics* 18, no. 1 (June 2020): 153–74. https://doi.org/10.1057/
s41253-020-00109-7.

Stephens, Philip. "Joe Biden Has a Lesson in Democracy for Angela
Merkel." *Financial Times*, February 25, 2021. https://www.ft.com/
content/9a1c0d07-8bb4-46b0-9dd1-b32762127f7c.

Stevenson, Alexandra, and Michael Forsythe. "Luxury Homes Tie
Chinese Communist Elite to Hong Kong's Fate." *New York Times*,
August 12, 2020. https://www.nytimes.com/2020/08/12/business/
china-hong-kong-elite.html.

Stevis-Gridneff, Matina. "E.U. Adopts Groundbreaking Stimulus
to Fight Coronavirus Recession." *New York Times*, July 21, 2020.
https://www.nytimes.com/2020/07/20/world/europe/eu-stimu-
lus-coronavirus.html.

Stirner, Max. *The Ego and Its Own*. The Perfect Library, 2015.

Stivachtis, Yannis, Chris Price, and Mike Habegger. "The European Union
as a Peace Actor." *Review of European Studies* 5, no. 3 (2013): 4.

Strayer, Joseph. *On the Medieval Origins of the Modern State*. Princeton, NJ: Princeton University Press, 1970.

Subsidy Tracker. "Koch Industries." Accessed February 11, 2021. https://subsidytracker.goodjobsfirst.org/parent/koch-industries.

Suetonius Tranquillus, C. *The Lives of the Twelve Caesars*. Translated by J.C. Rolfe. Cambridge, MA: Harvard University Press, 1913.

Surowiecki, James. *The Wisdom of Crowds: Why the Many Are Smarter than the Few*. New York: Random House, 2005.

Swaine, Jon, Dalton Bennett, Joyce Sohyun Lee, and Meg Kelly. "Video Shows Fatal Shooting of Ashli Babbitt in the Capitol." *Washington Post*, January 8, 2021. https://www.washingtonpost.com/investigations/2021/01/08/ashli-babbitt-shooting-video-capitol/.

Tabak, Mehmet. "Marx's Theory of Proletarian Dictatorship Revisited." *Science & Society* 64, no. 3 (2000): 333–56.

Tacitus. *The Annals*. Translated by J. Jackson. Cambridge, MA: Harvard University Press, 1925.

Talalay, Lauren E. "A Feminist Boomerang: The Great Goddess of Greek Prehistory." *Gender & History* 6, no. 2 (April 2, 2007): 165–83. https://doi.org/10.1111/j.1468-0424.1994.tb00001.x.

Teasley, Martell, and David Ikard. "Barack Obama and the Politics of Race: The Myth of Postracism in America." *Journal of Black Studies* 40, no. 3 (January 1, 2010): 411–25. https://doi.org/10.1177/0021934709352991.

Tennie, Claudio, Josep Call, and Michael Tomasello. "Ratcheting up the Ratchet: On the Evolution of Cumulative Culture." *Philosophical Transactions of the Royal Society B: Biological Sciences* 364, no. 1528 (August 27, 2009): 2405–15. https://doi.org/10.1098/rstb.2009.0052.

Thomas, Maria Angharad. "The Faith and the Fury: Popular Anticlerical Violence and Iconoclasm in Spain, 1931–1936." Royal Holloway University of London, 2012.

Thomson, David. *England in the Nineteenth Century*. London: Penguin Books, 1991.

Thucydides. *History of the Peloponnesian War*. Translated by Benjamin Jowett. Oxford, UK: Clarendon Press, 1881. https://www.perseus.tufts.edu/hopper/text?doc=Perseus:text:1999.04.0105.

Tilly, Charles. *Coercion, Capital and European States: AD 990–1992.* Oxford, UK: Basil Blackwell, 1990.

Tolstoy, Leo. *The Kingdom of God and Peace Essays.* World's Classics 445. London: Oxford University Press, 1936.

Tomasello, Michael, Ann Cale Kruger, and Hilary Horn Ratner. "Cultural Learning." *Behavioral and Brain Sciences* 16, no. 3 (1993): 495–511. https://doi.org/10.1017/s0140525x0003123x.

Trump, Donald. "Donald Trump Speech 'Save America' Rally Transcript January 6." *Rev.* Accessed February 8, 2021. https://www.rev.com/blog/transcripts/donald-trump-speech-save-america-rally-transcript-january-6.

Truth, Sojourner. *The Narrative of Sojourner Truth.* Boston: J.B. Yerrinton and Son, 1850. https://digital.library.upenn.edu/women/truth/1850/1850.html.

US Department of Defense, US Joint Forces Command (USJFCOM). "MC02 Final Report," 2002. https://www.esd.whs.mil/Portals/54/Documents/FOID/Reading%20Room/Joint_Staff/12-F-0344-Millennium-Challenge-2002-Experiment-Report.pdf.

US Department of Justice, US Attorney's Office, Southern District of New York. "Patrick Ho, Former Head of Organization Backed by Chinese Energy Conglomerate, Sentenced to 3 Years in Prison for International Bribery and Money Laundering Offenses," March 25, 2019. https://www.justice.gov/usao-sdny/pr/patrick-ho-former-head-organization-backed-chinese-energy-conglomerate-sentenced-3.

US Department of Labor, US Bureau of Labor Statistics. "Table 5. Quartiles and Selected Deciles of Usual Weekly Earnings of Full-Time Wage and Salary Workers by Selected Characteristics, Second Quarter 2020 Averages, Not Seasonally Adjusted," January 21, 2021. https://www.bls.gov/news.release/wkyeng.t05.htm.

Vásquez, Ian, and Fred McMahon. *The Human Freedom Index 2020,* 2020. http://www.deslibris.ca/ID/10105748.

Veselova, Oleksandra. "Famine in Ukraine after the Second World War." Translated by Marta D. Olynyk and Andrij Wynnyckyj. *Harvard Ukrainian Studies* 30, no. 1/4 (2008): 183–98.

Vico, Giambattista. *New Science: Principles of the New Science Concerning the Common Nature of Nations.* Translated by David Marsh. London: Penguin Classics, 2013.

Viswanatha, Aruna, and Melissa Korn. "Top Universities Took Billions in Unreported Foreign Funds, U.S. Finds." *Wall Street Journal,* October 20, 2020. https://www.wsj.com/articles/top-universities-took-billions-in-unreported-foreign-funds-u-s-finds-11603226953.

Wald, Abraham. "Statistical Decision Functions Which Minimize the Maximum Risk." *Annals of Mathematics* 46, no. 2 (1945): 265–80. https://doi.org/10.2307/1969022.

Weber, Max. "Politics as a Vocation." In *Weber's Rationalism and Modern Society,* 1–105. London: Palgrave MacMillan, 2015.

Wendt, Alexander. "Why a World State Is Inevitable." *European Journal of International Relations* 9 (2003): 491–542.

Winterhalder, B. "Diet Choice, Risk, and Food Sharing in a Stochastic Environment." *Journal of Anthropological Archaeology* 5 (1986): 369–92.

Wittfogel, Karl. *Oriental Despotism.* New Haven, CT: Yale University Press, 1957.

Wo-Lap Lam, Willy. "Has Xi Jinping Become 'Emperor for Life'?" Jamestown Foundation, November 10, 2017. https://jamestown.org/program/xi-jinping-become-emperor-life/.

Wollstonecraft, Mary. *A Vindication of the Rights of Woman: With Strictures on Political and Moral Subjects.* London: British Library, 1792. https://www.bl.uk/collection-items/mary-wollstonecraft-a-vindication-of-the-rights-of-woman.

World Bank. "GDP Data." Accessed February 9, 2021. https://data.worldbank.org.

———. "GDP Growth (Annual %) - China." Accessed April 20, 2021. https://data.worldbank.org/indicator/NY.GDP.MKTP.KD.ZG?locations=CN.

———. "Military Expenditure (Current USD) - European Union, United States." Accessed March 22, 2021. https://data.worldbank.org/indicator/MS.MIL.XPND.CD?locations=EU-US.

Wrangham, Richard, and Dale Peterson. *Demonic Males: Apes and the Origins of Human Violence.* Boston: Houghton Mifflin, 1997.

X, Malcolm, and Alex Haley. *The Autobiography of Malcolm X.* Harmondsworth, UK: Penguin Books, 2013.

Yao, Shujie. "A Note on the Causal Factors of China's Famine in 1959–1961." *Journal of Political Economy* 107, no. 6 (1999): 1365–69. https://doi.org/10.1086/250100.

Yellinek, Roie, and Elizabeth Chen. "The '22 vs. 50' Diplomatic Split between the West and China over Xinjiang and Human Rights." China Brief, December 31, 2019. https://jamestown.org/program/the-22-vs-50-diplomatic-split-between-the-west-and-china-over-xinjiang-and-human-rights/.

Yin, Robert K. *Applications of Case Study Research.* Thousand Oaks, CA: Sage Publishing, 2011.

Youssef, Nancy A., and Gordon Lubold. "Officials Discuss Return of Troops from Washington as Administration Mulls a Military Response." *Wall Street Journal,* June 3, 2020. https://www.wsj.com/articles/troops-await-orders-as-administration-mulls-a-military-response-11591183684.

Zagoria, Donald S. *Sino-Soviet Conflict, 1956–1961.* Princeton, NJ: Princeton University Press, 1962.

Zenz, Adrian. "Brainwashing, Police Guards and Coercive Internment: Evidence from Chinese Government Documents about the Nature and Extent of Xinjiang's 'Vocational Training Internment Camps.'" *Journal of Political Risk* 7, no. 7 (July 1, 2019). https://www.jpolrisk.com/brainwashing-police-guards-and-coercive-internment-evidence-from-chinese-government-documents-about-the-nature-and-extent-of-xinjiangs-vocational-training-internment-camps/.

Notes

INTRODUCTION: The Concentration of Power

1.   Luke Broadwater, "Militia Groups Want to 'Blow Up the Capitol,' a Police Chief Testifies," *New York Times*, February 25, 2021, accessed February 28, 2021, https://www.nytimes.com/2021/02/25/us/politics/capitol-attack-state-of-the-union.html; Adam Goldman, "Officer Attacked in Capitol Riot Died of Strokes, Medical Examiner Rules," *New York Times*, April 19, 2021, accessed April 20, 2021, https://www.nytimes.com/2021/04/19/us/politics/brian-sicknick-death.html.

       Jon Swaine et al., "Video Shows Fatal Shooting of Ashli Babbitt in the Capitol," *Washington Post*, January 8, 2021, accessed April 21, 2021, https://www.washingtonpost.com/investigations/2021/01/08/ashli-babbitt-shooting-video-capitol/; Evan Hill et al., "Officer Brian Sicknick Died After the Capitol Riot. New Videos Show How He Was Attacked.," *New York Times*, March 24, 2021, accessed April 21, 2021, https://www.nytimes.com/interactive/2021/03/24/us/officer-sicknick-capitol-riot.html.

2.   Robert A. Pape and Keven Ruby, "The Capitol Rioters Aren't Like Other Extremists," *Atlantic*, February 2, 2021, accessed February

24, 2021, https://www.theatlantic.com/ideas/archive/2021/02/the-capitol-rioters-arent-like-other-extremists/617895/.

3. Rebecca Ballhaus and Beth Reinhard, "Trump to Group of Law-Enforcement Officers: 'Please Don't Be Too Nice,'" *Wall Street Journal*, July 28, 2017, accessed February 26, 2021, https://www.wsj.com/articles/trump-to-group-of-law-enforcement-officers-please-dont-be-too-nice-1501273200.

4. Tiffany Hsu and Katie Robertson, "Covering Pro-Trump Mobs, the News Media Became a Target," *New York Times*, January 7, 2021, accessed February 7, 2021, https://www.nytimes.com/2021/01/06/business/media/media-murder-capitol-building.html; Domenico Montenaro, "Timeline: How One Of The Darkest Days In American History Unfolded," *National Public Radio*, January 7, 2021, accessed March 5, 2021, https://www.npr.org/2021/01/07/954384999/timeline-how-one-of-the-darkest-days-in-american-history-unfolded.

5. Unless otherwise noted, all italics within quotes in this book are from the original source. Philip Bump, "A Pillow Salesman Apparently Has Some Ideas about Declaring Martial Law," *Washington Post*, January 15, 2021, accessed March 12, 2021, https://www.washingtonpost.com/politics/2021/01/15/pillow-salesman-apparently-has-some-ideas-about-declaring-martial-law/.

6. Nancy A. Youssef and Gordon Lubold, "Officials Discuss Return of Troops from Washington as Administration Mulls a Military Response," *Wall Street Journal*, June 3, 2020, accessed March 29, 2021, https://www.wsj.com/articles/troops-await-orders-as-administration-mulls-a-military-response-11591183684.

7. Stacy Meichtry and Drew Hinshaw, "China's Greenland Ambitions Run Into Local Politics, U.S. Influence," *Wall Street Journal*, April 8, 2021, accessed April 9, 2021, https://www.wsj.com/articles/chinas-rare-earths-quest-upends-greenlands-government-11617807839.

8. While Michael Mann divides social power into four types—

namely, political, military, economic, and ideological—I combine political and military power for parsimony's sake. There is no real political power that is separate from military, economic, and ideological power, though there is arguably a strong distinction to be made among political-military, economic, and ideological forms. The combination of political and military power can be thought of as the power of force. For Mann's perspective, see *Sources of Social Power*, vol. 1–4 (Cambridge, UK: Cambridge University Press, 1986–2013).

9. Victor Mallet, "France Vows to Punish Military Signatories of Rightwing 'Call to Arms,'" *Financial Times*, April 29, 2021, accessed May 2, 2021, https://www.ft.com/content/00f89665-3c70-4a52-99ab-2790eeae4b94.

10. Jahara Matisek and Buddhika Jayamaha, "Turkish Breakup with the U.S. and NATO: The Illogical Logics," *Journal of Political Risk* 7, no. 5 (May 2019), accessed May 2, 2021, https://www.jpolrisk.com/turkish-breakup-with-the-u-s-and-nato-the-illogical-logics/.

11. Emilio Iodice, "Lessons from History: The Startling Rise to Power of Benito Mussolini," *Journal of Values-Based Leadership* 11, no. 2 (July 15, 2018), 1–32.

12. David Barboza, "The New Influencers," *The Wire China*, April 18, 2021, accessed April 21, 2021, https://www.thewirechina.com/2021/04/18/the-new-influencers/.

13. Hegel's cultural mind-spirit (*Geist*) and Marx's economic revolutions, then, are not the only force of change to the superstructure, but rather that superstructure is undermined over time as power of not only the economic and informational, but the political (Karl Popper, *The Open Society and Its Enemies*, London: George Routledge & Sons, 1947) aggregates into new and more concentrated hierarchies that absorb the old, diffuse, and disaggregating institutional forms. The argument for the overall historical dominance of any one type of power—whether ideological, economic, or political-military—is lacking in evidence. This book theorizes instead

a fusion and rough equality of effect from these three types of power.

14.   Marx used the term *dictatorship* here either in error, as the term should refer to an individual autocrat rather than a class, or as purposeful sophistry. Either way, the idea of a "dictatorship of the proletariat" was fallacious and enabled the communist and fascist dictatorships that followed. These dictators—in the USSR, Italy, Germany, and China—ultimately had little to do with the proletariat and, like other dictators, much to do with the elites. In his "Critique of the Gotha Program" (*Essential Writings of Karl Marx*, ed. Lenny Frank, St. Petersburg, FL: Red and Black Publishers, 2010), Marx distinguishes the "revolutionary dictatorship of the proletariat" from what he dismisses as "the old democratic litany familiar to all: universal suffrage, direct legislation, popular rights, a people's militia, etc." (250). Marx was thus jaundiced if not antagonistic toward democracy, and his "dictatorship of the proletariat" was decidedly not what we consider democracy. However, those who want to paint Marx as a supporter of—or, at least not antagonistic toward—democracy make much of Marx's description of the Paris Commune's democratic institutions in his *Civil War in France* (1871). See, for example, Mehmet Tabak, "Marx's Theory of Proletarian Dictatorship Revisited," *Science & Society* 64, no. 3 (Fall 2000): 338–53. Marx shows no particular affinity for democracy in his *Civil War in France*, but rather one for the communism of the commune, and perhaps a "democracy" that excludes all but the proletariat, which is no democracy at all. Had the commune been authoritarian, Marx could very well have been just as enthusiastic. Marx's frequent coauthor, Friedrich Engels, was likewise negative in his attitude toward democracy. He wrote, "That a host of somewhat muddled and purely democratic demands should figure in the [Lassallean] programme, some of them being of a purely fashionable nature—for instance 'legislation by the people' such as exists in Switzerland and does more harm than good, if it can be said to do anything at all. Administration by the people— that would at least be something." Administration by the people sounds very much like a dictatorship of the proletariat. See Engels's

letter to August Bebel, dated March 18–28, 1875, reprinted in Marx, *Essential Writings*, 234.

15. Pierre Asselin, "The Algerian Revolution and the Communist Bloc," Wilson Center, accessed February 26, 2021, https://www.wilsoncenter.org/publication/the-algerian-revolution-and-the-communist-bloc.

16. Todd Shepard, *The Invention of Decolonization: The Algerian War and the Remaking of France* (Ithaca, NY: Cornell University Press, 2006).

17. Claire Andrieu, "Managing Memory: National and Personal Identity at Stake in the Mitterrand Affair," *French Politics and Society* 14, no. 2 (1996): 17–32.

18. The subjectivity of historical analysis was recognized as early as the late eighteenth century by Johann Gottfried von Herder in his *Outlines of a Philosophy of the History of Man* (1784–91).

19. Anders Corr, "American Primacy and Offensive Posture: A Reply to Stephen Walt," Harvard Kennedy School of Government, 2002, accessed February 7, 2021, https://www.belfercenter.org/sites/default/files/legacy/files/corr_watl_response.pdf.

20. Cf. Louis Dumont, who sees hierarchy as a principle that ranks the value elements of a culturally specific whole, the good, rather than having to do with power, much less its institutionalization (Louis Dumont, "On Value: The Radcliffe-Brown Lecture in Social Anthropology, 1980," *HAU: Journal of Ethnographic Theory* 3, no. 1 (March 2013): 287–315).

21. J.H. Herz, "Rise and Demise of the Territorial State," *World Politics* 9, no. 4 (July 1957): 473–93; J.H. Herz, "The Territorial State Revisited: Reflections on the Future of the Nation-State," *Polity* 1, no. 1 (1968): 11–34.

22. Kimberlé Crenshaw, "Demarginalizing the Intersection of Race and Sex: A Black Feminist Critique of Antidiscrimination Doctrine, Feminist Theory and Antiracist Politics," *University of*

Chicago Legal Forum 1, no. 8 (1989): 31.

23. Peter J. Richerson and Robert Boyd, "Complex Societies: The Evolutionary Origins of Crude Superorganism," *Human Nature* 10 (1999): 253–289; See also, Claudio Tennie, Josep Call, and Michael Tomasello, "Ratcheting up the Ratchet: On the Evolution of Cumulative Culture," *Philosophical Transactions of the Royal Society B: Biological Sciences* 364, no. 1528 (August 27, 2009): 2405–15; and Michael Tomasello, Ann Cale Kruger, and Hilary Horn Ratner, "Cultural Learning," *Behavioral and Brain Sciences* 16, no. 3 (1993): 495–511, https://doi.org/10.1017/s0140525x0003123x.

24. Other authors have used the ratchet metaphor to describe path dependence, economies of scale, deconfliction, and superior economic technology. In "War, Technology, and Change: The Ratchet Effect and System Unification" (PhD diss., Harvard University, May 2008), which formalizes some of the theories in this book, I argue that the ratchet effect increases average political unit geographic size, albeit with some slippage to the ratchet.

25. Minor M. Markle III, "Macedonian arms and tactics under Alexander the Great," *Studies in the History of Art* 10, Symposium Series I: Macedonia and Greece in Late Classical and Early Hellenistic Times (1982): 86–111; Hugh Liebert, "Alexander the Great and the History of Globalization," *Review of Politics* 73, no. 4 (Fall 2011): 533–560.

26. Thomas Piketty, *Capital in the Twenty-First Century* (Cambridge, MA: Harvard University Press, 2017).

27. While I am critical of G.W.F. Hegel, there are occasional insights to be found in the coal mines of his voluminous writing. According to Hegel, "the ethical substance [or 'ethical order', depending on the translation of *Sittlichkeit*], potentially infinite, is actually a particular and limited substance … on its subjective side it labours under contingency, in the shape of its unreflective natural usages, and its content is presented to it as something *existing* in time and tied to an external nature and external world. The spirit, however, (which *thinks* in this moral organism) overrides and absorbs within

itself the finitude attaching to it as national spirit in its state and the state's temporal interests, in the system of laws and usages. It rises to apprehend itself in its essentiality. Such apprehension, however, still has the immanent limitedness of the national spirit. But the spirit which thinks in universal history, stripping off at the same time those limitations of the several national minds and its own temporal restrictions, lays hold of its concrete universality, and rises to apprehend the absolute mind, as the eternally actual truth in which the contemplative reason enjoys freedom, while the necessity of nature and the necessity of history are only ministrant to its revelation and the vessels of its honour" (*Philosophy of Mind*, trans. William Wallace, London and Oxford, UK: Oxford University Press, 1894, § 552).

28. Corr, "War, Technology, and Change," 1–43.

29. Robert K. Yin, *Applications of Case Study Research* (Thousand Oaks, CA: Sage Publishing, 2011).

CHAPTER 1. Theory Introduction

30. Colonial Office Information Department, "Singapore Police Capture Chinese Propaganda Press Then Issue Own Edition of Communist 'Freedom News'" (Oxford University Library, Fabian Colonial Bureau, MSS British Empire s365, Box 156/1, August 30, 1951): 35.

31. Starting in 1946, Freedom Press published communist books and pamphlets. *Freedom News* had been published since January 1949. Most of the *Freedom News* distribution was in Singapore, but some copies were sent to underground communist papers in the Malayan Federation (Colonial Office Information Department, "Singapore Police Capture," 35).

32. Carneiro defines a state in a manner that could just as well apply to an empire: "an autonomous political unit, encompassing many communities within its territory and having a centralized government with the power to collect taxes, draft men for work or war,

and decree and enforce laws." This hints at empire-building as a basis for state formation. A similar argument could be made for alliance-building as a basis for state- and empire-building. See: Robert L. Carneiro, "A Theory of the Origin of the State," *Science* 169, no. 3947 (August 21, 1970): 733.

33. Louis Dumont, *Homo Hierarchicus: The Caste System and its Implications*, trans. Mark Sainsbury, Louis Dumont, and Basia Gulati (Chicago: University of Chicago Press, 1980): xlvii. The original was published in 1966 in French under the title *Homo Hierarchicus: Essai sur le Système des Castes*.

34. The attempt to compare hierarchy across time and geography from prehistory to contemporary international organizations will rightly be questioned by regionalists and specialists. They would be correct in noting that we ought not to apply modern conceptions to earlier ones, or shoehorn the past into theories of the present. But I do not claim to be a historian or a regionalist. Rather, I am interested in how hierarchy works in many contexts. It is hoped that these critics will forgive the attempt to model something that is inherently more complex than any model could perfectly map, and will remember that all maps, models, thought, description, and language are abstractions from reality. Without necessarily inaccurate models for every particularity, we cannot approach a model of the whole, or take action based on that conception. Indeed, regionalists commit the same sin on their own turf, as human relations are always more complex than can be described even by the narrowest of ethnographies. Theorists, empiricists, specialists, and everyday folks are right to identify the inevitable inaccuracies and mistakes, and offer counter-theories. But we succumb to a nonscientific approach when we dismiss a model because it does not match every particularity. Others who address long-term historical change make similar observations on the need for overarching models despite the necessity of accepting some diverging particularities, and the inevitable pitfalls of addressing so much historical material. The measure of a model is the percentage of the particularities that it predicts. Good ones predict well. None

predict perfectly. For similar caveats, see introductions to works as diverse as John Maynard Keynes, *The General Theory of Employment, Interest and Money* (Cambridge: Cambridge University Press, 2012); Tilly, *Coercion, Capital*; and Francis Fukuyama, *The Origins of Political Order: From Prehuman Times to the French Revolution* (New York: Farrar, Straus and Giroux, 2011).

35. Samuel P. Huntington, *The Third Wave: Democratization in the Late Twentieth Century* (Norman, OK: University of Oklahoma Press, 1991).

36. Marx's historical theories have been collected together from his various writings. In the 1859 preface to *A Contribution to the Critique of Political Economy*, Marx writes, "In broad outlines we can designate the Asiatic, the ancient, the feudal, and the modern bourgeois methods of production as so many epochs in the progress of the economic formation of society." Here Marx follows Hegel in locating the beginning of history in Asia. Marx continues, "The bourgeois relations of production are the last antagonistic form of the social process of production—antagonistic not in the sense of individual antagonism, but of one arising from conditions surrounding the life of individuals in society; at the same time the productive forces developing in the womb of bourgeois society create the material conditions for the solution of that antagonism. This social formation constitutes, therefore, the closing chapter of the prehistoric stage of human society" (Trans. N.I. Stone, Chicago: Charles H. Kerr & Company, 1904, 14). For Marx, the new economic classes that new relations of production produce are instrumental in progressing history to each successive stage or epoch. He writes, "every class, as soon as it takes up the struggle against the class above it, is involved in a struggle with the class beneath it. Thus princes struggle against kings, bureaucrats against aristocrats, and the bourgeoisie against all of these, while the proletariat is already beginning to struggle against the bourgeoisie" (Introduction to the "Contribution of Hegel's Critique of Right," in *Early Writings*, 255). Each stage of economic development is reached as it discards the fetters of the prior stage that

have been outgrown. According to Marx and Engels, "the whole development of history [is] a coherent series of forms of inter-course, the coherence of which consists in this: an earlier form of intercourse, which has become a fetter, is replaced by a new one corresponding to the more developed productive forces and, hence, to the advanced mode of the self-activity of individuals—a form which in its turn becomes a fetter and is then replaced by another" (*German Ideology*, Amherst, NY: Prometheus Books, 1998, 91). By describing historical development as liberation from a series of fetters, Marx and Engels construct an inaccurately teleological purpose of the current moment as revolution, and inaccurately predict that such revolutions will lead to progress in the polit-ical and social conditions of humanity. For further material on Marxian ideas of history, see Anderson, *Passages from Antiquity*; Anderson, *Lineages*; and Gerald A. Cohen, *Karl Marx's Theory of History: A Defence* (Oxford: Clarendon Press, 1978).

37.   Steven Pinker, *The Better Angels of Our Nature: Why Violence has Declined* (New York: Penguin Books, 2011).

38.   According to Vico, writing in 1725, "In the family state, Jupiter's reign had been monarchical, but in the new city state it became aristocratic" (*New Science*, § 589). He also writes, "Governments began with the one in the unit of the family monarchies; passed to the few of heroic aristocracies; advanced to the many and the all in democracies, in which all the citizens or the majority make up the body politic; and finally returned to the one in civil monar-chies" (*New Science*, § 1026). A century later, Hegel followed in his published lectures with, "The abstract yet necessitated process in the development of truly independent states is as follows:— They begin with regal [or despotic] power, whether of patriarchal or military origin. In the next phase, particularity and individu-ality assert themselves in the form of Aristocracy and Democracy. Lastly, we have the subjection of these separate interests to a single power; but which can be absolutely none other than one outside of which those spheres have an independent position, viz., the Monarchical" (G.W.F. Hegel, *The Philosophy of History*, trans. J.

Sibree (Kitchener, ON: Batoche Books, 2001, 62).

39. Lars-Erik Cederman, "Modeling the Size of Wars: From Billiard Balls to Sandpiles," *American Political Science Review* 97, no. 1 (February 2003): 135–150.

40. Carneiro, "Political Expansion," 205–24; Marano, "Macrohistorical Trend," 35–40.

41. Richerson and Boyd, "Complexity Societies," 253–289.

42. Herz, "Rise and Demise," 473–493; Herz, "Territorial State," 11–34.

CHAPTER 2. Theory of Hierarchy and Hegemony

43. Marx overstates the case for the importance of avarice when he writes, "The only wheels which political economy sets in motion are *greed* and the *war of the avaricious—competition.*" He wrongly states that landed property is a "violent" consequence of "monopoly, of the guilds and of feudal property" (Karl Marx, *Economic and Philosophic Manuscripts of 1844*, in *Karl Marx: Early Writings*, trans. Rodney Livingstone and Gregor Benton, London: Penguin Books, 1992, 323), when in fact the violence of landed property stretches back to, in some but not all cases, the conquest and associated redivision of land by the conquerors. Thereafter, landed property generally changes hands through exchange, norm, or institution until the next advent of conquest or revolution, when land and other property may again be redivided among the conquerors, including revolutionists. Elsewhere, Marx acknowledges a violent basis for a "pre-economic" "distribution" of land when he states, "A conquering people divides the land among the conquerors, establishing thereby a certain division and form of landed property and determining the character of production; or, it turns the conquered people into slaves and thus makes slave labor the basis of production. Or, a nation, by revolution, breaks up large estates into small parcels of land and by this new distribution imparts to production a new character. Or, legislation perpetuates land ownership

in large families or distributes labor as an hereditary privilege and thus fixes it in castes" ("Introduction to the Critique of Political Economy," in *The German Ideology*, 12). Marx here inaccurately conflates legislation with violent conquest or revolution, in line with his jaundiced view of democracy.

44. Some Eastern European countries have, since the breakup of the Soviet Union in 1991, been going through this two-step process of disintegration and regestion.

45. In the context of a discussion about the transition from family to aristocratic power, Vico notes that "the name Minerva is derived from the Latin verb *minuere*, to diminish; and that the Roman legal phrase *capitis deminutio*, domination of the head, descended from the remotest age of poetic antiquity, since its meaning of 'change in status' recalls how Minerva changed the state of families to that of cities" (*New Science*, § 589).

46. Vico writes that "monarchs want all their subject nations made equal by laws, so that they will take an equal interest in the state" (*New Science*, § 39).

47. According to Vico, "monarchy can only spring from the people's unbridled liberty, to which in time of civil war the aristocracy subjects its power. For when power is divided into smaller units among the people, the whole of it is more easily seized by those leaders who, by championing popular liberty, eventually emerge as monarchs" (*New Science*, § 737). Vico argues that democracy leads to faction, sedition, and civil war (§ 1006). His analysis presages the French, American, Russian, and Chinese Revolutions, all of which claimed to liberate the individual, and all of which facilitated the long-term centralization of power at the expense of older, less powerful, autocracies. The new "monarchs" that emerged after these revolutions purchased their powers of the presidency, premiership, or chairmanship, by offering popular liberty in various forms, from equality before the law (§ 953), to liberty from arbitrary taxes, and socialist notions of "to each according to his needs," worker-owned production, and land to the tiller. The

post-revolution realities of the new "liberatory" governments were very different from what had been offered.

48.　Diogenes of Sinope allegedly said something similar. "He used to call the demagogues the lackeys of the people and the crowns awarded to them the efflorescence of fame." He also said that "bad men obey their lusts as servants obey their masters" (Diogenes Laërtius, *Lives of the Eminent Philosophers*, ed. Robert Aitkin, trans. Robert Drew Hicks, Kindle: 2014, 4026–181).

49.　*Hierarchical drift* is here defined as the aimlessness of hierarchy under a lack of leadership, in contradistinction to other definitions of hierarchical drift as "the extension of power from a specific, legitimate domain to other, illegitimate ones," which I would describe as "mission creep" or "power creep." For the alternate definition of "hierarchical drift," see Stephen C. Angle, Kwame Anthony Appiah, and Julian Baggini, "In Defense of Hierarchy," Aeon, March 22, 2017, accessed February, 8, 2021, https://aeon.co/essays/hierarchies-have-a-place-even-in-societies-built-on-equality.

CHAPTER 3. Defining Hierarchy

50.　David Graeber, "The Rise of Hierarchy," in *Hierarchy and Value: Comparative Perspectives on Moral Order*, eds. Jason Hickel and Naomi Haynes, (New York: Berghahn Books, 2018), 3432, Kindle.

51.　Oxford English Dictionary, "Hierarchy," accessed July 20, 2020, https://www.oed.com/view/Entry/86792?redirectedFrom=hierarchy#eid.

52.　According to Hegel, "the State is the universal spiritual life, to which individuals by birth sustain a relation of *confidence and habit*, and in which they have their existence and reality" (Hegel, *Philosophy of History*, 122).

53.　Frans B.M. de Waal, "The Integration of Dominance and Social Bonding in Primates," *Quarterly Review of Biology* 61, no. 4

(December 1986): 459–479; R. Dunbar and S. Shultz, "Evolution in the Social Brain," *Science* 317 (2007): 1344–7; R.M. Sapolsky, "A Natural History of Peace," *Foreign Affairs* 85 (2006): 104–21; *Biologism* is belittled by contemporary philosophy that attempts to escape the material world and ascribe the prime mover (ὃ οὐ κινούμενον κινεῖ) to the ideas with which philosophy is so conversant. Philosophy, like religion, is typically biased in its belief that the ideas it peddles matter above all else.

54. Ellen M. Burstein and Camille G. Caldera, "Harvard Took In $1.1 Billion from 63 Nations from 2013–2019, per Department of Education," *Harvard Crimson*, February 13, 2020, accessed April 15, 2021, https://www.thecrimson.com/article/2020/2/13/harvard-billion-foreign-funds/; Anders Corr, "China's Moneybag Friends at Harvard University," *Asia Sentinel*, August 17, 2017, accessed April 15, 2021, https://www.asiasentinel.com/p/china-moneybag-friends-harvard-university.

55. In *Homo Hierarchicus*, Dumont discusses hierarchy as "values and rank," "the gradation principle of the elements relative to the ensemble," and the "encompassing and encompassed"; Jason Hickel and Naomi Haynes, *Hierarchy and Value: Comparative Perspectives on Moral Order* (New York: Berghahn Books, 2018), 4, provide a literature review of Dumont, and other anthropological works on hierarchy, including clientistic relationships, seniority, and dependence.

56. Dumont makes a distinction in *Homo Hierarchicus* (xiv) between status (hierarchical) and power (political). But status is derivative of power more than position in the hierarchy because position alone can be symbolic, as, for example, in a constitutional monarchy. The Prime Minister of Britain has more power and therefore status than does the monarch, though some Britons—especially of the opposing party—might dispute this. Position within the hierarchy also provides status, but not as much as does real institutionalized power. Individuals without force, wealth, or knowledge at their disposal, but who still have positions in the hierarchy as minor bureaucrats outside the main flow of power, have some influence

merely from their positions within the institution, but relatively little. The flow of power, including along informal lines, is somewhere else. Where power flows, there flows the preponderance of status.

57. A.L. Kellermann and J.A. Mercy, "Men, Women, and Murder: Gender-Specific Differences in Rates of Fatal Violence and Victimization," *The Journal of Trauma* 33, no. 1 (July 1992): 1–5.

58. Cf. Rutger Bregman, *Humankind: A Hopeful History* (London: Bloomsbury, 2020).

CHAPTER 4. **Origins of Hierarchy**

59. See Jean-Jacques Rousseau, *Discourse on the Origin of Inequality* (Oxford: Oxford University Press, 1999); Lewis Henry Morgan, *Ancient Society: or, Researches in the Lines of Human Progress from Savagery through Barbarism to Civilization* (London: Routledge, 1998); and Friedrich Engels, *The Origin of the Family, Private Property, and the State* (London: Lawrence & Wishart, 1972).

60. Richard Wrangham and Dale Peterson, *Demonic Males: Apes and the Origins of Human Violence* (Boston: Houghton Mifflin, 1997).

61. For a survey of prehistory and different reading of it, see Herbert Gintis, Carel van Schaik, and Christopher Boehm, "*Zoon Politikon*: The Evolutionary Origins of Human Political Systems," *Current Anthropology* 56, no. 3 (June 2015): 327–53; Tennie et al., "Ratcheting," 2405.

62. Gintis et al., "*Zoon Politikon*," 327–53; Tennie et al., "Ratcheting," 2405.

63. Gintis et al., "*Zoon Politikon*," 327–53.

64. Gintis et al., "*Zoon Politikon*," 327–53.

65. As cited in Marx and Engels, *German Ideology*, 246. They mock Destutt without providing strong contradictory evidence.

66. William Tulio Divale and Marvin Harris, "Population, Warfare, and the Male Supremacist Complex," *American Anthropologist* 78, no. 3 (September 1976): 521–38.

67. Divale and Harris, "Population, Warfare," 524–32.

68. While the sex ratio of the groups Divale and Harris censused at a time warfare was present (mostly in South America and Oceania, but also in Europe, North America, and Africa) was, on average, 128 boys to 100 girls (14 years and younger), with fewer girls due to infanticide, that ratio equalizes to 101:100 for ages 15 years and older due to male mortality in war. Thus, female infanticide yielded, after taking into consideration male combat deaths, a roughly equal gender balance (Divale and Harris, "Population, Warfare," 526–9).

69. Ashley Kendell, "The Crow Creek Massacre: The Role of Sex in Native American Scalping Practices," *Archaeological Perspectives on Warfare on the Great Plains*, eds. Andrew J. Clark and Douglas B. Bamforth (Boulder: University Press of Colorado, 2018): 318–335.

70. B. Winterhalder, "Diet Choice, Risk, and Food Sharing in a Stochastic Environment," *Journal of Anthropological Archaeology* 5 (1986): 369–392; Lorna Marshall, "Sharing, Talking, and Giving: Relief of Social Tensions among !Kung Bushmen," *Africa: Journal of the International African Institute* 31, no. 3 (July 1961): 236–43.

71. Divale and Harris, "Population, Warfare," 526. There is some intriguing contrary evidence to the general patriarchal nature of the family in archaeological finds of hundreds of clay figurines of mostly females in Greece, some of which show symbols of power or godlike stature. While the figurines are sometimes taken as evidence of a rare goddess culture in human history, they have a number of other possible explanations, including as fertility talismans and fetishistic objects. See Lauren E. Talalay, "A Feminist Boomerang: The Great Goddess of Greek Prehistory," *Gender & History* 6, no. 2 (April 2, 2007): 165–83.

72. Émile Durkheim in his *De la Division du Travail Social* (*The Divi-

sion of Labor in Society, 1893) argued that the division of labor is inherited from animal ancestors and that it allows for larger social organization and thus coheres society and its social elements. As society develops, so does the division of labor. Human societies become more differentiated over time. However, the division of labor leads to strife between labor and capital. Class war results from individuals' dissatisfaction with their roles in the division of labor when forced upon them (trans. George Simpson, Glencoe, IL: Free Press, 1960). Cf. Herbert Spencer.

73. Divale and Harris, "Population, Warfare," 524.

74. Marx and Engels write, "The division of labour in which all these contradictions are implicit, and which in its turn is based on the natural division of labour in the family and the separation of society into individual families opposed to one another, simultaneously implies the *distribution*, and indeed the *unequal* distribution, both quantitative and qualitative, of labour and its products, hence property, the nucleus, the first form of which lies in the family, where wife and children are the slaves of the husband. This latent slavery in the family, though still very crude, is the first form of property, but even at this stage it corresponds perfectly to the definition of modern economists, who call it the power of disposing of the labour-power of others" (*German Ideology*, 51). Here Marx and Engels make their point abstract so that it fits their focus on economic, rather than a more generalized, history. They therefore fail to explicate how man's larger physical stature and organization into hunting parties prepared the way for his early physical and political, rather than economic, domination of women and children. Indeed, given ethnographic evidence for the greater contribution of women to the caloric intake of hunter-gatherer families, Marxists mistakenly focused on economic rather than physical power and socialization in early family hierarchies.

75. Vico, *New Science*, § 524–5.

76. Jane Goodall, *The Chimpanzees of Gombe: Patterns of Behavior* (Cambridge, MA: Harvard University Press, 1986).

77. According to sociologist Franz Oppenheimer, agricultural "peasants fight as undisciplined levies, and with their single combatants undisciplined; so that, in the long run, even though they are strong in numbers, they are no more able than are the hunters to withstand the charge of the heavily armed herdsmen. But the peasantry do not flee. The peasant is attached to his ground, and has been used to regular work. He remains, yields to subjection, and pays tribute to his conqueror; that is the genesis of the land states in the old world" (*The State*, New York: Free Life Editions, 1975, 21). While this story may be true in certain instances, it is evident from history that there is no single source for the formation of states and other political units. In addition to coercive forms of state formation, there are contractual forms, and some that include elements of both (e.g., political contracts agreed under duress in nineteenth-century Germany).

78. R. Brian Ferguson, "Violence and War in Prehistory," in *Troubled Times: Violence and Warfare in the Past*, eds. Debra L. Martin and David W. Frayer (Amsterdam, Netherlands: Gordon and Breach Publishers, 2014), 321–30.

79. R. Alexander Bentley, "Mobility and the Diversity of Early Neolithic Lives: Isotopic Evidence from Skeletons," *Journal of Anthropological Archaeology* 32, no. 3 (September 1, 2013): 303–12; Christian Meyer et al., "The Massacre Mass Grave of Schöneck-Kilianstädten Reveals New Insights into Collective Violence in Early Neolithic Central Europe," *Proceedings of the National Academy of Sciences of the United States of America* 112, no. 36 (2015): 11217–22.

80. Meyer et al., "Massacre Mass Grave," 11217–22.

81. Vico, *New Science*, § 526. Many nineteenth-century historical theorists agreed that scarce resources such as water were the sites of early state formation. China's irrigation system was a source of the genesis of its state, according to several (Joshua A. Fogel, "The Debates over the Asiatic Mode of Production in Soviet Russia, China, and Japan," *American Historical Review* 93, no. 1, 1988, 57).

Wittfogel's *Oriental Despotism* (New Haven, CT: Yale University Press, 1957) followed with the thesis that irrigation farming requires abundant water sources, which require mass labor that must be disciplined, coordinated, and led. Thus, irrigation farming tends to lead to state formation and administration; see David H. Price, "Wittfogel's Neglected Hydraulic/Hydroagricultural Distinction," *Journal of Anthropological Research* 50, no. 2 (Summer 1994): 187–204.

82.   Talalay, "Feminist Boomerang."

83.   Carneiro, "Theory," 734.

CHAPTER 5. **Functions of Hierarchy**

84.   Plutarch, "Pelopidas," 24.2–.4, in *The Parallel Lives*, trans. Bernadotte Perrin (Cambridge, MA: Harvard University Press, 1916), accessed March 9, 2021, https://penelope.uchicago.edu/Thayer/E/Roman/Texts/Plutarch/Lives/Pericles*.html.

85.   Naomi Haynes and Jason Hickel, "Hierarchy, Value, and the Value of Hierarchy," *Social Analysis* 60, no. 4 (Winter 2016): 1–20, cite evidence from numerous additional anthropological studies in which subjects value hierarchy.

86.   Graeber, "Rise of Hierarchy," 3567–77.

87.   G.W.F. Hegel, *Philosophy of Mind*, trans. William Wallace (London and Oxford, UK: Oxford University Press, 1894), § 502.

88.   Jared Diamond, *Guns, Germs, and Steel: the Fates of Human Societies* (New York: W.W. Norton & Co., 1997); Daniel A. Bell and Wang Pei, *Just Hierarchy: Why Social Hierarchies Matter in China and the Rest of the World* (Princeton, NJ: Princeton University Press, 2020).

89.   Vico, *New Science*, § 1029–30.

90.   Robert Owen and other utopian socialists were theoretical predecessors to Marx and Engels, including in their labor theory of value; symbiosis of worker collectives and industrial factories that would

transform society; utilization of a scientific framework to advocate for socialism; as well as their radical critique of individualism and support for utopianism that was, for Marx, an "anti-utopian utopianism," according to Steven Lukes. Marx and Engels departed from the utopians most clearly in the means they advocated to achieve socialism. The former advocated violent revolution, while the latter sought to persuade nonviolently through modeling socialism in small intentional communities. Advocacy for revolution by Marxists was at least, in part, due to the failure of actual socialist experiments, and was accompanied by advocacy against "dynastic" wars. See Karl Marx, "Critique of the Gotha Program," in *Essential Writings*, 228; Roger Paden, "Marx's Critique of the Utopian Socialists," *Utopian Studies* 13, no. 2 (2002): 67–91; and Gregory Claeys, "Paternalism and Democracy in the Politics of Robert Owen," *International Review of Social History* 27, no. 2 (1982): 161–207.

CHAPTER 6. Structure of Hierarchy

91.	Richerson and Boyd, "Complex Societies," 253–289.

92.	Richerson and Boyd, "Complex Societies," 253–289.

93.	A bank is a hierarchy of usually hierarchical investors, and a university is a hierarchy of hierarchical departments. Most sub-hierarchies are themselves meta-hierarchies that compete with one another in the climb upward.

94.	Matthew Leising, "Crypto Assets of $50 Billion Moved From China in the Past Year," Bloomberg, August 20, 2020, accessed September 10, 2020, https://www.bloombergquint.com/technology/crypto-assets-of-50-billion-moved-from-china-in-the-past-year.

95.	Michael Hasenstab, "China's Digital Currency Is a Threat to Dollar Dominance," *Financial Times*, April 14, 2021, accessed April 18, 2021, https://www.ft.com/content/3fe905e7-8b9b-4782-bf2d-fc4f45496915.

96. Hans J. Morgenthau, "The Nature and Use of Power and its Influence upon State Goals and Strategies: A lecture delivered at the Naval War College on 25 September 1963," *Naval War College Review* 16, no. 6 (February 1964): 19.

97. US Joint Forces Command (USJFCOM), "MC02 Final Report" (2002), accessed March 6, 2021, https://www.esd.whs.mil/Portals/54/Documents/FOID/Reading%20Room/Joint_Staff/12-F-0344-Millennium-Challenge-2002-Experiment-Report.pdf.

98. Weber, "Politics as a Vocation," 1–105.

99. Yuval Noaḥ Harari, *Sapiens: A Brief History of Humankind*, trans. John Purcell and Haim Watzman, (London: Vintage Books, 2015).

100. Laura Ashe and Emily Joan Ward, *Conquests in Eleventh-Century England: 1016, 1066* (Suffolk, UK: Boydell Press, 2020): 165–182.

101. Plutarch, "Romulus," 9.2. "For that the residents of Alba would not consent to give the fugitives the privilege of intermarriage with them, nor even receive them as fellow-citizens, is clear, in the first place, from the rape of the Sabine women, which was not a deed of wanton daring, but one of necessity, owing to the lack of marriages by consent; for they certainly honoured the women, when they had carried them off, beyond measure."

102. Irka Kuleshnyk, "The Stockholm Syndrome: Toward an Understanding," *Social Action & the Law* 10, no. 2 (1984): 37–42; Cecilia Åse, "Crisis Narratives and Masculinist Protection: Gendering the Original Stockholm Syndrome," *International Feminist Journal of Politics* 17, no. 4 (2015): 595–610; M. Namnyak, N. Tufton, R. Szekely, M. Toal, S. Worboys, and E.L. Sampson, "'Stockholm syndrome': psychiatric diagnosis or urban myth?" *Acta Psychiatrica Scandinavica* 117, no. 1 (January 2008): 4–11.

103. Wendy Brown, "Neoliberalized Knowledge," *History of the Present* 1, no. 1 (Summer 2011): 113–129.

104. Sojourner Truth, *The Narrative of Sojourner Truth* (Boston: J.B. Yerrinton and Son, 1850), accessed February 15, 2021, https://digital.library.upenn.edu/women/truth/1850/1850.html. Johann Gottfried von Herder wrote in 1784–91, "As nature has given him two free hands as instruments, and an inspecting eye to guide him, she has given him the power not only of placing the weights in the balance, but of being, as I may say, himself a weight in the scale. He can gloss over the most delusive errors and be voluntarily deceived, he can learn in time to love the chains with which he is unnaturally fettered, and adorn them with various flowers" (*Outlines of a Philosophy of the History of Man*, trans. T. Churchill and David G. Payne, n.p.: Random Shack, 2016, 203).

105. Sojourner Truth does a better job at describing the experience of slaves—including their ethics, agency, and diversity—than does Hegel in his *Philosophy of Right*. Hegel writes, with insufficient evidence, "The slave does not know his essence, his infinity and freedom; he does not know himself as an essence—he does not know himself as such, for he does not *think* [italics his] himself. This self-consciousness which comprehends itself as essence through thought and thereby divests itself of the contingent and the untrue constitutes the principle of right, of morality, and of all ethics." He continues, "If we hold firmly to the view that the human being in and for himself is free, we thereby condemn slavery. But if someone is a slave, his own will is responsible, just as the responsibility lies with the will of a people if that people is subjugated. Thus the wrong of slavery is the fault not only of those who enslave or subjugate people, but of the slaves and the subjugated themselves" (G.W.F. Hegel, *Elements of the Philosophy of Right*, ed. Allen W. Wood, trans. H.B. Nisbet, Cambridge, UK: Cambridge University Press, 2003, § 21–57).

106. Peter Fawcett, "'When I Squeeze You with *Eisphorai*': Taxes and Tax Policy in Classical Athens," *Hesperia* 85, no. 1 (January 2016): 182.

107. Intersectionality describes overlapping inequalities toward the bottom of the hierarchy and overlapping systems of oppression.

See, for example, Crenshaw, "Demarginalizing the Intersection," 1–31; and Helma Lutz, "Intersectionality as Method," *DiGeSt Journal of Diversity and Gender Studies* 2, no. 1–2 (2015): 39–44. For other related material, see bell hooks, *Talking Back: Thinking Feminist, Thinking Black* (New York: Routledge, 2014); Judith Butler, *Gender Trouble: Feminism and the Subversion of Identity* (New York: Routledge, 2006); Malcolm X and Alex Haley, *The Autobiography of Malcolm X* (Harmondsworth, UK: Penguin Books, 2013); Chinua Achebe, *Things Fall Apart* (Oxford: Heinemann, 2003); Chandra Talpade Mohanty, Ann Russo, and Lourdes Torres, eds., *Third World Women and the Politics of Feminism* (Bloomington: Indiana University Press, 1991); Eldridge Cleaver and Ishmael Reed, *Soul on Ice* (New York: Dell, 1999); and Paulo Freire, *Pedagogy of the Oppressed* (London: Penguin Books, 1996). For intersectional theory as applied to the academic discipline of international relations, see Brooke Ackerly and Jacqui True, "An Intersectional Analysis of International Relations: Recasting the Discipline," *Politics & Gender* 4, no. 1 (March 2008): 156–73.

108. James C. Scott, *Weapons of the Weak: Everyday Forms of Peasant Resistance* (New Haven, CT: Yale University Press, 1985).

109. Rufus E. Miles, "The Origin and Meaning of Miles' Law," *Public Administration Review* 38, no. 5 (1978): 399–403.

110. Charles M. Blow, "About the 'Basket of Deplorables,'" *New York Times*, September 12, 2016, accessed 28 February 2021, https://www.nytimes.com/2016/09/12/opinion/about-the-basket-of-deplorables.html.

111. Stephen W. Popper, *China's Propensity for Innovation in the 21st Century: Identifying Indicators of Future Outcomes* (Santa Monica, CA: RAND Corporation, 2020).

112. Max Stirner, *The Ego and Its Own* (The Perfect Library, 2015).

113. Friedrich Wilhelm Nietzsche, "Beyond Good and Evil: On the Genealogy of Morality," in *The Complete Works of Friedrich Nietzsche*, vol. 8 (Stanford, CA: Stanford University Press, 2014);

Friedrich Wilhelm Nietzsche, *Ecce Homo: How One Becomes What One Is*, trans. R.J. Hollingdale (London: Penguin Books, 1992).

114. Yvonne Sherratt, *Hitler's Philosophers* (New Haven, CT: Yale University Press, 2013).

115. Stirner, *Ego and Its Own*, 18.

116. For the most historically consequential applications of nonviolence, see Gandhi and Mahadev H. Desai, *Autobiography: The Story of My Experiments with Truth* (New York: Dover, 1983); Martin Luther King and Clayborne Carson, *The Autobiography of Martin Luther King, Jr* (London: Abacus, 2000); and Leo Tolstoy, *The Kingdom of God and Peace Essays* (London: Oxford University Press, 1936).

CHAPTER 7. Competition Introduction

117. Plutarch, "Pyrrhus," 14.2–.7. "Dionysius the Stoic says that after Chaeronea he [Diogenes of Sinope] was seized and dragged off to Philip, and being asked who he was, replied, 'A spy upon your insatiable greed.' For this he was admired and set free." Laërtius, *Lives*, 4036.

118. According to Herder, writing between 1784–91, "It is an old complaint that man, instead of cultivating the surface of the earth, has dived into its bowels and, to the destruction of his health and peace, has sought there, amid pestiferous vapors, the metals that subserve his pride and vanity, his avarice and ambition," (*Outlines*, 84). While Herder tends to center love and reason as the motivations of humanity, even he contradicts himself, writing, "In history every mode of vice and cruelty is exhausted, while here and there only a nobler train of human sentiments and virtues appears" (450). G.W.F. Hegel, who was influenced by Herder and Kant, wrote in *The Phenomenology of Spirit* (1807), "Just as stoical self-consciousness itself emerged out of mastery and servitude as the immediate existence of self-consciousness, personality emerges out of immediate spirit—emerges out of the universally dominating will of

all and their servile obedience" (trans. Terry Pinkard, Cambridge, UK: Cambridge University Press, 2018, § 478).

119. The three fundamental "moments" of human historical relations identified by Marx and Engels boil down to various kinds of avarice. They identify the need to live, the expanding nature of wants, and the need to reproduce in some form of social relationship. For them, the political and religious elements of history are dismissed as "nonsense" (Marx and Engels, *German Ideology*, 47–9). Marx and Engels fail to identify fear and reason as fundamental to human existence and action. "Consciousness" and "mind" are relegated to secondary and impure possessions of humanity that only transcend the animal level of "herd-consciousness" when human society achieves a division of material and mental labor. That results in "theory, theology, philosophy, morality, etc." that only has an effect by coming "into contradiction with the existing relations" of production because these relations have "come into contradiction with existing productive forces" (49–50). The philosophy of Marx and Engels failed, in part, because of this economic reductionism that refused to acknowledge the extent of political, military, and informational power.

120. Vico, *New Science*, § 503.

121. Vico, *New Science*, § 602.3.

122. Vico, *New Science*, § 603.

123. Vico, *New Science*, § 550.

124. Vico, *New Science*, § 592–5.

125. Vico, *New Science*, § 609.

126. Vico, *New Science*, § 1014.

127. James Surowiecki, *The Wisdom of Crowds: Why the Many Are Smarter Than the Few* (New York: Random House, 2005).

128. Vico, *New Science*, § 1008.

129. Popper, *Open Society*.

130. Cade Metz, "Who Is Making Sure the A.I. Machines Aren't Racist?," *New York Times*, March 15, 2021, accessed March 16, 2021, https://www.nytimes.com/2021/03/15/technology/artificial-intelligence-google-bias.html.

131. Herder, *Outlines*, 448–9.

132. Popper, *Open Society*.

133. Hegel, *Philosophy of Mind*, § 486.

134. Extended examples to illustrate the theories are explored here to provide process tracing that contributes to the gathering of causal evidence. Note that the examples are consciously drawn from a maximal reading of history in both time and geographic scope, rather than limiting understanding of today's hierarchies and concentration of power through considering just contemporary politics or those of a single region or period. By including in the analysis a diversity of historical examples from prehistoric archaeological evidence and anthropological research on hunter-gatherer political organization, through accounts of ancient Greece, Rome, and China, to the state- and empire-building that emerged from the wreckage of the Middle Ages, and finally to contemporary accounts of major power alliance politics and influence on international organizations, it is apparent, not only seeing the greed, concentration, and institutionalization of power throughout human history, but its enduring and universal result of conflict between freedom and control, and democracy and autocracy. Qualitative examples need not follow chronological order, but can rather follow theory in deductive order.

135. Suetonius, *Nero Claudius Caesar*; Dio Cassius, *Roman History*, 61–63; Tacitus, *Annales*, 12–16.

136. Suetonius, *Life of Nero*, XXXI; Federico Gurgone and Marco Ansaloni, "Golden House of an Emperor," *Archaeology* 68, no. 5 (September/October 2015): 37–43.

137. Suetonius, *Life of Nero*, XXXI.

138. See Book 1 of St. Augustine's *The City of God* (426 CE) and Fredrick Nietzsche's discussion of the will to power in *On the Genealogy of Morality* (1887).

139. Austin Ramzy and Tiffany May, "Hong Kong Arrests Jimmy Lai, Media Mogul, Under National Security Law," *New York Times*, August 9, 2020, accessed August 20, 2020, https://www.nytimes.com/2020/08/09/world/asia/hong-kong-arrests-lai-national-security-law.html.

140. Man Hoi Yan, Lu Xi, and Mudie Luisetta, "China-Backed Hong Kong Paper Calls For 'Ban' on Pro-Democracy Apple Daily," *Radio Free Asia*, accessed April 18, 2021, https://www.rfa.org/english/news/china/hongkong-appledaily-04162021084518.html.

141. Ramzy and May, "Hong Kong Arrests."

CHAPTER 8. **Competition Between Hierarchies**

142. Weber, "Politics as Vocation," 1–105.

143. Paul Kennedy, *The Rise and Fall of the Great Powers: Economic Change and Military Conflict from 1500–2000* (London: William Collins, 2017).

144. Mark R. Peattie and Ramon H. Myers, eds., *The Japanese Colonial Empire, 1895–1945* (Princeton, NJ: Princeton University Press, 1984), 8–13.

145. Azeem Ibrahim, *The Rohingyas: Inside Myanmar's Genocide* (London: Hurst & Company, 2018); Mohshin Habib, Christine Jubb, Salahuddin Ahmad, Masudur Rahman, and Henri Pallard, "Forced Migration of Rohingya: An Untold Experience," SSRN Scholarly Paper (Rochester, NY: Social Science Research Network, September 1, 2018).

146. Signe Howell, "Battle of Cosmologies: The Catholic Church, Adat, and 'Inculturation' among Northern Lio, Indonesia," in

Hierarchy and Value: Comparative Perspectives on Moral Order, eds. Jason Hickel and Naomi Haynes (New York: Berghahn Books, 2018), Kindle, 921–40.

147. Kennedy, *Rise and Fall*, 195–6; John H. Herz, "Idealist Internationalism and the Security Dilemma," *World Politics* 2, no. 2 (January 1950): 157–80.

148. Marx and Engels, *German Ideology*, 238.

149. William L. Shirer, *The Rise and Fall of the Third Reich: a History of Nazi Germany* (London: Secker & Warburg, 1960).

150. Stanley G. Payne, *Fascism in Spain, 1923–1977* (Madison: University of Wisconsin Press, 1999); Juan Avilés Farré, "Los socialistas y la insurrección de octubre de 1934," *Espacio Tiempo y Forma. Serie V, Historia Contemporánea* 20 (2008); Wireless, "Church Asks Spain to Pay Big Damages: Papal Nuncio Demands Indemnity for Fifty Buildings Burned in 1931 Riots," *New York Times*, June 10, 1932, 6; Paul Preston, "Spain's October Revolution and the Rightist Grasp for Power," *Journal of Contemporary History* 10, no. 4 (1975): 555–78; Maria Angharad Thomas, "The Faith and the Fury: Popular Anticlerical Violence and Iconoclasm in Spain, 1931–1936," Doctoral thesis (Royal Holloway University of London, 2012).

CHAPTER 9. **Division of Power**

151. Thomas, "Faith."

152. According to Dumont, Gandhi had an egalitarian theory of varnas (*Homo Hierarchicus*, xiii).

153. The *mutawaeen* system was moderated in 2016 to improve Saudi Arabia's investment climate. Najah Al-Osaimi, "Taming Riyadh's Religious Police," *The World Today* (Chatham House) 72, no. 3 (June 2016): 34–35.

154. Brown, "Neoliberalized Knowledge," 113–129.

CHAPTER 10. **Conflict Between Freedom and Organization**

155. Patrick M. Regan and Sam R. Bell, "Changing Lanes or Stuck in the Middle: Why Are Anocracies More Prone to Civil Wars?" *Political Research Quarterly* 63, no. 4 (December 2010): 747–759.

156. Yale H. Ferguson, "The Dominican Intervention of 1965: Recent Interpretations," *International Organization* 27, no. 4 (1973): 517–48.

157. Michael J. Kryzanek, "The 1978 Election in the Dominican Republic: Opposition Politics, Intervention and the Carter Administration," *Caribbean Studies* 19, no. 1/2 (1979): 51–73.

158. Luke Broadwater, "Militia Groups Want to 'Blow Up the Capitol,' a Police Chief Testifies," *New York Times*, February 25, 2021, accessed February 28, 2021, https://www.nytimes.com/2021/02/25/us/politics/capitol-attack-state-of-the-union.html; Rachael Levy, Ted Mann, and Andrew Restuccia, "Pro-Trump Mob Force Way Into Capitol; D.C. Orders Curfew," *Wall Street Journal*, January 6, 2021, accessed February 28, 2021, https://www.wsj.com/articles/as-rioters-again-dispute-trumps-defeat-d-c-police-make-arrests-11609945368.

CHAPTER 11. **International Hierarchy**

159. A. Ross Johnson, "The Warsaw Pact: Soviet Military Policy in Eastern Europe," *Rand Paper Series* (July 1981): 1–55.

160. Rush Doshi, *The Long Game: China's Grand Strategy to Displace American Order*, (New York: Oxford University Press, 2021).

161. David Reid, "Boeing Values China's Aircraft Business at Almost $3 Trillion over the next Two Decades," CNBC, September 17, 2019, accessed February 28, 2021, https://www.cnbc.com/2019/09/17/boeing-says-china-needs-to-spend-almost-3-trillion-on-new-planes.html.

162. David Barboza, Christopher Drew, and Steve Lohr, "G.E. to Share Jet Technology With China in New Joint Venture," *New York Times*, January 17, 2011, accessed February 17, 2021, https://www.nytimes.com/2011/01/18/business/global/18plane.html.

163. Matina Stevis-Gridneff, "E.U. Adopts Groundbreaking Stimulus to Fight Coronavirus Recession," *New York Times*, July 20, 2020, accessed July 25, 2020, https://www.nytimes.com/2020/07/20/world/europe/eu-stimulus-coronavirus.html.

164. William Barr, "Transcript of Attorney General Barr's Remarks on China Policy at the Gerald R. Ford Presidential Museum," Grand Rapids, US Department of Justice, July 17, 2020, accessed July 20, 2020,

https://www.justice.gov/opa/speech/transcript-attorney-general-barr-s-remarks-china-policy-gerald-r-ford-presidential-museum.

165. Secretary Michael Pompeo, "Communist China and the Free World's Future," Speech transcript, July 23, 2020, accessed July 24, 2020, https://2017-2021.state.gov/communist-china-and-the-free-worlds-future-2/index.html.

166. Spector, Stanley, Transcript of discussion, in *Colloquium on Overseas Chinese*, ed. Morton Fried (New York: Institute of Pacific Relations, 1958), 73.

167. Ann Kent, "China's Participation in International Organisations," in *Power and Responsibility in Chinese Foreign Policy*, eds. Yongjin Zhang and Greg Austin (Canberra: Australian National University Press, 2013), 132–166.

168. Commission on the Theft of American Intellectual Property, "Update to the IP Commission Report: The Theft of American Intellectual Property: Reassessments of the Challenge and United States Policy," National Bureau of Asian Research, 2017, accessed July 20, 2020, http://ipcommission.org/report/IP_Commission_Report_Update_2017.pdf.

169. World Bank, "GDP Growth (Annual %) - China," accessed April 20, 2021, https://data.worldbank.org/indicator/NY.GDP.MKTP.KD.ZG?locations=CN.

170. For example, China's "surface action strike groups can provide withering naval gunfire support for an amphibious landing force with their superior arsenal of anti-ship cruise missiles (ASCM)," US Navy Captain (ret.) James Fanell told the US House Permanent Select Committee on Intelligence in 2018. "They have greater range, speed and survivability." See "China's Global Naval Strategy and Expanding Force Structure: Pathway to Hegemony," testimony to the House Permanent Select Committee on Intelligence, May 17, 2018, accessed July 20, 2020, https://docs.house.gov/meetings/IG/IG00/20180517/108298/HHRG-115-IG00-Wstate-FanellJ-20180517.pdf.

171. Bruce Russett, *Grasping the Democratic Peace: Principles for a Post-Cold War World* (Princeton, NJ: Princeton University Press, 1994).

172. John Maynard Keynes, *The General Theory of Employment, Interest and Money* (Cambridge: Cambridge University Press, 2012), 238.

173. Clive Hamilton and Mareike Ohlberg, *Hidden Hand: Exposing How the Chinese Communist Party Is Reshaping the World* (London: Oneworld Publications, 2020).

174. While Turkic Muslim minorities in Xinjiang typically call the Xinjiang region East Turkistan, and are rightly sensitive about calling it China's preferred name of Xinjiang, the term *Xinjiang* is used here because China has military control over the territory, which is generally recognized as belonging to China by the international community. The same approach applies to Myanmar. This acknowledges the importance of military power and international recognition in state formation and control. It should not be construed as normative support for a particular government's control of a territory.

175. Francis Fukuyama, *End of History and the Last Man* (London: Penguin, 2020); Christopher Layne, "This Time It's Real: The

End of Unipolarity and the Pax Americana," *International Studies Quarterly* 56, no. 1 (March 2012): 203–213; Charles A. Kupchan, "The Normative Foundations of Hegemony and the Coming Challenge to Pax Americana," *Security Studies* 23, no. 2 (2014): 219–257.

176. Stuart Lau, "Xi Warns Biden and EU Not to Reignite Cold War," *Politico*, January 25, 2021, accessed January 27, 2021, https://www.politico.eu/article/xi-warns-biden-and-eu-not-to-reignite-cold-war/.

177. Fukuyama, *End of History*.

178. Dipanjan Roy Chaudhury, "India Nudges Shanghai Cooperation Organisation to Adopt English as Working Language," *Economic Times*, August 26, 2020, accessed October 8, 2020, https://economictimes.indiatimes.com/news/politics-and-nation/india-nudges-sco-to-adopt-english-as-working-language/articleshow/77749069.cms.

179. John Reed and Edward White, "Myanmar Protesters Accuse China of Backing Coup Plotters," *Financial Times*, February 17, 2021, accessed March 2, 2021, https://www.ft.com/content/43e6ecfe-081a-4390-aa18-154ec87ff764.

180. Roie Yellinek and Elizabeth Chen, "The '22 vs. 50' Diplomatic Split Between the West and China Over Xinjiang and Human Rights," *China Brief* 19, no. 22 (December 31, 2019), accessed February, 8, 2021, https://jamestown.org/program/the-22-vs-50-diplomatic-split-between-the-west-and-china-over-xinjiang-and-human-rights/.

181. Bell and Wang, *Just Hierarchy*.

182. Guo Shuqing, "Rejuvenation of China Is Unstoppable," speech by the Party Secretary and Deputy Governor of the People's Bank of China, Tsinghua PBCSF Global Finance Forum, Beijing, China, May 25, 2019, accessed August 6, 2020, https://www.bis.org/review/r190627m.htm.

183. Aruna Viswanatha and Melissa Korn, "Top Universities Took Billions in Unreported Foreign Funds, U.S. Finds," *Wall Street Journal*, October 20, 2020, accessed March 2, 2021, https://www.wsj.com/articles/top-universities-took-billions-in-unreported-foreign-funds-u-s-finds-11603226953.

184. Lorenz M. Lüthi, *The Sino-Soviet Split: Cold War in the Communist World* (Princeton, NJ: Princeton University Press, 2008); Sergey Radchenko, "The Sino-Soviet Split," in *Cambridge History of the Cold War: Crises and Détente*, eds. Melvyn P. Leffler and Odd Arne Westad (Cambridge: Cambridge University Press, 2010), 349–72; Donald S. Zagoria, *Sino-Soviet Conflict, 1956–1961* (Princeton, NJ: Princeton University Press, 1962).

185. US Department of Justice, "Patrick Ho, Former Head of Organization Backed by Chinese Energy Conglomerate, Sentenced to 3 Years in Prison for International Bribery and Money Laundering Offenses," US Attorney's Office, Southern District of New York, March 25, 2019, accessed July 19, 2020, https://www.justice.gov/usao-sdny/pr/patrick-ho-former-head-organization-backed-chinese-energy-conglomerate-sentenced-3.

186. Private communication, New York City, 2015.

187. Private communication, New York City, 2015; Horacio Sevilla Borja, "Development of an International Legally Binding Instrument Under UNCLOS on the Conservation and Sustainable Use of Marine Biological Diversity of Areas Beyond National Jurisdiction" (Opening Session of the 4th Prepcom Established by General Assembly Resolution 69/292, Group of 77), July 10, 2017, accessed March 8, 2021, http://www.g77.org/statement/getstatement.php?id=170710.

188. Horia Ciurtin, "The '16+1' Becomes the '17+1': Greece Joins China's Dwindling Cooperation Framework in Central and Eastern Europe," *China Brief* 19, no. 10 (May 29, 2019), accessed March 8, 2021, https://jamestown.org/program/the-161-becomes-the-171-greece-joins-chinas-dwindling-cooperation-framework-in-central-and-eastern-europe/.

189. Permanent Mission of the People's Republic of China to the United Nations, "CML/18/2009," Note verbale (New York: United Nations, 2009): 1–2, accessed March 8, 2021, May 7, 2009, https://www.un.org/Depts/los/clcs_new/submissions_files/vnm37_09/chn_2009re_vnm.pdf.

190. Cheng Leng, Zhang Yan, and Ryan Woo, "Chinese banks urged to switch away from SWIFT as U.S. sanctions loom," *Reuters*, July 29, 2020, accessed August 6, 2020, https://www.reuters.com/article/us-china-banks-usa-sanctions/chinese-banks-urged-to-switch-away-from-swift-as-u-s-sanctions-loom-idUSKCN24U0SN.

191. James Kynge and Sun Yu, "Virtual Control: the Agenda behind China's New Digital Currency," February 17, 2021, accessed February 19, 2021, https://www.ft.com/content/7511809e-827e-4526-81ad-ae83f405f623.

192. Javier C. Hernández, "Harsh Penalties, Vaguely Defined Crimes: Hong Kong's Security Law Explained," *New York Times*, June 30, 2020, accessed August 6, 2020, https://www.nytimes.com/2020/06/30/world/asia/hong-kong-security-law-explain.html.

193. Tony Cheung, "Beijing urges swift British response to burning of Chinese flag, Hong Kong pro-independence chants outside its London embassy," *South China Morning Post*, October 2, 2020, accessed October 6, 2020, https://www.scmp.com/news/hong-kong/politics/article/3103934/beijing-urges-swift-british-response-burning-chinese-flag.

194. Hegel writes, "In the game of war the independence of States is at stake. In one case the result may be the mutual recognition of free national individualities … and by peace-conventions supposed to be for ever, both this general recognition, and the special claims of nations on one another, are settled and fixed. External state-rights rest partly on these positive treaties, but to that extent contain only rights falling short of true actuality … partly on so-called *international* law, the general principle of which is its presupposed recognition by the several States. It thus restricts their otherwise unchecked action against one another in such a way that the

possibility of peace is left; and distinguishes individuals as private persons (non-belligerents) from the state. In general, international law rests on social usage" (*Philosophy of Mind*, § 547).

195. Philip Stephens, "Joe Biden Has a Lesson in Democracy for Angela Merkel," *Financial Times*, February 25, 2021, accessed April 21, 2021, https://www.ft.com/content/9a1c0d07-8bb4-46b0-9dd1-b32762127f7c.

CHAPTER 12. **Domestic Hierarchy**

196. Willy Wo-Lap Lam, "Has Xi Jinping Become 'Emperor for Life'?," Jamestown Foundation, November 10, 2017, accessed March 22, 2021, https://jamestown.org/program/xi-jinping-become-emperor-life/.

197. Sir Geoffrey Nice, QC, et al., "The Independent Tribunal into Forced Organ Harvesting from Prisoners of Conscience in China" (London: China Tribunal, March 1, 2020), accessed February 10, 2021, https://chinatribunal.com/wp-content/uploads/2020/03/ChinaTribunal_JUDGMENT_1stMarch_2020.pdf.

198. Adrian Zenz, "Brainwashing, Police Guards and Coercive Internment: Evidence from Chinese Government Documents about the Nature and Extent of Xinjiang's 'Vocational Training Internment Camps,'" *Journal of Political Risk* 7, no. 7 (July 1, 2019), accessed February 10, 2021, https://www.jpolrisk.com/brainwashing-police-guards-and-coercive-internment-evidence-from-chinese-government-documents-about-the-nature-and-extent-of-xinjiangs-vocational-training-internment-camps/.

199. "The struggle against the German political present is the struggle against the past of modern nations, which continue to be harassed by reminiscences of this past. It is instructive for them to see the [French] *ancien régime*, which in their countries has experienced its *tragedy*, play its comic role as a German phantom" (Introduction to the "Contribution of Hegel's Critique of Right," in *Early Writings*, 247–8).

200. David Thomson, *England in the Nineteenth Century* (London: Penguin Books, 1991), 40.

201. Marx and Engels, *German Ideology*, 52–65.

202. Anders Corr, *No Trespassing! Squatting, Rent Strikes, and Land Struggles Worldwide* (Cambridge, MA: South End Press, 1999).

203. US Bureau of Labor Statistics, "Table 5. Quartiles and Selected Deciles of Usual Weekly Earnings of Full-Time Wage and Salary Workers by Selected Characteristics, Second Quarter 2020 Averages, Not Seasonally Adjusted," January 21, 2021, accessed March 8, 2021, https://www.bls.gov/news.release/wkyeng.t05.htm.

204. Dezan Shira & Associates, "Minimum Wages in China 2020: A Complete Guide," *China Briefing News*, April 29, 2020, accessed February 10, 2021, https://www.china-briefing.com/news/minimum-wages-china-2020/.

205. Paul Avrich, "Russian Anarchists and the Civil War," *Russian Review* 27, no. 3 (1968): 296–306; Danny Evans, *Revolution and the State: Anarchism in the Spanish Civil War, 1936–1939* (London: Routledge, 2018).

206. Introduction to the "Contribution of Hegel's Critique of Right," in *Early Writings*, 251. Yet, Marx in a marginal note to *The German Ideology* contradicts himself by acknowledging that religion provides community. "To the 'community' as it appears in the ancient state, in feudalism and in the absolute monarchy, to this bond correspond especially the religious conceptions" (105, fn. 95).

207. *German Ideology*, 77. As it turns out, this figure of 72,000 hanged vagabonds is an elision if not fabrication of the facts. The original source was a French bishop in the sixteenth century. Nobody knows how the bishop would have received the data, but it was transmitted as a horoscope, of all things. According to the horoscope, "as many as seventy thousand persons were found to have perished by the hand of the executioner." This was not just vagabonds, and the source was questionable to say the least (Thorsten Sellin, "Two

Myths in the History of Capital Punishment," *Journal of Criminal Law, Criminology, and Police Science* 50, no. 2 (July 1959): 114-7).

208. Popper, *Open Society*.

209. Introduction to the "Contribution of Hegel's Critique of Right," in *Early Writings*, 246–7.

210. Introduction to the "Contribution of Hegel's Critique of Right," in *Early Writings*, 244.

211. Ian Vásquez and Fred McMahon, Human Freedom Index 2020, accessed February 10, 2021, http://www.deslibris.ca/ID/10105748.

212. Karl Marx, *The Civil War in France* (Kindle, n.d.), 1071–75.

213. Mehmet Tabak, "Marx's Theory of Proletarian Dictatorship Revisited," *Science and Society* 64, no. 3 (Fall 2000): 338–53.

214. Tabak, "Marx's Theory," 338–48.

215. "GDP per Capita (Current US$) - China," accessed February 9, 2021, https://data.worldbank.org/indicator/NY.GDP.PCAP.CD?locations=CN.

216. World Bank, "Military Expenditure (Current USD) - European Union, United States," accessed March 22, 2021, https://data.worldbank.org/indicator/MS.MIL.XPND.CD?locations=EU-US.

217. Marx and Engels, *German Ideology*, 52–65.

218. Marx and Engels, *German Ideology*, 52.

219. Marx and Engels, *German Ideology*, 53–9.

220. Daniel A. Bell, *The China Model: Political Meritocracy and the Limits of Democracy* (Princeton, NJ: Princeton University Press, 2015).

221. Marx and Engels, *German Ideology*, 69.

222. Oleksandra Veselova, "Famine in Ukraine after the Second World

War," *Harvard Ukrainian Studies* 30, no. ¼, trans. Marta D. Olynyk and Andrij Wynnyckyj (2008): 183–198.

223. Basil Ashton, Kenneth Hill, Alan Piazza and Robin Zeitz, "Famine in China, 1958–61," *Population and Development Review* 10, no. 4 (December 1984): 614–624; Shujie Yao, "A Note on the Causal Factors of China's Famine in 1959–1961," *Journal of Political Economy* 107, no. 6 (December 1999): 1365–1369.

224. Jamelle Bouie, "If There Was a Republican Civil War, It Appears to Be Over," *New York Times*, February 17, 2021, accessed February 17, 2021, https://www.nytimes.com/2021/02/17/opinion/trump-mconnell-republicans.html.

225. Chris Buckley, Doan Chau, and Thomas Fuller, "China Targeted by Vietnamese in Fiery Riots," *New York Times*, May 14, 2014, accessed March 2, 2021, https://www.nytimes.com/2014/05/15/world/asia/foreign-factories-in-vietnam-weigh-damage-in-anti-china-riots.html; Human Rights Watch, "Covid-19 Fueling Anti-Asian Racism and Xenophobia Worldwide," May 12, 2020, accessed February 16, 2021, https://www.hrw.org/news/2020/05/12/covid-19-fueling-anti-asian-racism-and-xenophobia-worldwide; "Coronavirus: Men Wanted over Racist Oxford Street Attack on Student," BBC News, March 4, 2020, accessed February 11, 2021, https://www.bbc.com/news/uk-england-london-51736755; John Reed and Edward White, "Myanmar Protesters Accuse China of Backing Coup Plotters," February 17, 2021, accessed February 18, 2021, https://www.ft.com/content/43e6ecfe-081a-4390-aa18-154ec87ff764.

226. In his introduction to the "Contribution of Hegel's Critique of Right," Marx notes, "What a spectacle! A society infinitely divided into the most diverse races which confront one another with their petty antipathies, their bad consciences and their brutal mediocrity and which, precisely because of their ambivalent and suspicious attitude towards one another, are dealt with by their *masters* without distinction, although with different formalities, as if their *existence* had been granted to them on *license*. And they

are even forced to recognize and acknowledge the fact that they are *dominated, ruled and possessed as a privilege from heaven!*" (*Early Writings*, 246).

227. Author's interview with General John Allen (USMC, Ret.), January 25, 2021.

228. Jack Nicas and Davey Alba, "Amazon, Apple and Google Cut Off Parler, an App That Drew Trump Supporters," *New York Times*, January 9, 2021, accessed April 21, 2021, https://www.nytimes.com/2021/01/09/technology/apple-google-parler.html.

229. "Largest Companies by Market Cap," accessed February 11, 2021, https://companiesmarketcap.com/.

230. Gary King, private communication, 2001.

231. "#2 Koch Family," *Forbes*, accessed February 11, 2021, https://www.forbes.com/profile/koch/.

232. Subsidy Tracker Parent Company Summary, "Koch Industries," accessed February 11, 2021, https://subsidytracker.goodjobsfirst.org/parent/koch-industries.

233. Jane Mayer, *Dark Money: The Hidden History of the Billionaires behind the Rise of the Radical Right* (New York: Anchor Books, 2017).

234. Jane Mayer, "The Danger of President Pence," *New Yorker*, October 16, 2017, accessed February 11, 2021, https://www.newyorker.com/magazine/2017/10/23/the-danger-of-president-pence; Susan B. Glasser, "Mike Pompeo, the Secretary of Trump," *New Yorker*, August 19, 2019, accessed February 11, 2021, https://www.newyorker.com/magazine/2019/08/26/mike-pompeo-the-secretary-of-trump.

235. This is a representative, rather than exhaustive, list of tax havens. Some American states like Florida that do not charge state tax could also be included, though they would still be subject to US federal tax.

236. Michael Forsythe, "As China's Leader Fights Graft, His Relatives Shed Assets," *New York Times*, June 17, 2014, accessed February 16, 2021, https://www.nytimes.com/2014/06/18/world/asia/chinas-president-xi-jinping-investments.html; Alexandra Stevenson and Michael Forsythe, "Luxury Homes Tie Chinese Communist Elite to Hong Kong's Fate," *New York Times*, August 12, 2020, accessed February 17, 2021, https://www.nytimes.com/2020/08/12/business/china-hong-kong-elite.html; Michael Forsythe, "Panama Papers Tie More of China's Elite to Secret Accounts," *New York Times*, April 6, 2016, accessed February 17, 2021, https://www.nytimes.com/2016/04/07/world/asia/china-panama-papers.html.

237. Sam Cooper, *Wilful Blindness: How a Criminal Network of Narcos, Tycoons, and CCP Agents Infiltrated the West* (Toronto: Optimum Publishing International, 2021).

CONCLUSION: The Deconcentration of Power

238. Niccolò Machiavelli, *The Prince*, trans. George Bull (Harmondsworth, UK: Penguin Books, 1961): 130.

239. Austin Ramzy and Raymond Zhong, "Hong Kong Protesters Defy Police Ban in Show of Strength After Tumult," *New York Times*, August 18, 2019, https://www.nytimes.com/2019/08/18/world/asia/hong-kong-protest.html.

240. Yannis Stivachtis, Chris Price, and Mike Habegger, "The European Union as a Peace Actor," *Review of European Studies* 5, no. 3 (2013): 4.

241. Joe Biden, "Biden's Speech to Congress: Full Transcript," *New York Times*, April 29, 2021, accessed April 29, 2021, https://www.nytimes.com/2021/04/29/us/politics/joe-biden-speech-transcript.html.

242. Laërtius, *Lives*, 4006. "But he claimed that to fortune he could oppose courage, to convention nature, to passion reason. When he

was sunning himself in the Craneum, Alexander came and stood over him and said, "Ask of me any boon you like." To which he replied, 'Stand out of my light.'"

243. Immanuel Kant, "What Is Enlightenment?," trans. Mary C. Smith, [1784], accessed March 9, 2021, http://www.columbia.edu/acis/ets/CCREAD/etscc/kant.html.

ACKNOWLEDGMENTS

244. Any opinions, findings, conclusions, or recommendations expressed in this work are those of the author and do not necessarily reflect the views of the National Science Foundation.

245. Alberto Alesina and Enrico Spolaore, "On the Number and Size of Nations," *Quarterly Journal of Economics* 112, no. 4 (November 1997): 1027–1056; Alberto Alesina and Enrico Spolaore, *The Size of Nations* (Cambridge, MA: MIT Press, 2003); Alberto Alesina and Enrico Spolaore, "War, Peace, and the Size of Countries," *Journal of Public Economics* 89 (2005): 1333–1354; Alberto Alesina and Enrico Spolaore, "Conflict, Defense Spending, and the Number of Nations," *European Economic Review* 50 (2006): 91–120.

246. Perry Anderson, *Passages from Antiquity to Feudalism* (London: NLB, 1974); Perry Anderson, *Lineages of the Absolutist State* (London: NLB, 1974).

247. Richerson and Boyd, "Complex Societies," 253–289.

248. Bear Braumoeller, "Systemic Politics: The Great Powers in General (Dis-)Equilibrium," Mershon Center at the Ohio State University, May 20, 2005; Bear Braumoeller, *The Great Powers and the International System: Systemic Theory in Empirical Perspective* (Cambridge, UK: Cambridge University Press, 2012).

249. Robert L. Carneiro, "Political Expansion as an Expression of the Principle of Competitive Exclusion," in *Origins of the State: The Anthropology of Political Evolution*, ed. Ronald Cohen (Philadelphia: Institute for the Study of Human Issues, 1978): 205–224.

250. Lars-Erik Cederman, *Emergent Actors in World Politics: How States and Nations Develop and Dissolve* (Princeton, NJ: Princeton University Press, 1997); Lars-Erik Cederman, "Generating State-Size Distributions: A Geopolitical Model," Center for Comparative and International Studies, Zurich, Switzerland, 2003.

251. Jared M. Diamond, *Guns, Germs and Steel: The Fates of Human Societies* (New York: W.W. Norton & Co., 1997).

252. Benoît Dubreuil, *Human Evolution and the Origins of Hierarchies: the State of Nature* (Cambridge, UK: Cambridge University Press, 2010).

253. Francis Fukuyama, *The End of History and the Last Man* (New York: Simon and Schuster, 2006).

254. Herz, "Rise and Demise," 473–93; Herz, "The Territorial State," 11–34.

255. Michael J. Hiscox and David A. Lake, "Democracy, Federalism, and the Size of States," Harvard University and University of California, San Diego, January 2002.

256. Samuel Huntington, *Political Order in Changing Societies* (New Haven, CT: Yale University Press, 2006).

257. Immanuel Kant, *To Perpetual Peace: A Philosophical Sketch* (Indianapolis, IN: Hackett, 2003).

258. Paul Kennedy, *The Rise and Fall of the Great Powers: Economic Change and Military Conflict from 1500–2000* (London: William Collins, 2017).

259. Hiscox and Lake, "Democracy, Federalism"; David A. Lake. "Escape from the State of Nature: Authority and Hierarchy in World Politics," *International Security* 32, 1 (Summer 2007): 47–79; David A. Lake and Angela O'Mahony, "The Incredible Shrinking State: Explaining Change in the Territorial Size of Countries," *Journal of Conflict Resolution* 48, no. 5 (October 2004): 699–722.

260. Mann, *Sources of Social Power*.

261. Louis A. Marano, "A Macrohistorical Trend Toward World Government," *Behavior*

Science Notes 8 (1973): 35–40.

262. Richerson and Boyd, "Complex Societies," 253–289.

263. Alesina and Spolaore, "On the number," 1027–1056; Alesina and Spolaore, *Size of Nations*; Alesina and Spolaore, "War, Peace," 1333–1354; Alesina and Spolaore, "Conflict, Defense Spending," 91–120.

264. Hendrik Spruyt, *The Sovereign State and Its Competitors: An Analysis of Systems Change* (Princeton, NJ: Princeton University Press, 1994); Hendrik Spruyt, "The Origins, Development, and Possible Decline of the Modern State," *Annual Review of Political Science* 5 (June 2002): 127–49.

265. Joseph Strayer, *On the Medieval Origins of the Modern State* (Princeton, NJ: Princeton University Press, 1970).

266. Charles Tilly, *Coercion, Capital and European States: AD 990–1992* (Oxford, UK: Basil Blackwell, 1990).

267. Max Weber, "Politics as a Vocation", in *Weber's Rationalism and Modern Society,* eds. and trans. Tony Waters and Dagmar Waters (London: Palgrave MacMillan, 2015): 1–105.

268. Alexander Wendt, "Why a World State is Inevitable," *European Journal of International Relations* 9 (2003): 491–542.

269. Giambattista Vico, *New Science: Principles of the New Science Concerning the Common Nature of Nations*, trans. David Marsh (London: Penguin Classics, 2013).

270. Hegel and Marx are rightly criticized by the neoliberal Popper (*Open Society*) as leaning too much toward the authoritarian and teleological, and lacking in empirical evidence. Popper himself lacked in empirical evidence for his claims against "historicism,"

and admitted as much. Hegel writes, "In the government—regarded as organic totality—the sovereign power (principate) is (a) *subjectivity* as the *infinite* self-unity of the notion in its development;—the all-sustaining, all-decreeing will of the state, its highest peak and all-pervasive unity. In the perfect form of the state, in which each and every element of the notion has reached free existence, this subjectivity is not a so-called 'moral person,' or a decree issuing from a majority (forms in which the unity of the decreeing will has not an *actual* existence), but an actual individual,—the will of a decreeing individual,—*monarchy*. The monarchical constitution is therefore the constitution of developed reason: all other constitutions belong to lower grades of the development and realisation of reason" (§ 542). Hegel writes, "Liberty and Equality are the simple rubrics into which is frequently concentrated what should form the fundamental principle, the final aim and result of the constitution. However true this is, the defect of these terms is their utter abstractness: if stuck to in this abstract form, they are principles which either prevent the rise of the concreteness of the state, i.e. its articulation into a constitution and a government in general, or destroy them" (Hegel, *Philosophy of Mind*, § 539). Hegel's notion of a benign monarch with a unitary consciousness is derivative of his predecessor, Vico, who in his *New Science* (1725) wrote that "monarchy is the form of government best suited to human nature when it possesses the most developed reason" (§ 1008). In other respects, too, Hegel is a Vichian thinker (Timothy Brennan, *Borrowed Light: Vico, Hegel, and the Colonies*, Stanford, CA: Stanford University Press, 2014, 4). Some, but not all, of Hegel and Marx's points on historical development are important and incorporated into the theory presented here. Vico's historicism is less teleological than that of Hegel, based as it is on causal mechanisms that he identifies in the text. Hegel and Marx can be self-contradictory, as well. Unless otherwise noted, all italics in this book are those of the author.

271. James C. Scott, *Weapons of the Weak: Everyday Forms of Peasant Resistance* (New Haven, CT: Yale University Press, 2000); James C. Scott, *Seeing like a State: How Certain Schemes to Improve the*

Human Condition Have Failed (New Haven, CT: Yale University Press, 1998); James C. Scott, *Domination and the Arts of Resistance: Hidden Transcripts* (New Haven, CT: Yale University Press, 1990).

272. Michel Foucault, *Discipline and Punish: The Birth of the Prison* (London: Penguin Books, 1991); Michel Foucault, *Madness and Civilization: A History of Insanity in the Age of Reason*, trans. Richard Howard (London: Routledge, 2007); Michel Foucault, *The History of Sexuality*, vol. 1 (London: Penguin Books, 1990); Michel Foucault, *The History of Sexuality*, vol. 2 (London: Penguin Books, 1992).

273. Crenshaw, "Demarginalizing the Criminalization," 1–31.

274. American Political Science Association Conference, Washington DC, August 31–September 4, 2005.

Index

academics, China's influence on, 9–10

Afghanistan, corruption and, 172

aggression, fear and avarice and, 105

Agrippina the Younger, 110

Alexander the Great, 18–19, 76, 187

Alexandra, Empress of Russia, 54

Algeria, fight for independence, 11–12

Allen, General John, 172

alliance blocs, sovereignty of subunits, 34, 221–22n32

altruism, individuals and, 51–52

Amazon, 173

America. *see* United States

anarchism

    far-left ideology, 161–62

    pacifist as unrealized ideal, 162

anarchists, 94–95

    reject chaos description, 97

anarchy, 128

anocracy, 128–29

    civil war and, 129

anthropological studies

    evidence supporting hierarchies, 70

anti-Chinese racism, 170

apartheid, China, 150, 158

Apple, 173

Apple Daily (Jimmy Lai), 112
aristocracy, views of, 32
armed combat and political power, 60
ascription-based bias, 91
ascriptive prescriptions, 156–58
ascriptive values, hierarchy and, 74
Asia Infrastructure Investment Bank, 152
Asia Society, 48
Athenian League, 133
authoritarian leaders, public avarice and, 110
authoritarian regimes
    capital flight and, 121
    examples of, 11
authoritarianism, vs. democracy, 12–13
authority, hierarchy and, 45
autocracy(ies)
    billionaires vs. 21
    challenge democracies' foundations, 124
    conflict with democracy, 72–73
    consequences of unfree press, 135–36
    global contest with democracy, 129
    stability of, 129–30
    war and, 141, 143
avarice
    competition, cause of, 104–105
    fear and, 105–106
    and human historical relations, 239n119
    leaders and, 110
    Nero example, 110–11, 240n134
    persistence of, 58
    ratchet theory and, 36, 110, 225–26n43

Babbitt, Ashley, 1
Balaguer, President Joaquín, 129
bandwagoning
    smaller countries, 140–41

Western elites with China, 183
Barr, William P., 139
basket of deplorables, 91, 98
Biden, Hunter, 173
Biden, President Joe, 144, 153
    domestic factionalism, warning of, 184
    global competition with China, 9
    inauguration of, 3
    biologism, 228n53
Bitcoin, 78
Black Lives Matter (BLM), 170
    Trump's opposition to, 3
Bolshevik Revolution (1917), 120
Bolsheviks, 11
Bosch, Juan, 129
Boyd, Robert, 18, 33
Brexit, 138
Brezhnev, Leonid, 134
Britain
    digital currency, considering, 78
    trade prioritized over genocide, 146
Britannicus, 110
British Empire, 76
    development of, 30–31
Brussels, power of nation-states and, 3
Buffett, Warren, 175
Burma, *see* Myanmar

capital flight
    labor conflicts and, 160
    from socialist-leaning democracies, 177
capital, concentration of power and, 20–21
Capitol Hill riot, 130
    precedents for, 11–13
Carneiro, Robert, 31, 33, 221n32+
Carter, President Jimmy, 129

Catholic Church
    Lio religious hierarchies and, 117–18
Chan, Ronnie, 48
channeling hierarchy, 180-81
China, 160-61
    airline technology transfer to, 136
    apartheid-like system, 150, 158
    competition with US and EU, 137–38
    contingency plans for international leadership, 152–53
    crypto-currencies capital flight, 78
    donations to Harvard, 48
    elite identify as humiliated, 86–87
    excluded from G7, 152
    failed American strategy re, 118–19
    failed communism, 169
    GDP, 138, T138
    GDP growth rate, 140
    global autocracy possible with, 141–42
    global corporations and, 8–9
    Han nationalism, 131
    hegemony, seeks, 142–43
    hierarchies in, 158
    influence and power growing, 139–40
    influence on US politics, 176–77
    invests in market democracies, 176
    leads country groupings, 152
    leads Sino-Russian partnership, 151
    linguistic influence failing, 145–46
    military spending, 140
    purchases of influence, 82–83
    replaces USSR as challenge to international system, 30
    state capitalism and, 96, 165, 166
    stealing intellectual property from US, 140
    sugar-coated Marxism of, 166
    supported by junior members of alliances, 151–52
    technological lead over US, 140, 242n170
    threat of war as coercion, 153

vs. US as hegemon, 143–45
uses influence to advance goals, 150–51
violations of international law, 152
wealth and power of, 9–10
Chinese Communist Party (CCP)
increasingly powerful, 3
one hundred years of humiliation and, 87
split from Russia in 1950s, 150–51
totalitarian meta-hierarchy, 151
Chinese language, promotion of failing, 145–46
civil wars, 94
class war myth in Marxism, 159–60
class wars
capital flight and, 160
democratic participation and, 160
myth of, 159–60
successful, 160–61
climate change, war and, 65
Cold War, 4, 117, 133, 143
close to, 141
military conflict and, 144
colonialism, rising, 13
communism, 158-66
anarchism and, 161–62
complete conformity to state required, 159
diverts blame to capitalism, 166
more hierarchical than democracies, 158
peakedness and Marxist philosophies, 158–59
rationalizing power, 58
reaction against democracies, 170
reliance on myths, 159–60
war against religion, 164
whether governments truly represent, 164–66
communist governments
poor metrics of, 164
communist revolution, 167–69
class wars and

160-61
    failure of, 168–69
    hurts lowest-skilled workers, 161
    no development as anticipated, 168
communists, 94
    utopian vs. state, 96
competition
    hierarchical relationships and, 108
    introduction to, 103–13
    Nero and avarice, 110–11
    rebellion, repression and, 112–13
    Vico's theory of religion, 105–108
competition between hierarchies, 115–21
    assets, seeking, 119
    bourgeoisie vs. aristocracy, 119
    breakup and regestion and, 117–18
    Catholic Church in Indonesia, 117–18
    extremist imbalances and, 120–21
    international level, at, 117–18
    Japan's cordon of sovereignty/advantage, 116–17
    military arms buildup and, 118
    state hierarchies and, 115–16
    state sovereignty and, 116–17
    US vs. China, 118–19
    winners and losers, 118–19
concentration of power, *see* power; power concentration, global
Crenshaw, Kimberlé, 17, 86
Cross-Border Interbank Payment System, 152
Cuba, 161
cultural resistance, 155
culture war, 93

de facto sovereignty, 38
de Gaulle, Charles, 11–12, 13
de jure sovereignty, 38
de Tracy, Antoine-Louis-Claude, Comte de, 61

decentralizing power
    ratchet mechanism prevents, 4–5, 6, 7
decolonization, regestion of power and, 142
deconfliction, structure of hierarchy and, 75–76
defeating hierarchy, 181–82
    alliances for, 182
democratic dyads consistently peaceful, 141
democracy(ies)
    capital needed, 20
    effort needed to support, 13–14
    egalitarian reforms in, 183, 184
    factionalism in, 13
    hierarchies and, 72–73
    historical trend toward, 32
    infighting as threat to, 10
    Marx and Engels on, 218–19n14
    as middle ground, 128
    moderate positions in, 98
    power and wealth, concentrating, 121
    threatened by hierarchical state power, 7
    transitioning to anocracy from, 128–29
democratic freedoms, need for, 20
democratic institutions, how they are weakened, 16–17
democratic leaders, satisfying security needs over avarice, 110
democratic values, 13
    institutionalizing and defending, 21–22
Denmark
    disaggregation threats to, 4–5
    transfer payments as pawl, 5
diffusing hierarchy, 181, 182
digital currencies, 78, 152
Diogenes, 187, 227n48, 238n117, 254–55n242
disincentives
    fear and, 105–106
    power concentration, maintaining, 4–5
    ratchet theory of, 4–5
Divale, William, 63, 64

domestic hierarchy(ies), 155–78
    communist authoritarianism, 157, 158–66
    competition among pluralistic, 156
    favorites, 157–58
    market authoritarianism, 157, 167–69
    market democracy, 157, 170–78
    peakedness of, 156–57
    primary, interlinked, 157
dominance
    persistence of, 58
    power, hierarchy and, 30
Dominican Republic, 129
Dumont, Louis, 32, 219n20
    hierarchy, 228n55
    status vs. power, 228–29n56
duopoly, 173

e-yuan, 152
economic hierarchy(ies)
    power of, 24
    subordination, privilege and, 87, T87, T88
    wealth and, 82–83
economic power, types of 40
egalitarian hunter-gatherers, 60–61
egalitarian principles, benevolent hierarchy and, 72
egalitarian values
    Greece, 19
    vs. power concentration, 19
egalitarianism, 94
    evidence lacking, 33
elites
    power concentrates among, 58
    ways to compete with China, 183–84
    Engels, Friedrich, 218–19n14
    avarice and human historical relations, 239n119
    economy and division of labor, 231n74

England, Danish conquest of, 81
English as common language, 145–46
equality of opportunity, myth of, 20
Erdoğan, Recep Tayyip, 7
Esper, Mark, 3
ethnic minorities
    China vs. US/EU treatment of, 158
European colonial empires, fall of, 30
European Union (EU)
    competition with US and China, 137–38
    consolidation of power in, 138
    democratic competition against China, 139
    English as language of choice, 145–46
    GDP, 138, T138
    as meta-hierarchy, 151
    as new hierarchy, 182–83
    support for US against China, 140
exchange, power and, 51
exploitation, ownership of humans and, 61

Facebook, 172–73
    as public good, 174–75
factionalism, dangers of, 91–92, 97–98
fake news, 83
Falun Gong, genocide against, 146–47, 152, 164
families
    capture and enslavement, 62–63
    patriarchal, development of, 61–62
fascism
    creation of, 11
    political instability and, 172
    power imbalances and, 118
    power seeking and, 58
    Western groups and, 8, 97, 179
fear
    checks avarice, 105–106

operation on leaders, 110

persistence of, 58

ratchet theory and, 36, 110

religion and (Vico), 105–106

fire, control of, 60

flattening hierarchy, 181

Flynn, General Mike, 3

force

can be bought, 82

political hierarchy and, 81

power and, 49

taxation and, 78

force hierarchy(ies), 77–78, T78

power, use of, 78–79, T79

France

fighting communism in Algeria, 11–12

Franco, General Francisco, 120

free speech

communist countries lack, 112, 164

drowning out, 20

protects societies, 135–36

freedom and organization, conflict between, 127–31

anarchy, 128

anocracy, 128–29

democracy, 128–29

expansionism, 131

nationalism, 130–31

patriotic vs. expansionist, 131

stable autocracies, 129–30

totalitarianism, 127–28

Freedom News, 221n31

retooling of (1951), 29–30

French empire, 76

Fukuyama, Francis (End of History), 143

functions of hierarchy, 69–74

civil sovereignty, enabling, 71

decision-making, 69–70, 71

list of, 71

winning vs. losing hierarchies, 73–74

Gandhi, Mahatma, 97, 242n152

Gates, Bill, 174

GDP

China, EU, and US compared, 138, T138

growth in and democracies, 160–61

per capita, communist *vs.* democracies, 161

gender, societal origins and, 65–68

gendered division of labor, 64, 230–31n72

genocides

communist, 164

current examples of, 146–47

German Ideology (Marx and Engels), 159

global corporations

CEO compensation and, 20–21

China's influence on, 9–10

Chinese influence on, 147–49

profit orientation vs. human rights, 146–47

profit seeking and China, 8–9

Google, 173

non-US CEO, 147

Graeber, David, 43, 70

Great Leap Forward (China), 169

Greece, egalitarian values of, 19

Greenland

secession threat and transfer payments to, 4–5

Group of 20 (G20), 152

Group of 7 (G7), 152

Group of 77 (G77), 151

Harris, Marvin, 63, 64

Harvard Business School professors

monetary incentives and bias, 47–48

Haynes, Naomi, 70

Hegel, G. W. F.

    aims of society and individual, 109–10

    ethical substance, 220–21n27

    hierarchy and nature, 70–71

    monarchy, view of, 32, 224n38

    personality, emergence of, 238–39n118

    power supporting monarchy, 107–108

    on slaves, 236n105

    state as spiritual life, 227n52

    states' independence, 248–49n194

hegemon, global

    military conflict and, 143–44

    single, close to, 142–45

    three contenders for, 40

hegemon(s)

    power relations and, 39–40

    regularizing laws and norms, 46

hegemonic power, institutionalization of, 10–11

hegemony

    China's expansion and, 141

    illiberal global,

        heading towards, 5–6

Hermogenianus, 106

Herz, John H., 17, 33

Hickel, Jason, 70

hierarchical drift, 42, 227n49

hierarchy(ies), 222–23n34

    as aggregation of power, 33

    benefits to individuals, 49–50

    conflict within, 24–25

    defining (*see* hierarchy, defining)

    dissolution of, 24

    domestic (*see* domestic hierarchy(ies))

    escaping, 186–87

    freedom of speech protection, 135–36

function of (*see* functions of hierarchy)
global, network theory of power and, 40–41
    global, changes to since 1951, 30–31
    and hegemony, theory of, 17–22
    individual liberation from rare, 68
    international (*see* international hierarchies)
    lack of is rare, 72
    man incapable of recognizing, 32
    nationalism and, 19–20
    optimistic theories of, 32, 33
    Oxford English Dictionary definition of, 43
    perceptions of, 31–32
    property in humans as early form of, 61
    ranking of, 79
    ratchet effect and, 22–25, 32
    ratchet theory and, 18
    ratchet used to maintain power, 4–5
    rebellion and repression in, 112–13
    structure of (*see* structure of hierarchy)
    success in, 185–86
    symbiosis of, 125
    totalitarianism and, 24
    unwritten, 51
    violent river, compared to, 179–80
    voluntarily adopted, 69–70
    weak, regestion/reincorporation into stronger, 37
    wealth and power concentration, 19
hierarchy, defining, 15
    altruism and power, 51–52
    authority and, 45
    benign, 44–45
    biological/materialist effects on power, 46
    climbing the hierarchy, 54
    conditioning and, 53
    egalitarian communities and, 45
    financial influences on, 47–48
    force, using, 52–53

group cohesion, maintaining, 53
ideas, influencing, 48–49
individual and family hierarchies as pattern for, 48
knowledge, systemizing power of, 53–54
legality and, 45–46
material forms of power and, 47
mutual dependence for sustenance, 48
perceivers and, 53
power essential to, 50–51
risk-acceptant and, 55
rules and norms, 51
theological context of term, 43, 44
hierarchy, origins of, 57–68
drive for power and position, 57–58
theories rejected, 68
Hierarchy, The, 77
hierarchy, theories of, 35–42
concentrating but punctuated equilibrium, 37–38
concentration of power, 36
dissolution of weak hierarchies, 37
division of power, 39–40
feminist and anti-racist theories, 41
hierarchical drift, 42
hierarchical skimming, 39
lack of leadership in hierarchy, 41–42
network theory of power, 40–41
oscillation of power imbalances, 36
preponderant sovereignty, 38
ratchet effect, 36
sovereign flux, 38–39
Hitler, Adolf, 11, 95
Hong Kong
National Security Law (NSL), 112, 142, 153
protests (2019), 180–81, 183
hooks, bell, 86
Howell, Signe, 117–18
Hui, apartheid and, 158

human rights violations ignored at global level, 146–47

ideas, influencing with money, 49
identity hierarchies, 81
identity politics, 98
ideology, loyalty and, 83–84
imperialism, rising, 13
incentives
    power concentration, maintaining, 4–5
    ratchet theory and, 4–5
    as subsidies, 36
India
    Hindu nationalism, 130
    separated hierarchies within, 123
individuals
    altruism and power, 51–52
    benefits from joining hierarchy, 49
    power expands within hierarchy, 50
influence
    derived from expectations, 53
    power and, 50–51
information, power and, 79
information technology (IT) sector
    top companies in, 173–74
informational hierarchies
    power of, 23
    power of knowledge and, 83
    subordination and privilege and, 87, T87, T88
informational power, types of, 40
Instagram, 173
international hierarchies, 133–54
    centralized vs. decentralized, 135
    China and global autocracy, 141–42
    China and Russia use influence, 150–51
    courting countries as allies, 139
    English common language of, 145–46

genocide and, 146–47
global concentration, growing, 141
global conferences and, 149
human rights violations ignored, 147
networking by global elite, 149–53
organizations and alliances, 145–54
science, flouting, 149
smaller countries and, 140–41
social and political hierarchies in, 147–48
universities part of, 148–49
value system profit-oriented, 14647
international organizations
examples of, 133–34
purpose of, 134–35
successful, 133
international trade
genocide and, 146–47
profits trump human rights, 146–47
intersectional theory, 86, 236–37n107

Japanese empire, collapse of, 116–17
Jinping, Xi, 3, 144, 146, 149, 158
Johnson, President Lyndon B., 129

Kant, Immanuel, 141
autocracies and war, 143
democracy, widespread adoption of, 187
Keynes, John Maynard
economic cause of war, 141
rationalizing power, 58
Khrushchev, Nikita, 150
King Agis (Sparta), 106
King, Martin Luther, 97
Kissinger, Henry, 54
knowledge

informational hierarchies and, 83
power and, 49
power concentration and, 19
production controlled, 136
vs. totalitarian power, 127–28
knowledge hierarchies
knowledge of their structure, 84–85
love and, 84
Koch family, 175
Korean War, 144
!Kung tribe, 64

labor, *see* workers
Lai, Jimmy, imprisonment of, 112
language development among hominids, 60
leaders
bought off by foreign powers, 136
two types, 90
leadership, individual illusion of, 24
leftists
least offensive outcomes and, 96
mobilizing in reaction to, 95
moderate, 92–93, 95
recognizing property value, 172
social movements and, 93
true communism and, 164–65, 166
legality, hierarchy and, 45
liberal principles, building new hierarchies on, 182–83
libertarians, 95–96
liberty, pursuing on multiple fronts, 98–99
Linearbandkeramik Culture (LBK), 66
LinkedIn, 173
Lio indigenous religious hierarchies supplanted by Catholic Church, 117–18
love, and knowledge hierarchies, 84
Luther, Martin, 109

Machiavelli, Niccolò, 179
Macron, Emmanuel, 138
Magna Carta, 109
Malayan Communist Party (MCP), 29–30
Mao, Chairman
    Great Leap Forward, 169
    hierarchical pumping by, 115
Marano, Louis, 33
marginalized groups, 91–98
market democracies, 170–78
    buying political influence in, 175–76
    vs. communist standard of living, 161
    competition for investment, 177
    economic conflicts in, 159
    elites, role for, 171–72
    extreme ideologies, rise of, 170–71
    greed and, 172, 175
    leftists, role for, 172
    luck and, 172, 173–75
    monopolies and, 172–73
    monosopony in, 172
    outperform communist countries, 161
    wealth inequality in, 171
    workers in, 172
marriage, property and, 61
Marx, Karl
    avarice, 225–26n43, 239n119
    culpability of, 165
    dictatorship of proletariat and, 158–59, 218–19n14
    economy and division of labor, 231n74
    on French revolutions, 159, 249n199
    historical theories, 223–24n36
    Paris Commune and, 165, 219–19n14
    on racism, 252–53n226
    religion, criticism of, 162, 250n206
    religion as opium of people, 164
    total revolt of, 163–64

vagabondage, 163

violence, support for, 162–63

withering away of hierarchy, 32

Marxism

    class war myth, 159–60

    theory of class bigotry, 167

    worker alienation, 167–68

median voter and left-right-wing political spectrum, 92

men

    combat effectiveness of, 62–63

    competitive dominance of, 62–63

    socialized as leaders, 63

meta-hierarchy(ies), 23–24, 73, 77, 234n93

    China taking advantage of, 145

    current, 151

    international organizations, China and, 153–54

    Sino-Russian against NATO, 151

    subalterns within, 151

    universities and, 149

methodology of book, 25–26

Meyer, Christian, 66

micro-hierarchies, 86

Microsoft, 173, 174

Miles, Rufus Edward, 91

Miles's Law, 91

military, political control and, 137

Mitterand, François, 12

Mohanty, Chandra Talhade, 86

monarchy

    benign (Vico), 107–108

    democratic revolutions and, 109

    hierarchical association and, 32

monogamy, property and, 61

monopolies, 172–75

monopolistic exchange, 51

monopsonistic exchange, 51

Morgenthau, Hans J., 79–80

Mussolini, Benito, 8, 95
Myanmar (Burma), 117
    genocide in, 146–47

National Security Law (China, 2020), 112, 142, 153
national sports team analogy, 73
nationalism
    concentration/deconcentration of power and, 130–31
    cultural resistance and, 155
    hierarchies and, 19–20
NATO (North Atlantic Treaty Organization), 5, 34
    Chinese market access worries, 139
    hierarchy, as, 135
    voluntary defensive alliance, 133–34
nature, hierarchy as escape from violence of, 70–71
Nazi Party, Germany, 11
Nero, avarice of, 110–11
network theory of power, 79
networking by global elite, 149–53
New Cold War (US and China), 143
Nicholas II, Emperor of Russia, 54
Nietzsche, Friedrich, 95
Ninety-five Theses (Luther), 109
Nixon, Richard, 54
nonviolence and reform in democracies, 181
norms, unwritten, of hierarchies, 51
North Atlantic Treaty Organization, *see* NATO
nuclear weaponry, 33

Oppenheimer, Franz, 232n77
optimism vs. realistic pessimism, 57–58
optimistic theories of power and hierarchy, 32, 33
Owen, Robert, 72, 233–34n90
Owenite experiments, 72

Parler, 173
patriarchal family
    contrary evidence re, 230n71
    endurance of, 67
    first political unit, 61–62
hierarchical association and, 32
    non-performers weeded out, 67–68
patriotism. *see* nationalism
pawl
    defined, 4–5
            hierarchy and, 18–19
    incentive/disincentive, as, 36–37
Pax Americana, 118, 143
penalties, as disincentives, 36–37
Pence, Mike, 175
People's Republic of China (PRC), *see* China
PepsiCo, non-US CEO, 147
perceivers
    reason and fear, 53
    relation to powerful and, 50–51
Philippines, the, 161
Plutarch, 69–70, 103–104, 235n101
political hierarchy, defined, 81
political power, 80–81
    armed combat and, 60
    climate change and instability of, 65
    dominance over females and, 60–61
    egalitarian hunter-gatherers, 60–61
    fire, hominids gain control of, 60
    hereditary leadership and sovereignty, 62
    human beings as property, 61–62
    language development, 60
    legitimacy and, 80
    male competitive dominance, 62–63
    men socialized as leaders, 63–64
    organized violence and, 65–68
    patriarchal family and, 61–62

physical force, as, 80
polygyny and, 63
primate dominance hierarchies, 59–60
sharing not egalitarian, 63–64
slow aggregation of, 59–60
types of, 40, 216–17n8
war, contract, and state formation, 65–68
weapons, development of, 59–60
political-military hierarchies
power of, 23
subordination and privilege and, 87, T87, T88
politicians, China's influence on, 9–10
politics
all global, 183
anarchists, 94–95
communists, 94
factional linguistic squabbles, 96–97
identity-based, 51–52
left-right spectrum of, 92
lethality of, 33
libertarians, 95–96
moderate left-right, 92–93
origins of, 58–65
power and, *see* political power
radical right, 93–94
reactionaries, 95
socialists, 93
violence vs. nonviolence, 97–98
polygyny, 63
Pompeo, Michael, 139, 175
Popper, Karl, 163,257–58n270
population, political control through revolution, 137
power
concentrating, 33
de facto/de jure, 39
defined for book, 49–50
essential to hierarchy, 50–51

force and, 77–78, T78
Freedom News and, 29–30
illegal/gray utilization of, 46
influence and, 50
institutionalization of, 30–31, 49–50
interlinked hierarchies and, 85–86
intersections' loss of, 86
network theory of, 40–41, 79
nine level-types of, 40, 217–18n13
optimistic theories of, 32, 33
politics and, *see* political power
reinstitutionalization of, 112–13
trade and coercion and, 50–51
power concentration, global
book argument and, 10–11
examples of, 3–4
lack of restraints on, 21
maintaining, 23–24
name changes, 23
ratchet theory of, *see* ratchet theory
reification of, 22–23
slippage, 18–19
power, deconcentration of, 179–87
defeating hierarchy excesses, 180–84
escaping hierarchy, 186–87
success in the hierarchy, 185–86
power, disaggregation of
monarchies and, 109
ratchet theory and, 4–5
Turkey's hoax coup and, 7–8
power, division of, 123–25
knowledge, importance of, 124–25
mutually and self-reinforcing hierarchies, 124
religion and, 123–24
wealth and power not separated in, 124
PRC (People's Republic of China), *see* China
primate dominance hierarchies, 59–60

intragroup behaviors, 59–60
women denied weapons, 60
privilege
hierarchy and, 86–87, 88, T87
power and, 89, 90
ratchet theory of, 89
subordination, regestion and, 89–90
property
hereditary as sovereignty, 62
human beings as, 61–62
men as means to power, 64–65
origins in patriarchy, 62
ownership of one's body, 60
Roman, fear and, 106
violent conquest and, 60–61
Proud Boys, 1, 2, 170
prudence, fear and, 105
Putin, Vladimir, 149
Pyrrhus, 103–104

Rasputin, Grigori, 53–54
ratchet effect
hierarchy and, 22–25
slippage and, 15, 23
ratchet theory *see also* pawl
concentration of power and, 4, 6–7, 14–16
Denmark/Greenland example, 4–5
human elements that engage pawl, 36
lower taxes and, 36
Richerson and Boyd on, 18
reactionaries, 95
reason
of hierarchy, Nero and, 111
mediates between fear and avarice, 105
operation on leaders, 110
ratchet theory and, 36

reforms, piecemeal. and hierarchy evolution, 72
religion
    communists' war against, 164
    fear and (Vico), 105–106
    secular power and (Vico), 106
reproduction, control and, 58–59
Richerson, Peter J., 18, 33
Rohingya, genocide against, 146–47
Roosevelt, Franklin Delano, 4
Russia, 160. *See also* USSR
    invests in market democracies, 176
    uses influence to advance goals, 150–51
Russian Revolution (1917), 11

16+1 group, 152
Sabine women, 81
Sanders, Bernie, 96
Saudi Arabia
    closer to Beijing, 140
    mutaween system, 124, 242n153
    separated hierarchies within, 123–24
Shanghai Cooperation Organization (SCO), 34, 146
sharing in primitive societies, 63–64
Shoshone tribe, 63
Sicknick, Brian, 1
Singapore Police retooling of *Freedom News* (1951), 29–30
slavery
    economic hierarchy and, 82
    as ownership of humans, 61
social complexity
    hierarchy and, 71
    power concentration and, 18
social justice, hierarchy and, 71
social media
    luck of founders, 173–75
    monopolies in, 172–73

power concentration and, 19
    wiping out hierarchy, 32
social movements
    defeating hierarchy, 181–82
    factionalism, risk of, 184
    global politics and, 183
nonviolent, 16–17
    violence wrong strategy for, 162, 181
socialist, Warren and Sanders reject term, 96
socialists, 93
Socrates, 80
Southeast Asia, GDP per capita, 161
sovereign flux, 38–39
sovereign hierarchy, Roman state and, 107
sovereignty, *de facto,* 38
Soviet Union, 11
    economic hierarchy, as, 139
Spanish empire,120
Sparta, 69–70
Spartans at Thermopylae, 73
Spector, Stanley, 139
Stalin, Joseph, 169
state capitalist, China and USSR as, 96
state communists, 96
state sovereignty, 116
state, individual loyalties and, 109–10
Stirner, Max, 95
structure of hierarchy, 75–98
    deconfliction and, 75–76
    deterrence and, 85
    factionalism at the margin, 91–98
    familial/clan structure more successful, 75
    flattening, 98
    intersection of privilege and, 86–87
    knowledge of, 84–85
    loyalty, ideology and, 83–84
    meta-hierarchies, organizing into, 77

scarce resources and, 75
subordination and privilege, 86–90
tension between dominant and subordinate units of, 76–77
types of hierarchy, 77–86
unitary value system and, 76–77
sub-hierarchies, 86 234n93,
    diffusion of hierarchies and, 181
subalterns in alliance systems, 151
subordination
    disintegration and regestion and, 89
    hierarchy and, 87, T88
    oscillation of power imbalances and, 88–89
    power siphoning and, 90
    ratchet theory of, 89
subsidies
    as pawl in ratchet theory, 36, 37
    ratchet mechanism and, 4–5
Suetonius, Nero's Golden House, 111
SWIFT international banking system, 152

3M, non-US CEO, 147
Tabak, Mehmet, 165–66
Taiwan, 183
tax havens, capital flight and, 177
taxation as institutionalization of force, 78
terrorism, romanticization of, 162–63
Tether, 78
think tanks, China's influence on, 9–10
Thomson, David, 159
Thucydides, 107
Tibet, 142, 158
too big to fail, 9
totalitarian hierarchies
    unify primary elements of power, 136–37
    Warsaw Pact (Soviet Union), 134
totalitarianism

hierarchies and, 24
knowledge constrained in, 127–28, 136
rationalizing power, 58
transactional manifestations of power, 50–51
transfer payments
ratchet mechanism and, 4–5
triopoly, 173
Trump supporters
Capitol Hill, 1–3
civil war talk, 7
Trump, President Donald, 14, 153
avarice and, 112
Capitol Hill riot and, 2–3, 7
censorship of, 173
compared to Mussolini, 8
martial law plans, 3
supporters, 170
Truth, Sojourner, 83–84
slave experience, describing, 236n105
Turkey, 2016 hoax coup, 7–8
Twitter, 172–73
as public good, 174–75

Ukrainian genocide, 164
United Nations (UN)
China and, 153, 154
influence threatened, 147
only US can shore up, 141–42
United States
vs. China as hegemon, 143–45
competition with EU and China, 137–38, 139
factors weakening its power, 8–9
freedom of speech and press, 135
GDP, 138, T138
has strength to shore up UN, 141–42
as meta-hierarchy, 151

military power and influence in Asia eroding, 140
political divisions in, 170
racism in, 170
rise of as superpower, 30
voting structure, 130
working-class anger and, 170
universities, part of emerging international elite, 148–49
US Joint Forces Command (PMESII), 79
USSR, Russia
China's split from, 150–51
failed communism, 168–69
replaced by China, 30
state capitalism, 96, 165, 166
US failed strategy re China and, 118–19
utopia, religious hierarchies and, 32
utopian beliefs, Robert Owen, 72, 233–34n90
utopian communists, 96
utopians
illegal regimes' adoption of technology and, 92
Uyghurs
apartheid and, 158
genocide against, 146–47, 152, 164

vagabondage, Marx claimed increase in, 163, 250–51n207
Valerius Publicola, 107
value hierarchies, 85
Vico, Giambattista, 65, 67
aristocracy, function of, 107, 224n38
egalitarian morality in Sparta, 107
hierarchy and civil sovereignty, 71
Minerva's name change, 226n45
monarchy, view of, 32, 107, 226nn46, 47
origin of property theory, 106
religion and fear, theory of, 105–107, 108
state formation and scarce resources, 67, 232–33n81
Vietnam, 135, 161

violence
    bad strategy, as, 162
    as disincentives, 36–37
    vs. nonviolence, 97–98
    patriarchal family and, 61–62
    perceived decrease over time, 32
    political factions and, 96
    revolutionary, 94
    at service of hierarchies, 33
    state monopoly on use of (Weber), 80
    subordination of those not adept at, 75
    wrong strategy for social movements, 162, 181
von Herder, Johann Gottfried, 108–109, 219n18, 236n104, 238n118

wage labor and ownership of humans, 61
war
    female infanticide and, 63
    as foundation of government in Europe, 108–109
    organized violence, as, 65–66
    resources needed to support, 67
    as storm at sea (Plutarch), 69–70
Warren, Elizabeth, 96
Warsaw Pact, 34, 134
wealth, *see also* market democracies
    power and, 49
    power concentration and, 19
    power of, 81–83
wealth hierarchy, 81–83
    physicality and, 78–79
    power and, 81
    slavery and, 82
weapons in primate dominance hierarchies, 59–60
Weber, Max, 80
    state monopoly on use of violence, 80
Western airline companies and technology transfer, 136
Westphalia, Treaty of, 109

WhatsApp, 173
women
    captured to become wives, 62
    China vs. US/EU treatment of, 158
    clay figures of, 230n71
    denied use of weapons, 60
    excluded from male-centered socializing, 62–63
    female infanticide, 63, 230n68
    gendered division of labor, 231n74
    male conquest of as sexual partners, 60–61
    patrilocal exogamy, 64
    subordinate socialization conditions, 63
workers
    democratic means to betterment, 160–61
    Marxist alienation from product, 167–68
    religious persecution and, 164
World Bank, 152
World Trade Organization, 140

Xi Jinping, 3, 144, 146, 149, 158
    family wealth in tax havens, 177
    Xinjiang (East Tibet), 142, 245n174

Zuckerberg, Mark, 174